ies, and larceny.
I just root them out.''

Veteran private eye Arthur Manweiler is a hunter in the seamy, secret underside of contemporary life. The hours are long and unpredictable. Sex, violence, and degredation are all in a day's work. A pair of binoculars, a nondescript car, and someone else's business card are tools of the trade.

In this gripping, first-person narrative, Manweiler reveals the startling truth about his profession. With more than 40 years in the field, he blows the lid wide open on the secret sins and weaknesses of society's lost souls: men, women, and children who can't get anyone else to care.

There's the missing seventeen-year-old who was kidnapped by her father; the prominent businessman whose homosexual tendencies threaten to destroy him; the distraught parents out to discover the truth about their daughter's death; and a cast of dispairing couples—husbands and wives whose marriage vows have collapsed under the weight of suspicion, betrayal, and illicit desire.

Here is a behind-the-scenes look at real-life crimes and the explosive passions that lie behind them—a world where morality is questionable and emotions are deadly.

IF IT WEREN'T FOR SEX... I'D HAVE TO GET A JOB

ARNOLD MANWEILER

As told to James Burke

KNIGHTSBRIDGE PUBLISHING COMPANY

NEW YORK

This paperback edition of *If It Weren't for Sex . . . I'd Have to Get a Job* first published in 1990 by Knightsbridge Publishing Company

Originally published by McClelland & Stewart, Inc. in 1984.

Published in the United States by
Knightsbridge Publishing Company
255 East 49th Street
New York, New York 10017

ISBN 1-877961-30-2

10 9 8 7 6 5 4 3 2 1
FIRST EDITION

Contents

Introduction

LET'S SUPPOSE you were taking part in a word-association test. What would be the first thing to pop into your head when you heard "private detective?" Chances are, it'd be something like "shyster" or "window-peeper," right? And if you tried to conjure up a picture to match, it'd probably be of a shifty-eyed slob who'd do anything for a buck, uses a lot of four-letter words, smokes cheap cigars, drinks like a fish, and wears a baggy suit and a trench coat whose collar is pulled up so high it almost shakes hands with the brim of his slouch hat.

The conventional wisdom about private eyes includes the profession's methods of operation which most people seem to think range from shoving forty-fives up people's noses to bedding down curvaceous blonde socialites who are bored with their effete husbands and/or boyfriends and want to sample the sexual wares of a quick-fisted macho man who drinks danger on the rocks.

Let me tell you, it's not easy to dispel these myths. For example, I'm past sixty, packing about forty pounds of excess baggage, and barbers no longer ask me if I want any off the top, but a lot of my businessman friends still look at me with envy as though my job guarantees me unlimited excitement and a daily invitation to a sexual smorgasbord.

Of course, most of this stereotyping is due to the way private investigators have been popularized in fiction over the years, particularly in Mickey Spillane's stuff which I personally enjoy if only because I get some laughs out of it. The trouble is, most people don't laugh. They take it seriously and the advent of television sure as hell didn't help matters any. To the average television addict who's bug-eyed from watching "Remington Steele" or "Magnum P.I.," being a private eye means slug-fests, fast cars, and equally fast women who are always slinking about in bikinis, throwing what's already falling out of their swimsuits at some gumshoe so he'll take their cases which usually involve blackmail, forgery, incest, and three or four murders, depending on how hard the censors are hitting violence that week.

Still, there's a reason for the mystique of the private eye surviving for so long because I have to admit that it originates in a kernel of truth. Private detectives do encounter some or all of the above-mentioned dangers and delights and, in the thirty-five years I've been in the business, I've seen my share of both. So what am I crying about then? Just this: the stuff that's commonly identified with guys like me is just the surface flash and the real goods, the essence of what it takes to be a good private investigator – is seldom discussed and rarely understood. I guess that's the main reason for me talking about my career now. I want to set the record straight – if not for the profession in general, at least for myself.

The traits that separate the successes from the fly-by-night failures in this business aren't a quick trigger-finger and quicker fists. They are dogged determination, patience, powers of deduction, and acting ability. Along with the last, goes the gift of gab which, thank God, I have in some abundance. As a result, I've been able to talk my way into a lot of places and information and con my way out of a lot of tight spots.

But there's also one other thing you've got to have if you're going to last in this business and that's the ability to keep from becoming emotionally involved. You've got to be a real ice-man because if you're not, there isn't going to be much left of your insides after a couple of years. Of course, that's easier said than done and there've been times when even I couldn't see past my heart. The lonely, the mentally ill, the psychologically and physically abused: I get them all and it's not easy to keep your distance when someone is pouring their guts out onto your desk.

There were also times when I wanted to reach out and throttle some sleazy would-be client who proposed that I perform some equally sleazy assignment involving blackmail or strongarm stuff. But instead of tossing the scumbag out on his ear, I just quietly asked him if he wouldn't mind leaving before he had an unfortunate accident.

Over thirty years in the business. I could've done a lot better financially if I'd gone into some other line. I could've had a lot more security too. But I've stuck with it for over half my life. I wouldn't change it if I had to do it over again either but don't ask me why.

Freedom? Yeah, I've got that alright – at least, I'm not tied to a desk. I make a decent living too. But the hours are long and unpredictable and what happens within those hours doesn't engender any deep-seated love for humanity because, most of the time, I see people at their worst. I lift the lids off their morals and pick up their sins after them the way a mother retrieves her kid's hastily discarded clothes.

Some might say people like me are parasites feeding off evil and weakness and maybe, to a degree, they're right. But isn't that what priests and ministers do? And don't they perform a useful service? And how about doctors? Don't they thrive on other people's pain and sickness? A cop-out? Maybe so. But I didn't invent lust, lies, and larceny. I just root them out and by doing it, I think I perform a useful public service. At least, most of the time I think that way. But there are other times when I wake up in the middle of the night and wonder. And I guess that's one of the reasons for this book.

ONE

'Til Death Us Do Part

I F YOU HAD to make a list of people whose professions carry a helluva lot of responsibility, chances are you'd include doctors, nurses, airline pilots, firemen, and, maybe, ambulance drivers. They'd all be good choices too because each of them trades in that most precious commodity of all: human life. One slip and today's living, breathing, human can become tomorrow's corpse.

Take doctors, for example. In spite of what we like to believe, especially when we're due to go under the knife, doctors aren't miracle workers and there are times when they've done their damnedest and still had patients cash in on them. But that doesn't mean they throw in the towel because being a professional means you have to deal in realities and what greater reality is there than death?

Now, you're probably saying to yourself: Where does a private eye get off philosophizing about professional responsibility and life and death? And to be truthful, years back I probably would have said the same thing. But not any more. Not since a spring afternoon more than ten years ago when, for the first time in my life, I seriously thought about chucking the whole thing and forgetting I was ever a private investigator.

It began in the summer of '79. I was on what I figured was just another case but it turned out to be anything but. It wasn't until the following spring that it finally came to a head but the poison had been building up for a long time, long before Edward Gant shuffled into my office and poured out some of the pain he'd bottled up for so long.

A bookkeeper with a large Winnipeg grain company, Gant perpetually wore an apologetic expression, as though he suspected he'd done something wrong but wasn't quite sure what. Both his posture and his mannerisms contributed to his hang-dog appearance. Tall and gangly, he was so stoop-shouldered he looked like he had curvature of the spine. And talk about fidgety! The guy was a walking neurosis. If he wasn't tugging at his earlobes or scratching his neck, he'd be biting his nails or squirming in his seat and looking everywhere but at me.

He was in his mid-fifties and still had about three-quarters of his hair. If it hadn't been for a slightly hooked nose and a prominent Adam's apple, he wouldn't have been bad looking. But then, he didn't come to see me because of his looks. No, his problem was his wife.

"Elaine goes out at least twice a week, Mr. Manweiler, and doesn't come home until two or three in the morning." His voice dropped. "Last Wednesday, she stayed out all night."

"You think she's got a boyfriend?"

He looked at his hands for a good ten seconds. "I don't know. I can't think of any reason why she'd want to cheat on me. We have a nice home, two beautiful daughters. . . ."

That was his cue to take out his wallet and show me photographs of two smiling teenagers.

"The one on the left is Joanne. She's fourteen. And the dark one there, that's Dianne. She's seventeen. Next year, she'll be going into nursing." He took one last, fond, look before putting the billfold away.

"Where does she say she's been when she stays out late like that?"

"With her friend, Lil."

"Did you ever check with this Lil to see if she was telling the truth?"

He let out a deep sigh. "Oh yes, a number of times and

she always says she and Elaine were at bingo or just visiting but there's something about the way she says it – like she's nervous or scared or something – that makes me think she's lying; that she's covering up for my wife."

Suspicion. That's how it always starts. First a seed and, later, a full-grown plant that sucks all the nourishment out of a relationship, leaving it to feed off its own bitterness and jealousy. Suspicion alone is never enough though. Not for people who think their spouses may be engaging in a little extramarital recreation. No, they're never satisfied with half a loaf of masochism if they can have the whole thing – the knowledge that strips them of every last shred of pride and convinces them they're nothing, zeroes, unloved and unlovable.

That's what they seem to want and need and, as a private investigator, that's what I try to give them. Before he left, I got Gant to give me a couple of photos of his wife. He had quite a collection. His wallet could have passed for a family album and I had to smile and nod at all of them before I could get the ones I wanted.

"This one was taken at the lake," he said, handing me a picture of a fleshy redhead in halter and shorts, squinting into the sun. "I rent a cottage for the summer. Or at least I used to. The girls want to spend their holidays in the city with their friends now they're older and this year, Dianne got on with McDonald's. And Elaine, well, she doesn't seem to take to the outdoors like she used to. Says the sun's bad for her skin."

A couple of them were reasonably good closeups. They showed a round-faced, plain-looking woman with a good headstart on a second chin. She was just shy of her fiftieth birthday and far from a knockout as far as I was concerned, but to Ed Gant, she was all a woman should be.

"Just as pretty as the day I married her," he nodded.

And he really believed it because, as strange as it may sound, this quiet, meek-looking man was still crazy about his wife after more than twenty years of marriage. Where most long-married types had the occasional flickering ember among a lot of dead coals, he still had a flame burning high and hot.

And that was what made this case as difficult as it was unique. You see, most of the time when someone wants to get evidence of adultery, it's strictly for divorce purposes. But not in Ed Gant's case. He wanted to find out if his wife was fooling around alright but he didn't, at least that's the way it seemed to me, want to take the next logical step and cut her loose.

Strange alright. But that was nothing compared to what came later. Now, I wasn't in on this one right from the start. I was up to my ass in a big industrial crime caper at the time. A shipper with a large garment manufacturer was doing some freelance work on the side, shipping out stuff to customers the company didn't even know it had. So I delegated the surveillance to one of my operatives whom I'll call Ernie. The case couldn't have been in better hands, though, because he was one of the best bird-dogs around. When he got on someone's trail, you couldn't shake him loose with a charge of dynamite. After a couple of weeks, he knew Elaine Gant's movements almost as well as she did herself. You see, when you tail someone, the first thing you look for is a pattern; where the subject goes and when and the frequency of the visits. That way, you've got a kind of predictability profile so you're not flying blind when you try to figure out where a subject might be at any given time.

In Mrs. Gant's case, the pattern was only too clear because if she wasn't an alcoholic, she was well on the road. And like most heavy drinkers, she liked to get pissed in familiar surroundings – bars she frequented so often they were almost like second homes. In a way, that was a bonus for Ernie because if he ever lost her, he could pretty well count on picking up her trail in one of the four downtown bars in which she did most of her serious drinking. Few weeks went by when she didn't pay at least one visit to all four. The hour of the day didn't matter either. Anytime after opening was good enough for her. But she wasn't a solitary drinker. No, Elaine Gant liked company. Male company. And most of the time, she got it. As a matter of fact, the only thing in pants that she didn't seem particularly fussy about was her husband.

For the first couple of weeks though, in spite of the fact Ernie kept her under constant surveillance, he couldn't come up with any hard evidence that she was playing around, at least to the point of sleeping with anyone, and on the single occasion when she didn't make it back home, she actually did spend the night with her friend, Lil. Of course, it wasn't as though she was acting like a nun either. She drank with all kinds of guys and danced and had a good time, but if she made it with anyone it must've been in the women's can because that was the only place she went without Ernie tagging along. I couldn't figure it and I started to think that either she was onto us and playing it cool or her husband was just another poor bugger who was so jealous he couldn't think straight.

Both of those theories went right out the window on the third week. Elaine started meeting the same guy two or three times a week, sometimes in one bar, sometimes in another, but always the same man. Not a bad-looking guy either. Early forties probably. Six feet tall and well-built aside from the beginnings of a paunch, he had black wavy hair with just a touch of grey at the temples. Well-dressed too, given to three-piece suits and sports jackets. With his pencil moustache, he looked a little like Errol Flynn and the fact that Flynn had a reputation for hitting the sauce didn't hurt the comparison either because Elaine's boy-friend had the watery eyes and florid complexion of a practising pisstank.

We traced him through his license plate and found that his name was Harry McWilliams. Some discreet checking revealed he was a real estate salesman although considering all the time he spent in bars, he couldn't have been doing it on more than a part-time basis. At least, he didn't let it get in the way of his more serious pastime which consisted of knocking back double rum-and-cokes. That was also probably why Elaine paid for most of the rounds. As Ernie put it, the guy had all the makings of a C.O.D. stud.

Elaine Gant sure seemed hung-up on him too. She was forever touching him. Playing with his hair, stroking his cheek, or holding his hand. A couple of real lovebirds alright – except one of them belonged in another nest.

I didn't jump into the case with both feet until mid-August, even though I still hadn't wrapped up that industrial job. There were some big bucks on the line there too and I hated to hand it over to one of my agents but I felt I had no choice. It was because of something in one of Ernie's reports. Something that made me think the Gant case might turn out to be a whole lot more than either I or my client had bargained for. You see, after you've been in this business for a while, you develop a kind of intuition – a feeling about cases and people – and, after reading Ernie's report of August 12th, 1979, a warning signal sounded inside me and stayed there off and on throughout the entire case. And here's what set it off.

Attended at subject's home at 3:00 p.m. At approximately 3:45, she was picked up by a taxi which I followed. Lost subject in traffic at 3:55 p.m. After checking pubs and lounges in downtown area, I finally located subject in the cocktail lounge of the Marlborough Hotel. She was seated at a table with Harry McWilliams. Both were drinking doubles and appeared to be feeling good.

The lounge was fairly empty and I took a seat two tables away from them. They continued to drink doubles one after another and spoke in very loud voices. Although I had my back to them, I could hear them quite clearly. There was considerable discussion about a holiday with each saying where they'd like to go. Hawaii and Mexico were mentioned. Then the conversation turned to life insurance. At this time, some people came in and sat at the table between myself and the subject. The conversation of these new arrivals drowned out some of the discussion between the subject and McWilliams but I did manage to pick up further references to insurance and heard the sum of $50,000 mentioned.

Subject also said something to the effect that she'd "finally got him to sign the papers." Talk reverted to holidays and shortly afterward (5:55 p.m.), subject and McWilliams went into the hotel dining room where they had a meal.

Now, if someone were to say that I sometimes let myself get carried away by nothing more than a hunch or suspicion, he wouldn't get that much of an argument from me although, in my own defence, I'd have to say that most of my hunches turn out to be a lot more than that. At that point in the Gant case though it was still strictly suspicion. Suspicion based on some loose talk about fifty grand in insurance which was quite a sum in those days. That's why I thought it was time I got into the act and, the next day, I laid on a meeting with Edward Gant. I told him I wanted to review the case but what I really wanted to do was talk to him about insurance. Since, at this point, I was doing nothing more than playing a hunch, I led up to it gradually.

"Aside from the fact your wife likes to step out on her own, how's your relationship? Do you get along alright?"

"Oh yes," he said quickly. "We get along fine." He hesitated for a moment, staring down at his hands. "Oh, we have our squabbles – what couple doesn't – but just over small things. Nothing serious."

"Well, I don't want to pry but it might help if you told me about some of those squabbles. For a start, have you had any recently?"

He thought for a moment. "Just one, really, but it was kind of an ongoing thing." He gave his usual apologetic smile. "Probably all my fault. I do tend to get a little pig-headed sometimes."

It turned out that what he'd been "pig-headed" about was an insurance policy – a $50,000 policy on his life. His wife had been pressing him to take it out, arguing that his company policy was insufficient. Ed had resisted, saying the premiums on a policy that size were more than he could afford. He'd suggested a compromise, a $25,000 policy, but she wouldn't hear of it. She'd even gone so far as to contact an insurance agent and have him prepare a policy for the higher figure. The whole thing had been her brainchild and, finally, after several weeks of badgering, she'd gotten him to sign the form which named her as the sole beneficiary.

"Elaine, well, when she gets something in her head, she's not about to let it go and she thought I should be thinking about the girls and their future." He rubbed his chin reflectively. "I guess she's right but, like I said, sometimes I get my back up and just won't budge."

"But you budged this time?"

He smiled sheepishly. "If you had to listen to her day after day, you would too. It's something like the Chinese water torture with words. So I figured, well, what's a few more bucks if it'll keep peace in the family."

"Fifty thousand is quite a piece of change."

"Yes, that's true but the way inflation's going, it might not be all that much by the time they plant me."

If my hunch was correct, inflation would be the last thing he'd have to worry about for I now knew that Elaine Gant hadn't just been engaged in booze talk when she blabbed to McWilliams about the $50,000 policy. It was the straight goods and she'd made no secret of the fact that she would've liked to get her hands on the dough. Of course, this was a long way from a conspiracy to knock someone off because people are known to say a lot of things they don't mean and if shooting off your mouth was a crime, most of us would've seen the inside of a jail cell by now. So, even though I had an uneasy feeling about the whole case, I kept my mouth shut and stuck to the business at hand which was finding out if Elaine was spreading her sexual wares around. I told Ed what we'd turned up so far.

"The only regular male companion we've seen your

wife with is a fellow named Harry McWilliams. The name ring a bell?"

He shook his head vigorously. His features softened as the tension drained from his body. "They were just drinking together, weren't they? I mean she didn't go anywhere with him, did she, like up to his place or a room or anything?"

"No. When they left whatever bar they happened to be in, they went their separate ways."

His tentative smile widened. "Then I guess I was wrong about . . . what I thought. Elaine says I have a jealous streak a mile wide and I guess she's right. But I suppose that's what it's like when you've loved a woman for so long. It tears you up to even think of her with another guy."

Even though we hadn't nailed her, I still wasn't prepared to give Elaine Gant a clean bill of health but I also didn't want to sound as though I was trying to drum up business.

"Well, like I said, we haven't turned up any hard evidence that your wife's been unfaithful with McWilliams. . . ."

"Or anyone else." He was so eager to believe in his wife that he rushed to complete the sentence.

It was funny. He'd paid me a good buck to get the goods on his old lady yet was relieved that we'd come up empty. In a way, I was kind of glad we didn't catch her in the sack with someone. I didn't think Ed would've been able to take it. He really loved that woman and yet that love, strong as it was, had been at war with his self-respect, with the sense that he was being played for a sucker. Part of him wanted to know and another part didn't. The fact that he was so mixed up bothered me. It made me wonder if he was capable of levelling with me. Maybe he'd deceived himself for so long that he wouldn't know the truth if it came up and grabbed him by the balls. I was almost relieved when he called off the surveillance and paid me off.

"You know," he said, stopping in the doorway on his way out of my office, "it wasn't easy for me to come here. I mean, I'm basically a very private person and, well, I've had to tell you some pretty personal things. But I feel it was well worth it, both the expense and the . . . rest. Those suspicions were eating me up so bad I had to go to the doctor to get something to help me sleep. I can't tell you what a weight it is off my mind now."

But in the next instant, relief gave way to worry as he added: "I know people in your business are supposed to be discreet but. . . ."

"Don't worry," I said, "no one will ever know you hired us."

A minute later he was out of sight. But not out of mind. And not, as it turned out, out of my life. It was early in the new year – mid-January of 1980 – when I heard from him again. He sounded agitated and wanted to make an appointment to see me. He said it was urgent.

It'd only been about five months since I'd seen him last but the change in his appearance was almost unbelievable. Formerly a neat, almost impeccable dresser, he was now decked out in a baggy suit that looked like it'd been slept in. There was a couple of days stubble on his chin and his thin hair was long and unkempt. We'd barely gotten started when he began to sob, burying his face in his hands.

The story was that he was now firmly convinced that his wife was having an affair and he wanted us to put her under surveillance again, around the clock if necessary.

"Maybe it's none of my business, Mr. Gant," I said, "but you don't look that well. Have you seen a doctor recently?"

"Doctors," he snorted. "Every time I go to one, he just gives me more pills. Pink pills, yellow pills, pills to sleep, pills to wake up. One of them was even talking about shock treatments. Shock treatments!" His voice became shrill. "As though I'm crazy or something. I'm not crazy! I'm just . . ." his voice cracked. ". . . just nervous."

That was an understatement if I ever heard one. What with his constantly blinking eyes and a twitch at the corner of his mouth, his face was an exercise in perpetual motion. Figuring he was about ten seconds shy of a nervous breakdown, I told him to get a grip on himself.

"How could she do that to me – to us?" he asked plaintively. "For Christmas, I bought her a fur coat – a full-length one, not just a jacket – and then on New Year's Eve, she didn't even come home. Didn't call either. I was worried sick. Then when she finally showed up, she wouldn't give me any explanation. Told me it was none of my business!"

Since then, she'd been staying away from home one or two days at a time and any illusions that Gant had harboured about her fidelity were long gone. I gave him a cup of coffee and a little pep-talk and told him we'd put a tail on her that night. When he was getting ready to leave, I also told him I could put him in touch with a good lawyer if he didn't already have one. He said he'd think about it and left.

I began my stakeout at the Gant residence at 7:00 p.m. A taxi showed up shortly after eight and Elaine, all dolled up in her loving husband's Christmas gift, got in. I followed the cab downtown where Elaine was dropped off in front of the St. Charles Hotel. Now, there are certainly a lot of hotels in Winnipeg seedier than the St. Charles but it still wasn't the kind of place a "lady" would go to alone, or for that matter, with someone else. Along with a heavy blue-collar clientele, the bar catered to a mixed bag of bikers, hookers, and small-time hoods. The only time you had a chance to have a quiet drink was when all the rowdies passed out or got carted away in a paddy wagon.

As usual, the place was smokier than hell. Coming in from the front, you could see a thin grey haze extending the full length of the beer hall. Drab and cavernous, the room was partly bisected by a line of pillars that looked like they might have been salvaged from a Roman coliseum. In the middle, against the left wall, was a small, semi-circular stage where a big-assed coloured broad was grinding and thrusting to the beat of some recorded rock music. She looked like a fullback who'd taken the wrong kind of hormone shots. She had huge swelling thighs and you could see the muscles shifting under the smooth chocolate skin. You could see a lot more than that too. The only thing separating her from total nudity was a filmy scarf that she was sliding back and forth between her legs as though she were polishing her pussy. A real class act alright. And all the while she was giving herself this silk massage, her eyes were rolling in mock ecstasy and her tongue was caressing her full, glistening lips.

For a moment, I almost forgot what the hell I was doing there but then I got back down to business and refocused my attention on Elaine. She was standing in the middle of the aisle, craning her neck, trying to spot someone. Or maybe she was just searching for an unoccupied table because the place was pretty full. In that joint, her fancy fur coat stood out like an honest man at a used car dealers' convention. She finally located a vacant table in the middle of the room and plunked herself down, unbuttoning the coat but keeping it around her shoulders.

Hoping to get a seat where I could keep an eye on her and whoever might join her, I passed in front of the stage, sneaking one last look at the dancer. Her twirling melons and grinding hips were picking up speed as the music – and probably half the guys watching – built to a climax.

"Christ, man, why doncha watch where you're goin'?"

I was so caught up in the broad's act, being a big fan of interpretive dancing, that I wasn't looking where I was going and would've walked right into a biker on his way to the john if he hadn't sidestepped at the last second. I mumbled an apology and picked out a table. It was far enough away from Elaine that she wouldn't be able to recognize me if she saw me again yet close enough for me to get a make on anyone who joined her. There was another guy at my table but for all the attention he paid

me, we could have been on different planets. His eyes were
following the stripper's box like a pair of heat-seeking
missiles. Having discarded both her scarf and false modesty, she was aiming her midnight patch at anyone who
looked even vaguely appreciative. The music was just
winding down when my table-mate, a grey-haired, shriv-
elled-up old guy of about seventy-five, with either beer or
saliva running down his chin, turned to me and said with
fervent conviction: "I like dis kind moosic."

"Yeah, me too," I said.

The spotlight had died and the dancer prowled the
stage in semi-darkness like a big, kinky-headed panther,
picking up the parts of her costume. There was a scatter-
ing of applause and a lone cry of "We want pussy" drew a
few hoots and whistles.

Figuring he'd had enough excitement for one day, the
old geezer at my table slapped on his ski-cap, buttoned his
old, black, double-breasted overcoat and weaved his way
toward the door. Thank God for that. Having to make
small-talk with the old bugger would've been both a chore
and a needless distraction. Now I was able to turn all of
my attention to Elaine Gant. Between sips of what looked
like a double rye, she alternated between gawking around
the room and peering at her wristwatch. It was obvious
that she was waiting for someone. I hoped it wasn't as
obvious that I was doing the same thing.

As an afterthought, I glanced over to the bar. Nick was
on duty. Nick Seeposh. A former client in a divorce case,
he'd managed to get rid of his wife on the basis of evidence
that I'd dug up and was so grateful that he always sent me
over a free drink or two whenever I dropped into the St.
Charles. Since Elaine looked as though she was planning
to hang around for a while, having just latched onto
another double, I thought I'd at least touch base with him.

"Well, if it isn't my old friend, Arnold!" he boomed,
shooting out his hand.

"How ya doing, Nick?"

"The same. No better, no worse," he smiled. "Can't

complain though. Things could be a helluva lot worse, if you know what I mean."

I knew. His ex had been a real bitch. Besides screwing around on him, she'd spent his dough like it was going out of style.

"Where you sitting?" he asked. "I'll send you over a drink. You still drinking rye and seven?"

"C'mon, Nick, business isn't that bad. I can still pay for my own hangovers."

He shook his head. "You gotta have at least one on Nick. You saved my life, man. I mean, you goddamn-well saved my life. That twat was driving me to an early grave. Either that or I would've ended up behind bars because it was getting to the point where it was either her or me."

"Bullshit. You're a pussycat, Nick."

"Oh yeah?" he snorted, "even a pussycat has claws. That bitch was begging for it. You know that better than anyone."

All the while, I kept my eyes on Elaine Gant. She was still alone, still knocking back the booze. Her fancy coat had slid off her shoulders and was draped on the back of her chair, dusting the bar's grubby floor. She didn't seem to mind though. So what if it had cost her husband a month's pay? She was some dame alright.

I'd no sooner gotten back to my table when the drink Nick promised arrived. I saluted him with it and he responded with a friendly wave. It was good to have friends like Nick. Not just because of the free booze but because bartenders are usually a wealth of information. They always look as though the only things they're concerned with are pouring out shots of booze, cracking open bottles of beer, and giving the waitresses shit, but most of them are like sponges, soaking up just about everything that goes down in their bars. And what they pick up sometimes comes in handy. For them and for me too.

Another good thing about Nick was that he never asked me questions about business, probably realizing I wouldn't answer them anyway. So, even though he must've known I wasn't in his bar either to socialize or to get plastered, he didn't try to pump me.

It wasn't until after nine that Elaine got some company. There were two of them. The first one to the table was good old Harry McWilliams who, whatever else you might say about him, at least wasn't treating Elaine Gant like a one-night stand. Trailing along behind him was another guy, a big, rough-looking sonuvabitch. About six-two and well over two-hundred, he had the face and build of an over-the-hill heavyweight. He was wearing a stylish brown leather coat but on him it looked completely out of place because he sure as hell didn't look anything like those unisex types you see lounging around in fashion magazines. With that beetle-brow and those craggy features, he looked like a contestant in a Neanderthal of the Year competition.

His hair was something else too. He had one of those fancy razor cuts that guys named Philippe or Bruce charge twenty bucks for. The only thing was he looked like the kind of guy who'd go in for those seventy-five cent specials at Moler's Barber College. A strange looking bird alright.

I watched Harry introduce him to Elaine then order a round of drinks. Until the waitress set their drinks down and left, it looked like they were making small-talk. But that changed as soon as she was out of earshot. Harry and the heavy looked around kind of furtively while Elaine checked out her make-up in her compact mirror then all three leaned forward, forming a tight triangle, and I could tell from their expressions that what they were discussing was more business than pleasure. But what kind of business? I would have given a bundle to have had a wireless mike planted at their table. I felt kind of helpless, sitting there stealing glances through a haze of smoke that seemed to grow thicker by the minute. Christ I thought, at this rate, by eleven, I'll need a seeing-eye dog to get to the can. The red neon sign over the rear exit already looked fuzzy, like a water-colour that was starting to run.

Rather than just sit there like a dummy, I slipped back to the bar where Nick was dispensing shots of booze with cool precision and little wasted movement. The only time he showed any emotion was when one of the waitresses screwed up an order and he had to try and find a home for the orphaned booze.

When I got there, he was chewing out a tough-looking chick with dyed red hair that went at least half-way to her black roots and make-up so thick you would've thought it would crack if she smiled. Not that there was any danger of that right then because her mouth was tight and only the muscles of her jaws were working, trying to keep from spitting out a retort to the static Nick was giving her.

"Christ, that's the third time tonight, Jean. If you don't know what they want, ask for Chrissake. Guessing games. That's what you broads want to play. Guessing games."

She whisked a full tray off the bar and bustled away, muttering under her breath. "Drop dead, you goddamn hunky."

Nick spotted me and his expression softened.

"What's up, dick?" he said, laughing in appreciation at his own line. "Hey, that's not bad, eh? What's up, dick instead of what's up, doc? You know, dick, as in detective?"

I mustered up a smile. "Yeah, that's pretty funny, Nick. You've got a quick mind." Then, to myself. "For a Uke."

I leaned forward, keeping my voice as low as I could without having it drowned out by the country-and-western trio that'd taken over for the stripper.

"Don't look over there right away but there's three people – a broad and two guys – sitting over by the juke-box. The broad's got on a cream-coloured sweater and one guy's wearing a brown leather coat. The second guy. . . ."

"I see them. What about 'em?"

"Do you know them?"

He squinted in their direction. "Don't know the broad – at least not by name. She's been in before though."

"How about the guys?"

"The guy in the grey topcoat, him I know a little – Harry something-or-other. Comes in maybe once, twice a week. The other guy, the mean-looking one, him I know too well."

"What do you mean, 'too well?' "

"Just that guys like him it's better not to know at all. He's trouble. A heavy. Got a record a mile long and not for jaywalking either. I hear he just got out of the joint a couple of weeks ago and look at him. The coat must be worth a couple of hundred bucks and you can bet your ass he didn't work for it."

"What's his name?"

"Prinzek. Emil Prinzek. I think he's Hungarian or Czech. Came over from the old country in the mid-fifties. Before he went to the slammer this last time, he was working for a firm of bailiffs."

As soon as he started talking about Prinzek, Nick had suddenly seemed to be hit with an attack of nerves and by now, he showed a distinct lack of enthusiasm for discussing the guy at all. I made a mental note to check Prinzek's record through a pal at the police department but curiosity got the better of me and I asked Nick one last question. "What kind of beefs did that poor, misunderstood lad get sent up for?"

He gave a furtive glance toward the table where the trio were still deep in conversation and said, almost in a whisper, "Strong-arm stuff. Collecting debts by leaning on people, usually with a baseball bat or his size twelves. On his last beef, the cops just happened to come by when Prinzek was tapdancing on some poor bugger's chest. Do yourself a favour, Arnold. Do not get within a city block of him if he's not smiling. He is not a nice man."

Then he turned away abruptly and made a big show of wiping the counter.

"I'll try not to, Nick. Thanks."

He rubbed at a non-existent smudge and without bothering to look up, said: "Yeah, sure."

Since Elaine and her friends looked as though they'd be

hanging around for a while, I thought it'd be a good time to show my kidneys some mercy. Standing at a urinal and breathing a sigh of relief, I heard the door swing open and who the hell comes in but the gorilla, Emil Prinzek. And of all the urinals in the place, he has to pick the one next to me to piss into. I kept my face averted and not just because I didn't want him to think I was some fag checking out his plumbing. I didn't know what the story was with him and Elaine and Harry but there was a little warning voice inside me that said it'd be best if he didn't suspect I was on their case. I snuck one look at him though and, up close his map looked even more menacing. It was a face that'd seen violence from both sides.

I got out of there fast and made my way back to my table, watching for Prinzek to rejoin Elaine and Harry. But he never showed and I guessed he took off out the back door. So now it was just the two love birds and their conversation seemed to have lightened up accordingly. Either that or the doubles they were pushing back had finally started to take effect because the furrowed brows and frowns of concentration had given way to relaxed smiles and laughter.

Elaine threw her head back and I could hear her throaty laughter halfway across the room. I could also see Harry sliding his hand up under her skirt while she went through the motions of fending him off. They hung around for another twenty minutes and two doubles apiece and then stumbled out of the room arm-in-arm. It was 11:30 p.m.

Waiting until they got a slight headstart, I left my table and half a shot of whiskey that tasted as though it had been distilled that morning. Before following them out, however, I made a brief detour, stopping at their table. Elaine had been doodling on an empty cigarette package which she'd subsequently discarded. For some reason, probably because I'm a natural packrat, I decided to pick it up. It was a habit I'd gotten into over the years because you never knew when something could come in handy, even something as harmless as a cigarette package carrying some squiggles and scrawls. I shoved it into my coat pocket and stepped into the lobby. Harry was at the vendor picking up a case of beer while Elaine was plugging coins into a cigarette machine. I brushed by them and hustled over to my car which was parked in the adjacent lot. By the time they came out and made their way to Harry's ten-year-old Buick, I was poised and ready to roll.

It was a blustery night. Snow was swirling around the streets and gathering in pockets against the curbs and buildings. By morning, it would be another Winnipeg winter wonderland with senior citizens dropping dead from shovelling their walks and motorists cursing the condition of the streets and wondering why all the city snowplows were parked in front of coffee shops.

Harry took off, his headlights beating a path through a thickening curtain of snow. I tried to keep about fifty or sixty yards behind but even at that distance, I lost sight of his tail-lights now and then as they flickered in and out of the building blizzard. I had my wipers on full blast but they didn't help much. The poor visibility smoothed angles into curves and made distance an illusion. It was like looking out through a layer of gauze. It would be only too easy to lose them. I tramped on the gas having once again lost sight of his tail lights. Where did they go? Suddenly, the wind died momentarily and with it the driving snow, and I found out. The Buick was stopped for a light no more than thirty yards ahead. And there I was on a direct collision course. I pumped my brakes and tried to ease over to the side, afraid of going into a skid. Beads of sweat popped onto my forehead as my headlights measured the glare ice between me and Harry. Twenty yards. Fifteen. I finally got some traction and started to slow down. Ten yards. Just as I'd begun to think there was no way I could stop in time, the light changed, Harry started off, and I ended up in the middle of the intersection, with just enough time to mop my brow and take a deep breath before getting back on the trail again.

The Buick covered another dozen blocks before turning left on a residential street and stopping in front of a small, three-storey apartment block. Harry and Elaine got out and went inside without so much as looking over their shoulders so I was reasonably sure they hadn't spotted me. I got to the door in time to see their feet disappearing up the stairs and I waited on the main floor landing, hearing their footsteps ascend then level off as they headed down the second-floor hallway. As I started up the stairs, a muttered curse wafted down. Harry was having trouble finding his key.

A door creaked open then closed a few seconds later and the building was silent. I tried to keep it that way as I tip-toed up the stairs. I couldn't be sure but it had sounded as though they'd gone into one of the front suites. Listening at doors along both sides of the hall, I heard voices coming from the first one to my right – one, a man's; the other belonging to a woman, Elaine. I picked up her boozy contralto right away. Harry's voice was harder to recognize – maybe he was a little further gone than she was. And to complicate things, the TV was on pretty loud which Elaine seemed none too happy about.

"Listen, we've got things to talk about. Can't you do without the TV for one night?"

"As long as I don't have to do without anything else." It was Harry alright.

The TV clicked off and I pressed my ear to the door, hearing Elaine lead off. Some of the conversation was inaudible and other parts didn't make much sense – just booze-talk – but one of their topics came through loud and clear and it made me feel like someone was playing tic-tac-toe on my back with an icicle. The fifty thousand. It'd come up again and I was sure it was no coincidence that it was the amount of Ed Gant's insurance policy.

"With fifty grand, I could set up my own business," Harry rhapsodized.

"You mean, *we* could," Elaine corrected. "And it's not fifty, it's forty-five, thanks to you."

"You're damn right it's thanks to me. If it wasn't for me, you'd be waiting for twenty years to see one red cent."

"But five thousand. . . ."

"If you think you can get someone for minimum wage, go right ahead."

"Well, we could do it ourselves."

"Maybe *you* could," he laughed, "but not old Harry. I'm a lover not a. . . ."

I heard footsteps coming up the stairs and was distracted just long enough to miss the last word but you didn't have to be a genius to guess what it was. I beat it to the back stairs and waited until the coast was clear. The footsteps belonged to a hippie-type kid on his way up to the third floor. He looked so stoned I could've probably stood right in front of him and he wouldn't have noticed me. A door slammed above me and I figured it was safe to return to my listening post. When I re-glued my ear to Harry's door, Elaine, as usual, was complaining.

"I don't like him. I don't like the way he talks. He's so . . . crude."

"What the hell did you expect – a college graduate? You're goddamn right he's crude! If he wasn't, he sure as hell wouldn't be any good to us."

"Well, you don't have to yell," she pouted. "I was just worried about getting involved with someone like that."

"Nobody's getting involved, honey. It's just business."

"Well, I guess you know best, baby," she cooed. "I love you so much, I couldn't stand it if anything happened to you."

"I love you too, doll."

His comment was punctuated by some rustling and heavy breathing, after which Elaine said huskily, "That's enough business talk. Let's go to bed."

Harry said something inaudible that she responded to with a high-pitched, sensual laugh, then there was a sound of receding footsteps. I plucked a match from a matchbook and inserted it between the door and the jamb, about a third of the way up. Then I headed home for a couple of hours of shut-eye. It was close to one a.m. and there wasn't much chance they'd be stepping out anymore that night. If the match was there when I came back in the morning, it would be pretty conclusive proof that Elaine and Harry had been shacked up for the night. To make it stick in court, I'd need a little more but, at this point, I really didn't know what Edward Gant's intentions were. He wanted to find out if his wife was playing around, that's for sure. But why? So far, a divorce action hadn't even been mentioned.

As I left the building, I glanced up at the windows of Harry's suite. They were all dark – dark as the souls of the pair inside. They were made for each other alright. I climbed into my car, reached into my pocket for the keys, and felt the empty cigarette package that I'd picked up in the bar. I'd forgotten all about it. I flicked on the dome light and looked it over. Elaine's handwriting was no model of penmanship, that's for sure. There wasn't much there. Just some figures and a couple of names – or, to be more accurate, the same name written two different ways. The first version was "Mrs. Harry McWilliams" and the second, "Mrs. Elaine McWilliams." And the figures? "50,000 – 5,000 = 45,000." The pieces were coming together. I shoved the package back in my pocket. I hoped it would never come to that but if Elaine and Harry succeeded in getting my client's name engraved on a slab of granite, that scrap of cardboard might turn into a powerful piece of evidence. Of course, I had no intention of letting that happen which is why I immediately set up a meeting with Ed.

We met at a Burger King restaurant not far from his residence since he'd started to worry that someone might see him coming to my office. He'd been coaching a kids' hockey team earlier in the evening but, in spite of being on an outdoor rink for a couple of hours, there was still little colour in his face. His features were haggard and his skin had a sickly greyish look. The only time he had any life was when he talked about "his" kids.

"They're a great bunch of kids. A little shy on talent maybe but great diggers." He interrupted himself to spoon some sugar into his coffee with a quavering hand. "And it's great to watch them improve, even if it is just a little. In a way, it's like watching them grow." Then he added hastily. "Oh, I love my girls. A man couldn't be blessed with two finer daughters. But I guess deep down, I always wanted a son too and the kids on the team, well, I kinda feel that, in a way, they're all my boys."

For a while, he looked almost happy and I hated to bring him down but I had no choice. I handed him a report of his wife's escapades of the night before. Instead of reading it, he started stirring his coffee fiercely, trying to delay the inevitable. He took a deep, steadying breath before starting to read. A couple of times, he stopped and looked at me questioningly but he didn't say a word until he finished the whole thing and even then, it was a while before he said, half to himself: "She called and said she was at Lil's. Said it was snowing so hard she figured she might as well spend the night." Then he looked at me sharply. "That match could've fallen out and been replaced, couldn't it?"

"Sure, and Raquel Welch could come down my chimney in a Santa Claus suit but it's not very likely."

You see, like I said, I'd placed a match between the door and the jamb at Harry McWilliams' apartment and when I went back at about six a.m., it was still there. That meant just one thing: Elaine Gant had spent the night with the third member of a love triangle that had some sharp and dangerous edges.

"Maybe she. . . ." His voice faltered as he struggled to come up with an alternate explanation. "Could she have gone out another way?"

"One way in and one way out."

"Maybe Lil was there. Maybe this McWilliams is Lil's boyfriend and Elaine was just . . . just. . . ." He didn't have enough conviction to finish the sentence but he kept on grasping for non-existent straws – some not-too-transparent lies he could tell himself.

"I called Lil at about two and she said Elaine was sleeping and she didn't want to wake her up."

I didn't say anything while he kept throwing out possibilities the way a poker player tosses away cards when he's trying to fill a winning hand.

"Maybe you were following the wrong woman. Those pictures I gave you of Elaine aren't that good. In one of them, she's standing in the shadows – they come right down over her face – and in that other one, her hair was a lot lighter than it is now."

By then I was getting tired of his self-imposed con job and I said abruptly: "If I were you, I'd get myself a good lawyer."

If he heard me, he didn't show it. He seemed to be looking right past me and his voice sounded like it was coming from a long way off.

"I don't know if I told you but I come from a small family – in fact, I was an only child."

"Is that right?" I said, trying to appear interested and wondering where the hell he was heading.

"Maybe that's why I always wanted a family of my own – y'know, to have people around that care about you. When Dianne came along and then Joanne, well, I was the happiest man in the world. They're beautiful girls too – a man couldn't ask for a finer pair of daughters. Smart and well-liked too. Always got friends over."

He was silent for a moment, staring at the ceiling. Behind the counter, a tired-looking waitress was clattering dishes into a sink. The place was empty except for ourselves and an off-duty bus driver who was taking tentative sips of a steaming cup of coffee. I don't know who was more surprised – the waitress, the bus driver, or me – when Ed slammed his fist down on the table. It was like a cannonshot, a magnet of sound that pulled every eye in the place toward us.

"Take it easy, Ed," I said, wanting to be any place but there.

"You work your ass off to make something – something to last, something to make it all worthwhile – and then, all of a sudden you find out you haven't got a thing, not one goddamn thing!"

His raised voice insured us of an audience. The waitress had stopped washing her dishes, the bus driver was letting his coffee get cold, and a short-order cook had come out of a back room where he was doing whatever short-order cooks do when they're not cranking out burgers and fries.

"Listen, Ed," I soothed, "you've got a lot. You've got a couple of great daughters and things like this – this problem with your wife – well, they happen all the time, believe me. It's my business to know."

He shook his head slowly, in a long, looping arc. "I don't know. I don't know."

I had no idea what it was he didn't know but I was afraid to ask for fear of setting him off again. We left a couple of minutes later and he walked me over to my car where he paid me off and thanked me for my services. After shaking hands, I told him I could give him the names of a couple of good divorce lawyers if he wanted them. He said he'd let me know then turned and walked slowly away. I sat there for a couple of minutes, feeling a little troubled – not just about him but the case itself and that's a cardinal sin for a private eye because, like I said before, getting emotionally involved is something to avoid at all costs.

You see, I had mixed feelings about the whole thing. I knew I'd driven the final nail into the coffin of his marriage but on the other side of the ledger, I just might've saved something even more important – Ed Gant's life. Now ordinarily, that would've been a pretty good tradeoff but in Gant's case, I wasn't all that sure because it just might be that without his wife – without the dream of home and family he'd nurtured for so long – what I was trying to preserve no longer meant a damn thing to him.

You see, while Gant had shown a fanatical interest in whether his wife was screwing around, he'd just skimmed over those parts of the report that touched on what I thought was a conspiracy to knock him off. Maybe he was just whistling past the graveyard but it's more likely he was such a nice, inoffensive guy that he couldn't conceive of anyone wanting to take his life. That's what scared me because I'd hoped he'd get his ass in gear and cut his old lady loose right away – before deadly plans flowered into fatal acts. Now, you may ask, if I was so concerned, why didn't I go to the police myself?

Two reasons: first, I didn't really have all that much to go on in terms of hard evidence and I was afraid the cops might laugh me right out of the station. And, second – and this was the most important factor – whatever I'd found out – everything in my reports on the case – belonged to Ed Gant. He'd paid for it and it was his sole property so there was no way I could breach client-investigator confidentiality without his sayso – even if there might be a life in the balance. But when I saw him again some three months later, I began to wonder if I'd made the right decision in going by the book.

It was the end of March. A three-month build-up of ice and snow was softening into grey slush and there was a rumor spring might hit Winnipeg sometime before June. It was like seeing a ghost when Ed Gant dropped into my office – and it wasn't just his appearance although, God knows, he'd gone downhill since I'd seen him last. Maybe it was because, considering the circumstances, I'd had my doubts whether I'd ever see him alive again. But there he was alive and in almost-living colour. And, after hearing that he and Elaine were still together, I started to think I might've been wrong and that my conspiracy theory had been just a product of an overactive imagination. My sense of relief was short-lived though because right about then, I noticed a bulge in the front of his topcoat, the right sleeve of which was hanging empty. When he unbuttoned his coat and sat down, I found out why. His arm was in a cast from his fingertips almost to his shoulder and suspended from a sling.

"Christ, what happened to you?"

"An accident. Got hit by a car." He gave his familiar apologetic smile. "Could've been worse," he said, fingering the cast. "It just grazed me and knocked me down. Aside from a few scrapes and bruises, this flipper's the only damage."

My mind galloped ahead of my question. "How did it happen?"

He stroked his chin thoughtfully. "I don't really know. I was walking back home from the community club after practice – you remember, I told you I coach the pee-wees – when this car came out of nowhere. The headlights were right in my face, blinding me. I jumped back more out of reflex than anything else and managed to get out of the way." He smiled ruefully at the trussed-up wing. "At least most of me did. The guy must have been drunk, driving live that. He couldn't have helped but see me. I mean, there was a lamp-post right there."

"Did you get a look at him?" From out of nowhere, Emil Prinzek's menacing face flashed in my mind.

"No. Like I said, the lights blinded me for a while and by the time I got up, he was long gone."

"Then you don't even know for sure it was a 'he.'"

"No, I guess you're right. I don't."

"Did you report it to the police?"

"Oh yes but they didn't think there was much chance of making an arrest. There wouldn't have been any damage to the car."

As it turned out, he hadn't told the police about Elaine, Harry, and Prinzek and, in spite of my trying to convince him that his accident might've been anything but that, he didn't seem to want to do anything about it. What he did want was for me to put Elaine under surveillance again.

"Sure I can do that. No problem. But what's the point? We had her dead to rights the last time and you didn't follow through."

"I just wasn't sure in my own mind," he said. "I've got to be sure – there's so much at stake. One way or the other, I've got to be a hundred percent sure. I can't take a chance on making a mistake. I have to think of the girls. They're the ones who'll be hurt the most."

Looking at him, I doubted that. They'd have to go a long way to feel the pain he'd kept hidden for so long. He leaned forward, almost begging for reassurance. "You don't think they'll blame me, do you?"

The next afternoon, for the third time, I was back on a case that I'd hoped I'd seen the last of. Why did I take it then? Well, aside from the obvious reason, meaning dollars, there was still that suspicion gnawing away at me. Gant had refused to go to the police even after I'd told him I thought his so-called accident was part and parcel of a conspiracy to take his life. He'd scoffed at the idea but I felt that deep down he knew I was right and that he was just trying to rationalize his refusal to let the cops in on the caper and let *them* decide if there was anything to it.

The way I saw it, the quicker I got the goods on Elaine, the quicker Ed could cut her loose, and the quicker he got rid of his would-be widow, the greater his chances of avoiding another "accident." So, in a way, I thought of my renewed investigation as a kind of race; one that I – and more, particularly, Ed – couldn't afford to lose.

By then, at least I knew all of Elaine Gant's watering holes by heart and tracking her down was a piece of cake. This time, I found her in the Marlborough, a once-elegant downtown hotel that had been allowed to go to seed. A new wing had recently been added and with the two contrasting architectural styles side-by-side, the place reminded me of one of those pictures you see on the social pages of the newspapers – those group shots of different generations of the same family. The old wing of the hotel was like the family patriarch: wrinkled, liver-spotted, but dignified, while the new section was akin to the third generation kid in his twenties whose cocky smile is stuck in the middle of a face that doesn't look as though it's been lived in yet.

When I came in, she was sitting at a table with a middle-aged guy whom I hadn't seen before. I wondered if she'd broken up with McWilliams but I didn't have to wonder long because just then, Harry himself showed up and there was blood in his eye. He started chewing out Elaine and then turned his anger on the poor stiff she was sitting with. He was a mousey little guy who looked as if he'd have to use both hands to hoist a soup-spoon and, when Harry lit into him, he lost no time in grabbing his coat and heading for the nearest exit.

After he left, Elaine and Harry exchanged some heated words and then, a couple of minutes later, they were all lovey-dovey again, toasting each other with double ryes. I sat down a couple of tables away and for the next couple of hours, I nursed my drinks while keeping them under surveillance. Finally, after quite a while had passed and they had taken on a pretty good load, they left the hotel and got into Harry's car. I lost them in traffic and made a bee-line for Harry's place, hoping that was where they were going. I struck it lucky. The lights were on in his apartment and Harry's car was parked in his stall. Ed Gant had requested that I call him the minute it looked like something spicy might be taking place. I made the call at about seven-thirty p.m.

"I'll be right down," he said.

"I don't think that's a very good idea, Ed. It'd be better. . . ." The next second, I was giving my advice to a dial tone.

He showed up about twenty minutes later and I immediately tried to talk him into going back home but it was no dice.

"She's with him?"

"Yes."

"Are you sure?"

"Positive."

"There's no way you could've made a mistake? You're sure it's Elaine?"

I led him over to my car which was parked directly across the street from the building. Once we were inside, I took my binoculars out of the glove compartment and handed them to him.

"See that picture window to the right, up there on the second floor? That's his living room." I tapped the binoculars. "Go ahead. Take a look. You might not see anything and then again, you just might."

He looked at the binoculars warily as though trying to decide if they could be trusted, then, in one quick, decisive motion, he lifted them to his eyes and trained them on the rectangle of light. The curtains hadn't been drawn and even without the field glasses, I could see figures passing in front of the window. One had stopped and was standing almost in dead centre. I saw Ed Gant stiffen.

"It's her." His voice quavered but not half as much as his hands. Instinctively, I reached out to grab the glasses, expecting them to fall from his hands at any moment. But he kept holding onto them, staring at the window like a morbid voyeur peeping in at his own funeral. Then the single silhouette grew into two. Two figures closely entwined. That was when he finally surrendered the binoculars and buried his face in his hands. His shoulders heaved and his muffled sobs filled the whole car.

I grabbed the field glasses and aimed them at the window. They were still there, Elaine and Harry, clinging to each other in a boozy embrace, his mouth hungrily seeking hers. She was wearing just a bra and a pair of panties, the inside of which Harry was starting to explore when I lowered the glasses. Poor Ed still had his face cupped in his hands and he repeated over and over in a choked voice: "How could she do this to us?"

It was a good twenty minutes before he settled down enough to be able to drive. By then, all the lights in McWilliams' place had been doused. I told Gant that if he wanted I could make him an appointment with a lawyer for the following day. He muttered something about it not being necessary then got out and went over to his own car. And that was the last time I saw Edward Gant . . . alive.

He phoned me the next afternoon and sounded so calm and composed that I figured he'd finally got his act together and decided to do something about Elaine's playing him for a sucker. And, as it turned out, I was right but not in the way I thought.

"I put a cheque in the mail this morning to settle your account," he said, "and I want to tell you that I appreciate all of your help and patience." He hesitated and I heard a deep intake of breath. "There's one last thing. I don't want to trouble you but there's really no one else I can ask. . . ."

"Shoot."

"Well, I was wondering if you could see that the police got here before . . . before my girls come home from school. I'd call them myself but they might think it's some kind of joke and not do anything."

"What the hell do you want with. . . ." He didn't even let me finish the question.

"You once said that you knew some policemen. I'm sure they'd listen to you if you told them to come over here. Dianne and Joanne get home at about 4:30. If the police come over right away, they'll have plenty of time to do what they have to."

"Ed, listen to me," I pleaded, trying to keep him talking, sensing and fearing he was about to do something no clock could turn back.

"I've got to go now. Thanks again for everything."

As soon as he broke the connection, I dialed the police, threw on my coat, and charged out of my office. I wasted little time getting to Gant's place but even that was too much. His car was in the driveway. I knocked at the front door, not really expecting an answer but holding my breath just the same. Nothing. I headed to the back of the well-kept bungalow, trying to run on legs that'd suddenly grown rubbery. Just then a cruiser car pulled up and I waved the officers over. After filling them in on who I was and what I suspected, I stood aside while one of the constables knocked. When there was no answer, he tried the door. It swung open at his touch. Both officers called out, identifying themselves and, failing to get a response, they stepped inside with me following close behind. While I accompanied one of the constables on a search of the main floor, the other one checked out the basement.

"Down here! Hurry up! He's down here!" We took the steps two at a time, reaching the basement before the last echo of his shout had died.

The officer had his arms around Edward Gant's thighs, hoisting him up, trying to take the weight off the noose that was looped around his throat. Without wasting a second, his partner grabbed a chair that had been lying on its back a couple of feet to the left of Ed Gant's dangling legs. Hopping up on it, he worked frantically, prying at the slip-knot in a noose fashioned from a long electrical cord. Anchored to an overhead beam, the cord had carved an angry red fissure into Gant's neck.

While the two officers cursed and sweated, I stood there like a goddamn statue unable to take my eyes off Gant's face. His eyes were swollen, glassy, and seemed to be staring right at me and his face was frozen with anguish. It was as though all the pain that'd been building up inside him for so long had finally erupted, displaying his inner torment for all to see.

They got him down in less than a minute but it was already a lifetime too late. Mouth-to-mouth resuscitation and heart massage were administered by the ambulance attendants who were on the scene by the time the officers laid Gant on the tile floor of his utility room. I could see from the attendants' expressions that they thought it was a lost cause but that didn't stop them from giving it their best shot. And while they worked over Ed, I kept looking at my watch, hoping his girls wouldn't show up early and see their father all sprawled out and horrible-looking. The poor bastard. With that broken arm of his, even if he'd changed his mind after kicking the chair from under himself and feeling the noose tighten, he wouldn't have been able to do a damn thing to save himself. Finally, the attendants threw in the towel and it was only then that we noticed the note pinned to his chest.

While the attendants loaded the body into the ambulance, the cops studied the scrap of paper then passed it to me. It was addressed to Elaine and read:

"I know you were counting on the insurance money but I understand they don't pay off on suicides. I would've taken my life in some way that would've looked like an accident if I thought the girls would benefit but I knew you'd only end up giving the money to your boyfriend. That's why I chose this way. Kiss the girls for me and ask them to forgive me for taking the easy way out." It was signed: "Your Loving Husband."

The easy way out. If that was the easy way, I'd hate to see a difficult one. But I guess for him, even death was preferable to facing life knowing that the one he loved was playing him for a fool. And the final blow must've been the realization that Elaine hated him so much she not only wanted him dead but was willing to take a hand in arranging it.

I guess that's what bothered me the most because if that was the final blow, I'd had a helluva lot to do with delivering it. He might never have known if it hadn't been for me. If I'd kept it to myself, he might be alive today. If. Yeah, if wishes were horses, then beggars would ride. But they aren't and they don't. And people still keep killing each other and themselves a day at a time or all at once. And I make a living watching them do it.

TWO

Fairy Tail

Now, MOST people think a private eye's best friend is his automatic but guns are probably the least necessary tools of an investigator's trade. The only time I carry one is when I act as a body guard for jewellery company couriers who need armed protection when they transport high-value items. It's a good thing too because, to tell the truth, I'm not that good a shot with a handgun and, besides, during the war I saw first-hand the damage a lousy little slug of lead could cause and I wouldn't wish it on anyone – well, almost anyone.

There was at least one other time that I had to pack a piece though and it haunts me to this day, in spite of the fact that, financially, I came out smelling like a whole bouquet of roses. But there was a lot more to it than just money.

Just money. I sure wasn't downplaying the importance of the green stuff on this one particular day in the mid-sixties when I went over my books and found the debits leading the credits by a good length-and-a-half. Right about then, the market for private eyes was anything but bullish and, for the first time, I was genuinely worried that I wouldn't be able to keep my business afloat.

But just when things appear the darkest, it seems a little ray of hope shines through to con you into thinking that life really is worth living. And, one morning, in the early fall of 1967, one lit up the doorway of my office.

He was tall, slim, with thinning blond hair combed straight back. I would have guessed him to be in his late thirties but it was hard to tell because he had a boyish face that belied the loose folds of skin under his blue eyes. Nattily attired in a navy blazer and grey slacks, he carried himself with a confidence that bordered on arrogance.

He looked familiar but it wasn't until he introduced himself that I placed him. Robert Van Helton was a very prominent man in Winnipeg business and social circles. A director of a number of prestigious companies, he was also chairman of a well-known charity and served on the executive of a variety of fraternal organizations. His was old money. The roots of the family fortune were planted in the days of the Red River fur trade and the subsequent tree was large enough to buy status and respect – not to mention a ritzy mansion and a chauffeur-driven Rolls. Even though I've always tried to treat all of my clients the same regardless of their social standing, I have to admit I turned on more than my usual amount of charm.

"Have a seat, sir. Would you care for a coffee?"

"I think not."

He had a clipped, supercilious manner of speech, the kind affected by a lot of Americans and Canadians who, having spent some time abroad, start to think of their own countries as somehow beneath them.

"What can I do for you, Mr. Van Helton?"

"I'd like you to locate someone for me, if you could be so kind."

He crossed his legs carefully, making sure the razor-sharp creases in his flannel slacks stayed that way. I flipped open my note-pad, ready to take down any pertinent data when he waggled a reproving forefinger.

"No notes. There must be no record of our conversation. As far as you're concerned, I have never been here and you have never seen me."

"My notes are completely confidential, sir," I said. "No

one sees them but me and I keep them locked in my safe.
There's no possibility your privacy will be breached."

That still wasn't good enough for him.

"No notes," he said, his tone convincing me that it was
a closed subject.

"O.K., no notes. But if you retain me, I'm sure you'll
want progress reports . . . won't you?"

"We shall see about that in due course."

Then, without any prompting, he laid his story on me
and it didn't take a bulb to light up over my head to make
me realize why he was so hung up on confidentiality. You
see, one of Winnipeg's perennial contenders for the city's
Citizen-of-the-Year award was being blackmailed. He
didn't use the term though. Oh no, he was much too
refined and sensitive to use such a crude word. The way he
put it was:

"Some. . . ." His face clouded as he searched for the
right word. "*Persons* have intimated that my reputation
will be compromised unless I provide them with substan-
tial financial considerations."

His inflated rhetoric was getting under my skin but I
tried to hide my annoyance.

"Are you saying somebody's trying to extort money
from you?"

"No," he said crisply, "I am decidedly not saying that.
And you are not to say that either. To me or anyone else."

O.K., you smug bastard, I said to myself, if that's the
way you want to play it, go ahead but you've already let
the cat out of the bag. I had the upper hand regardless of
how superior he considered himself.

"Alright, sir. I won't say that but I would like to hear
what *you* have to say."

It was quite a story. And if it got out, it would've done
more than compromise his reputation. It would've pretty
well destroyed it and him. You see, Van Helton had everything a man could ask for: wealth, status, an attractive,
intelligent wife, and two healthy children. But he also had
something that most men wouldn't ask for: a penchant for

jumping in the sack with members of his own sex – the younger the better.

He was still in the closet though. So far in that almost everyone, including his family, was in the dark. It turned out there were others who weren't though. Those who cruised the city's gay subculture knew Robert Van Helton very well indeed. In their vernacular, he was a chicken hawk, an older gay who preyed upon young male flesh. He was something else alright, coming on like the All-Canadian captain of industry to the straight world and studying Greek culture with any punk who needed a few bucks and didn't care which orifice he had to use to get it.

Like a number of other homosexual predators in the city, Van Helton made a lot of his pick-ups during evening visits to the grounds of the provincial legislature which slope up from the north side of the Assiniboine River. It's a picturesque spot by day. By night, it's a place where deviant sex is cheap and easy with no questions asked – where orgasms are given and received in the shadows of bushes bordering the river and the front seats of parked cars. C.O.D. or gratis. Furtive satisfaction with no consequences. But that isn't quite the way it turned out for Robert Van Helton. One of his encounters, as it turned out, hadn't been by chance. It'd been a set-up by someone who knew what and who he was and it had very serious consequences. So serious that he had to let me in on the whole story in spite of the fact that he obviously considered me – and probably most other people – his inferior.

What it added up to was this: One night, a month or so back, he'd been cruising the legislative grounds "looking for a friend" and had been approached by "a slim, darkly-attractive" youth who, according to Van Helton, was a spitting image of Sal Mineo. One word led to another which, in turn, led to the kid inviting him up to his place for a drink or whatever.

Shortly after Van Helton was ushered into a small basement apartment, things got in and out of hand and into bed. Robert and the kid, who said his name was Kerry

Alden, were in the buff with their limbs twined around
each other when Van Helton was suddenly blinded by a
burst of light – then another. Three more flash bulbs went
off before he had the presence of mind to avert his face
and grab for his clothes – much too late, of course. Counting the naked bodies of Robert and his erstwhile lover,
that added up to seven exposures and big trouble for one
of Winnipeg's leading citizens.

Before he'd gotten half-way through the story, I needed
a drink real bad. It wasn't that I was thirsty – more like I
needed something to wash the bad taste from my mouth.
It's not that I have anything against homosexuals or feel
they shouldn't have the right to love each other up but the
way the whole thing is promoted and hyped, it's getting so
a guy starts to feel there's something wrong with him if he
likes girls. Besides, if God wanted men to screw each
other, he would've created Adam and Bruce.

I kept my feelings to myself though because, what the
hell, there might be a good buck on the line. Still, I didn't
see what I could do for the guy and I didn't want to waste
his time or mine, so I came right out and told him:

"Mr. Van Helton, this is a very serious matter and, to
my mind, the only ones who can assist you are the police.
Now, I know a number of the senior men there and I can
assure you they'll be very discreet."

"Oh, I'm sure they will," he smirked, "after all, policemen are renowned for their sensitivity toward gays, aren't
they?"

He pursed his lips primly and shook his head.

"If the police get involved, there will be charges, a court
case. A man in my position makes a lot of enemies – there
are so many envious people in this world – and they'd just
love to see my . . . indiscretion exposed. The muckrakers
would be even worse. They'd positively salivate over the
story. Do you think it would bother them if it destroyed
me and my family? Not a bit. Well, that is something I can
well do without and I intend to. But I can also . . ." his

eyes narrowed and his voice dripped venom ". . . do without paying for the silence of human garbage."

"Just when did they make their first demand?"

"A few days after the . . . incident."

"And did you pay them?"

He nodded.

"How much?"

"A thousand dollars." Then, as an afterthought. "In small, used, bills. Those were my instructions."

"How were they delivered?"

"He phoned. Not Kerry. The other one – the one with the camera. He said I should call him Gypsy. I don't know what his real name is."

"How did you make the drop?"

"Drop?"

"The pay-off. How did you get the money to them?"

"They didn't want me to come to their place. They told me to put it in a locker at the bus depot and tape the key under the lid of one of the toilet tanks. I followed their instructions and a couple of days later, I got one of the photos in the mail."

Pretty elaborate. I wondered if the punks who were putting the squeeze on Van Helton had been watching too much TV.

"Do you remember where they live? The address?"

"They're not there anymore," he frowned. "I went back there the day after to warn them. . ." his voice dropped as, for the first time, his bravado slipped, ". . . to plead with them not to do anything thoughtless. But they'd left already. The suite was vacant. You can't imagine how frustrated and desperate I felt, not knowing where they were and what they might do. It was almost a relief when their call came even though I knew it was the beginning of a nightmare."

You didn't have to be psychic to know he'd heard from them again. A couple of weeks after he made the first drop, he got another call. This time it was two thousand and Van Helton had delivered the pay-off to the railway station, once again depositing it in a locker and leaving the key in a designated spot. And a couple of days later, picture number two showed up in the mail. Two down and three to go. Or maybe a lot more because, for all we knew, they could have run off lots of negatives.

As expected, there was a subsequent call and, predictably, the ante was raised once again. The day before Van Helton came to see me, the guy who called himself Gypsy demanded five thousand dollars and that was when my would-be client realized they'd never stop bleeding him.

He finished his story and sat there, looking at me expectantly. I didn't know what to say, mainly because I didn't know whether I wanted anything to do with the case at any price. As far as I'm concerned, blackmail is one of the lowest forms of crime, down there with child-molesting, and even though he was an arrogant s.o.b., I sympathized with him. But extortion is heavy business and by rights, I should have reported it to the police myself. But then there was also the matter of the client's confidentiality which is something I never take lightly. I walked over to the window, weighing the pros and cons and stalling for time. I felt his eyes on me with every step. Since, even in those days, I was middle-aged and more-than-slightly overweight, I comforted myself with the belief that he was more interested in my investigative skills than my ass.

Looking down at the traffic darting from one stoplight to another, I was pondering the options for the umpteenth time when his voice slashed through my deliberations like a straight razor.

"What seems to be the difficulty, Mr. Manweiler? Do you find this matter too distasteful for your sensibilities?"

"Not at all, Mr. Van Helton," I blurted. "In my job, I live with crap. Whether it's yours or someone else's makes no difference to me. It all smells the same."

He grimaced.

"Must you be so . . . so . . . graphic?"

"That's my style," I shrugged. "But for the time being, suppose we leave my shortcomings alone and concentrate on . . ." I was about to say "yours" but caught myself and finished with ". . . the matter at hand."

"Well?"

"Well what? Just what do you want me to do?"

His voice was taut as a bow string.

"I want you to find those bastards. I want you to find them and make them stop tormenting me."

"Oh, sure," I said breezily. "No problem. I'll just let them know you're upset by their behaviour and ask them if they'd mind blackmailing someone else."

"I told you not to use that word," he hissed.

"I know you did. You told me a lot of things but what you didn't tell me was how I'm supposed to get your pals to back off, assuming, of course, that I'm able to track them down."

"I'll leave that to you, Mr. Private Detective. I don't care what you have to do to get them out of my life. Just do it." He smiled mockingly. "And just so you'll have sufficient incentive, I will pay you five thousand dollars if you bring this assignment to a satisfactory conclusion."

"Five thousand?"

"Get them to leave me alone and it's yours."

Five grand was a lot of money in those days, when a dollar was still worth about ninety cents. Not only did I jump at the bait, I just about swallowed the rod and reel as well. It would be a gamble but at least the stakes were high enough to make it interesting.

Time wasn't on my side though. Usually, I like to plan a job as complex as this one but that was out of the question since I had to start the assignment immediately if not sooner. You see, Van Helton was scheduled to make the five-thousand-dollar drop that very night which meant that to pick up his blackmailers' trail, I'd have to stake out the payoff site. And then? I still wasn't quite sure. All the options had their own personal pitfalls, including the one I finally selected, more out of desperation than anything else.

Maybe it was the vision of dollar signs dancing in my

head or just the challenge of pulling the thing off. I didn't
know – still don't – but finally, I convinced myself that the
end justified the means and jumped into one of the diciest
propositions I've ever been involved in, with my eyes wide
open. A proposition that involved me playing the role of a
hit man imported from the East to take care of Van Helton's limpwristed leeches. Sound far out? It did to me too,
even while I rehearsed all that afternoon with one of my
agents whom I'd picked to play the part of my partner in
crime.

Slope-shouldered, with a barrel chest and large meaty
hands, Fred Karpo didn't look like he'd need a piece to
snuff somebody. And that craggy face of his gave you the
feeling he was the kind of guy who'd whistle while he
worked someone over. That map was really the icing on
the cake. Swarthy and beetle-browed, he had a jutting,
gun-metal chin that always looked as though it sported a
day's growth. His eyes were probably his most menacing
feature though. Habitually slitted and glinting, they
looked like they were lying in wait behind his heavy lids. I
don't think I saw them blink more than half a dozen times
in the more than two years he worked for me.

The only thing was that while Karpo looked like a
gorilla, underneath, he had all the toughness of a hot
fudge sundae. And those eyes of his? They were so narrowed and mean looking because the poor bugger was so
nearsighted he could barely see without squinting. Some
heavy. I nicknamed him "The Magician" because whenever it looked like there was going to be trouble, he made
himself disappear.

Well, at least we'd look the part. We even decked ourselves out in what we thought was the latest style for
mobsters: grey suits with dark shirts and narrow ties and
wide-brimmed fedoras pulled low over our foreheads.
And to top it off, I strapped on a shoulder holster that I
borrowed from a pal of mine, making sure that my gun
was empty.

I really had no idea what kind of guys we were dealing

with and even though I had no intention of flashing the weapon, I figured it wouldn't hurt to sort of accidentally on purpose arrange for them to see it, just to show them we meant business.

This time, the drop was to be made at the airport. The five grand was to be placed in a flight bag and left under the bench nearest the Tilden Car Rental booth at exactly 9:45 p.m. I didn't much care for the arrangement because there was always the chance that someone other than the extortionist could take off with it. But I guess the black-mailers were getting tired of the locker routine and wanted to try something different.

Van Helton showed up at 9:40, trying so hard to avoid looking suspicious that he stood out like a sore thumb. He was carrying a small blue flight bag and looked over his shoulder so many times you'd have thought he was check-ing his coat collar for dandruff.

I leaned against the end of the Tilden counter and watched him out of the corner of my eye. At 9:45 on the nose, he got up and walked briskly out of the terminal. He was empty-handed. The drop had been made. While all this was going on, my partner, Fred, was parked in the loading zone in front, making like he was there to pick up a deplaning passenger.

Their timing was good, I'll say that for them. At 9:49, a guy matching the description Van Helton had given me of Kerry Alden brushed past me. Slim, fine-featured, with a shock of brown, wavy hair, he was dressed in a pair of tight black slacks and a waist-length, fashionable-looking brown leather jacket. Without stopping, he reached down and plucked the flight bag in a single motion. As he headed for the exit, he looked back anxiously a couple of times. He didn't look like a pro, that's for sure. I followed him onto the sidewalk and gave the high sign to Fred. Alden got into the passenger side of an idling sedan and before the vehicle could pull away, I jumped into the back and snarled at the driver: "Get moving. Both of you keep looking straight ahead and nobody'll get hurt."

Alden and his buddy froze in their seats and the driver was so shook up he almost stalled the car when he took off. I shot a quick backward glance. Fred was right behind us and, so far, at least, everything was going like clockwork. The driver, a blond, curly-headed kid in his mid-twenties, guided the car through the airport grounds and out the main exit.

"Wha –"

"Don't talk. Just drive," I ordered.

I directed him onto a highway leading north then, a couple of miles later, had him turn onto a road that led past a community college and a number of industrial buildings. At night, it was lightly travelled and the glow from the streetlights barely made a dent in the surrounding darkness.

"Slow down. O.K., now turn into that driveway up ahead on your right."

The vehicle slowed, as the driver glanced to the right, then pulled to a shuddering halt.

"There? You want me to go in there?" he asked incredulously.

He started to turn around then thought better of it, saying through gritted teeth: "But that's a cemetery. Why do you want to go in there?"

I didn't answer, letting his imagination do my dirty work. As scared as he was, he certainly hadn't lost his powers of perception because that was exactly what we were in front of: the Brookside Cemetery, a sprawling, city-owned graveyard which at 10:00 p.m. was as quiet and empty as one would've expected. You couldn't have come up with a better setting for act two of my little scenario.

As we passed between the white stone pillars at the entrance, I prayed that Fred remembered his lines and wouldn't screw up the deal. That was only a part of the prayer though. The rest was a plea that no one wandered in on us because, as good a con man as I am, if a watchman or a cop crashed the party, there was no goddamn way I could even come close to bailing us out of that caper and I had visions of my investigator's license sprouting wings and taking off for parts unknown.

"Take it easy," I cautioned, feeling the wheels stray onto the gravel shoulder.

All we needed was for him to lose control and send the car careening into a maze of monuments.

"O.K., pull over," I commanded.

We were in the outermost section of the cemetery. To the north and west lay uncultivated farm land and we were a good half mile from the main road. The only sound was from a massed choir of frogs ribitting from a nearby creek. I made the guy behind the wheel douse the lights right away. Fred eased up behind us and did the same. There was a full moon shimmering down, giving everything a luminous quality. In the older section, the towering trees and dense decorative shrubbery supplied a parklike atmosphere but where we were, there was nothing but sterile rows of headstones and beyond them, vacant tracts that would someday be filled with a contingent of dearly beloveds.

"Out!"

The pair exchanged frightened glances and did as they were told. By this time, Fred had joined us and I almost dropped my load when I saw that the crazy bugger was packing a piece. Not a real one, mind you. It was just one of those compressed-air target pistols but from a distance, it looked like the real McCoy. I reminded myself to give him shit later on. It had the desired effect though. When the two punks spotted it, I thought they were going to faint.

"Is your name Gypsy?" I asked the driver.

He nodded.

"I can't hear you," I snapped.

"Y-y-y-e-e-e-s-s-s," he said tremulously.

"Well, Gypsy, you're in a whole lot of trouble and so's your pal, Kerry." I turned to the other punk. "That is your name, isn't it? Kerry Alden?"

He started to nod, then piped clearly: "Yes sir, that's right." Then without missing a beat, asked: "Are you guys police officers?"

"Did you hear that," I chuckled, turning toward Fred, "this punk wants to know if we're cops."

Fred snickered and I turned back to Alden, spooning out some sarcasm: "Now, why would you get an idea like that?" I pulled my jacket open, revealing the holster. "Could it be because of this? Well, let me tell you sonny, bulls ain't the only ones that carry pieces." I patted the gun lovingly. "Without this baby, I'd be like a plumber without a wrench."

Beside me, Fred was warming to his role.

"C'mon," he snarled, "let's get it over with."

"Who's calling the shots around here, you or me?"

"You are," he said glumly, "but the flight leaves first thing in the morning and I want to get some shut-eye."

"Hear that," I said to Gypsy and Kerry. "My partner's in a hurry."

The Alden kid finally got up enough nerve to ask: "What's this all about? Who are you guys? What do you want with us?"

"What do we want with you?" I sneered. "The same thing you wanted with Van Helton. You wanted to bleed *him* and, now, we're going to bleed *you*."

They started to shake and blubber, pleading for their lives and saying that it was all a mistake and that they didn't know any Van Helton.

"And I guess you picked up that flight bag by mistake," I jeered.

Fred butted in on cue, saying: "Christ, let's can the talk and finish the job."

"Maybe you're right," I said. "These punks ain't worth wastin' time over."

I gave Gypsy a shove and herded him and his buddy toward a newly-excavated grave. The cloying scent of freshly-turned earth rose from the mound beside it.

"Boys," I intoned, "meet your new home."

With that, Alden dropped to his knees, wringing his hands and pleading: "No, please don't! Please! We weren't going to bother him again. This was gonna be the last time. Honest! You've got to believe me!"

"I've only gotta believe one thing, punk and it's that I'm getting paid to do a job and you're it. You ladies sure picked the wrong guy to lean on but I guess you had no way of knowing Van Helton had good connections with the syndicate."

His pal, Gypsy, stood there petrified, his jaw hanging open and his fear-stricken eyes alternating between Fred's air pistol and the bulge under my jacket. But not for long. With an explosion of desperate energy, he took off like a sprinter leaving the starting blocks. Telling Fred to watch Alden, I bolted after him, knowing that if he made it to the road, we were all in big trouble.

I never ran so fast in my life but the kid was whippet-swift and it was all I could do to keep him in sight. Darting in and out of the rows of headstones, he was like a flitting shadow. My chest was heaving and I could hardly feel my legs. It was all over. I could already see the five grand waving bye-bye and the cops asking some very embarrassing questions. He was half-way to the main entrance. There were headlights on the road and he'd be able to flag down a ride. I was ready to pull up and go back and tip Fred off so we could get the hell out of there when I finally got a break.

Gypsy, still running full-out, glanced back over his shoulder to see if I was picking up ground, and ran smack into a large granite cross. The monument hit him chest high, knocking the wind out of him and when I reached him, he was hunched over, holding his stomach, and gasping for air. I had to half-carry him back to where Fred still had the drop on Kerry Alden. Gypsy flopped on the ground next to his partner, whimpering like a whipped dog.

"Let me go, please. It was Kerry's idea. I didn't want to do it. He made me."

"My idea?" Alden flared. "You're the one who said he had mountains of money! You're the one who said he'd be too scared to go to the police!"

They'd been reduced to quivering lumps of meat who'd sell out each other or anyone else for a chance at the brass ring of survival. The stage was set for act three.

I checked Fred who was prodding Gypsy with the barrel of the pellet gun.

"Hold on a sec."

"What for? Let's get it over with. If these bastards keep crying their fruity little eyes out, we're all liable to float away."

"Yeah, well just listen for a minute. If we knock them off, the cops'll come nosing around their place and chances are they'll come up with the blackmail pics."

"So?"

"So there's a tie-in with Mr. V. and, through him, to us."

"Yeah," Fred mused, stroking his lantern chin contemplatively. "I never thought of that. So what do we do?"

"That depends on our friends here." I nudged Gypsy with the toe of my shoe. "Whattaya think, punk? Do ya wanna go on breathin'?"

His hands dropped from his tear-stained face.

"Oh yes. Please. Please."

And his pal chimed in with: "I'll do anything. Anything. Just let me live."

"O.K., get up," I said brusquely.

On the way to their place, I was once again in the back seat of their car, with Fred bringing up the rear.

"O.K., girls," I said, "now what are we going to do when we get there?"

Alden recited eagerly.

"We're going to give you the photographs and all the money we've got left."

"And?"

"And we're going to get out of town."

"And you're going to dummy up about everything that happened tonight, is that right?"

"That's right," they quavered in unison.

I heaved a sigh of relief. It looked like it was going to work out. By this time, I was sorry I'd ever laid eyes on Van Helton and these two terrified faggots. Even though I was performing a worthwhile service in getting a couple of blackmailers off the back of their victim, I'd taken the case against my better judgement. I never should have let my money problems elbow my ethics aside and convince me that the end justified the means. Gypsy could've been seriously hurt when he smashed into that grave marker and it would've been on my conscience. Never again, I told myself. Never again. And I've kept my word, too, although that's at least partly due to what happened later on in this case.

After picking up the remainder of the very candid shots of Robert Van Helton, I once again advised Gypsy and Kerry to make themselves scarce for at least the next decade and they affirmed that they would. I even gave them a couple of hundred bucks out of what was left of their stash for travelling money. They'd blown about half of the original pay-off money but I was still able to retrieve the five grand in the flight bag plus another fifteen hundred and I figured that ought to warm my client's profit-oriented heart. As Fred and I were leaving, Kerry Alden promised they'd be out of town within forty-eight hours.

I called Van Helton as soon as I got home and we set up a meeting at his residence for the following morning. It was a massive Tudor mansion, the grey stone softened by a fresco of clinging ivy. When I arrived, the chauffeur was polishing a Rolls Silver Cloud in the driveway. The finish gleamed and threw back a distorted image, the kind you see in a midway funhouse, when I walked by.

Mrs. Van Helton had taken the Jaguar and gone shopping, which was why her husband allowed me to come to his home. A petite Japanese maid in a navy dress and crisp white apron led me up a curving flight of marble steps to his second-floor study. The place was wall-to-wall books, most of them bound in the finest leather. There was a massive stone fireplace against one wall and the room was furnished with highly-polished antiques. Van Helton was seated at a roll-top desk and grunted without looking up when I was announced. Above the desk, on the oak-panelled wall was a collection of scrolls and plaques, all attesting to his service to this or that charity. The maid padded away but it was a good couple of minutes before he turned toward me and, even then, he didn't so much as say "good morning."

"The pictures," he said curtly.

He extended his hand and I gave him the envelope containing the three photos and five negatives I'd obtained from Kerry Alden. He studied them in the light from the desk lamp, seemingly reluctant to give them up. Finally, though, he fanned them like cards, took out a long gold lighter and set them ablaze. Within seconds, they were transformed into a bouquet of twining ribbons of red, blue, and yellow. In a swift motion, he got up, strode over to the fireplace, and tossed the half-consumed prints onto the hearth. He fed the fire with the negatives and the room was laced with an acrid smell. He didn't say a word until the ceremony was over then asked: "Where are they living now?"

I told him, adding: "But they won't be there long. I gave them until the week-end to blow town."

"Fine," he smiled. "That'll be plenty of time."

"For what?"

"For you to pay them another visit?"

"Me? What for?"

"To hurt them the way they hurt me with their vicious greed. The law can't punish *them* without destroying *me* so you'll have to do the job for me."

The upshot was that he wanted me to arrange for Kerry and Gypsy to have an accident – nothing serious, just a couple of broken arms and legs. Well, I told him to stick it in his ear, collected my pay, and stormed out feeling as righteous as a virgin in a whorehouse. The feeling didn't last long though.

A couple of days later, the newspapers carried a story about a young man who had been savagely beaten by some unknown assailants. It turned out he'd been worked over the day after I'd met with Robert Van Helton. The victim of the brutal beating was Kerry Alden and he spent three weeks in the hospital before recovering enough to leave town. I checked with a buddy on the force and learned the kid refused to spill a thing about who did it or why. His pal, Gypsy, had, luckily, been absent and the cops had been unable to find and question him. It was a messy end to a decidedly messy case for everyone except Robert Van Helton who kept his image intact as someone the youth of this country could look up to. And me? I learned a lesson about means and ends that has stayed with me ever since.

THREE

The Girl Who Never Missed Choir Practice

LIKE ANY other business, the private detective field has become pretty competitive over the years and the fact that you don't need a hell of a lot of qualifications to get a license probably accounts for part of it. And that's too bad because for every competent, ethical, private eye, there's a fly-by-night type who'd sell his own mother to make a buck. But, thank God, guys like that never last too long because a private detective's reputation is his most important asset and, as that goes, so goes his clientele.

Like most private investigators, I advertise in the yellow pages and hand out cards to anyone I think might do me some good but you'd be surprised how much business I get just through word of mouth. Like, I may have done a good job for someone and he lets his friends know about it. As a matter of fact, that was how I got hired for one of my more interesting and, in a way, most difficult cases. Not difficult in terms of carrying out the assignment though. No, aside from a couple of dead ends, that was a piece of cake. The problem came later and it made me do a helluva lot of soul-searching about my role as a private snooper.

It began in late August of 1976 and started out, like most of my cases, with a telephone call. The caller had heard about me from a friend who'd retained me to check on pilferage from his lumber yard some years back. I'd managed to nail the thief, who just happened to be his head shipper, and earned the owner's undying admiration as well as a nice bonus, both of which were greatly appreciated. Both the lumber yard owner and the caller lived in a small town in southern Manitoba where the latter had been a minister until recently, when he'd been taken seriously ill and sent to Winnipeg for treatment.

That was why he couldn't come to my office and why, for the first time, I met with a client in a hospital room – a room, which I later found out, was located in a wing reserved for the terminally ill. You see my caller, whom I'll call Reverend Willis Barlow, was dying of cancer and indirectly, that was why he needed my services.

As far as I'm concerned, terminal wards should be fumigated or have really strong air fresheners or something because the smell of death is so thick you can just about slice it. Maybe that's why I get so turned off by them because in the back of my mind, sometimes, I think I might end up in one myself, staring up at people who know I'm drawing my last breath but are trying to pretend I'll be up and about by next week at the latest. Did you ever wonder why it's so hard to look someone in the eye when you know they're dying? I don't know either but that's the way it was when I came to see Reverend Barlow. Of course, his appearance might've had something to do with that because he was no more than a skeleton by then, a skeleton kept alive by pills and tubes shoved into him when it looked like he might cop out and commit the unpardonable sin of dying. He was only a little more than fifty but looked a helluva lot older, with his skin a sickly white, tinged with blue where his veins stood out.

There was a nurse flitting around trying not to appear as nosy as she actually was, while I talked to the poor bugger. If she thought she was going to hear anything though, she must've been disappointed because Barlow whispered more than spoke and I had to lean right down to pick up what he was saying. What it boiled down to was that he was a widower with two kids, both girls. The older daughter, Susan, was married and living in Vancouver while Gail, who'd just turned twenty, had left Winnipeg about a year earlier and, as far as my client knew, was working for an insurance company in Toronto.

A couple of months earlier, when he'd got the news the cancer had spread through his stomach and was inoperable, he'd wanted to get in touch with Gail but didn't have her address or phone number. I wondered why but didn't ask him about it until later when he told me he and his younger daughter had had an argument and she'd packed up and left without so much as a good-bye. Anyway, he'd called a bunch of her former friends and learned that one of them had gotten a letter from Gail sometime in May. Through the return address, Reverend Barlow had managed to find out his daughter's phone number but when he tried it, he learned her line had been disconnected. He also sent her a letter but it came back marked "Return to Sender" so either the girl had moved without leaving a forwarding address or she just wanted her old man to think so. After that, Barlow placed ads in the personal columns of the Toronto newspapers asking his daughter or anyone who had any information about her whereabouts to contact him but there were no takers.

So that's where I came in. Reverend Barlow wanted me to go to Toronto, find his daughter, and lay the bad news on her so he could spend some time with her before cashing in his chips. That sounded reasonable. After all, if you're going to be packing it in, the least you can do is have your loved ones around to see you off.

In a way, I didn't like to take off for Toronto right then because I knew I could be away for several days and I had some unfinished business in Winnipeg to take care of. But I felt sorry for the guy plus I hadn't been East for a couple of years and figured it'd be a good chance to kill two birds with one stone and look up some old war buddies.

Before leaving, I called some of Gail's friends to see if anyone had heard from her recently but came up empty so all I really had to go on was a three-month-old address and some wallet-size photographs of a pretty girl with long blonde hair and clear blue eyes. A real Nordic type.

Based on information from her father, I put together a profile on her to see if I could find out what made her tick. But there wasn't much to go on: In most ways, she seemed like your average small-town girl who'd had a strict but decent upbringing. She'd been a good student and a member of the 4-H club in her area, winning awards for sewing and cooking. After graduating from high school, she'd taken a job as a clerk in the local real estate office. But that was just a stop-gap since, according to her dad, she'd been planning to go into missionary work in Africa or South America. Before she suddenly pulled up stakes, she'd been a part-time Sunday school teacher and had sung in the church choir. As a matter of fact, Reverend Barlow said music was her main love and in six years, she'd never missed a choir practice.

So why then had she upped and left for Toronto, a place where she'd never been before and had no ties? What happened to the missionary plans and her family and community roots? Reverend Barlow couldn't – or wouldn't – say. His story was that she'd begun to act somewhat strangely just before she left. He said she'd become even quieter than usual and seemed quite withdrawn but, as for any problems she might've had, well, he had no idea. She hadn't been going out with any boys at the time, so romantic entanglements seemed to be pretty well out of the picture and none of her former girlfriends were able to shed any light on her sudden departure either.

It was a mystery alright but it wasn't the one I was getting paid to solve. My job was to find a needle in a great big haystack called Toronto and I didn't kid myself it'd be easy. I also didn't think I had that much time either because Willis Barlow didn't look like he was too long for this world which, incidentally, was why I got a five hundred dollar advance before taking the assignment. Now, that may seem a little callous but, believe me, collecting from someone's estate is far from the easiest thing in the world.

Something else that isn't so easy is getting a cab at the Toronto Airport. Talk about a lack of organization! Islands of baggage and a couple of hundred of us and not a single cab in sight. The problem, so we were told, was that we'd had a tail-wind and had arrived ten minutes ahead of schedule which meant that the cabbies were caught with their flags down. Why they couldn't have showed up a little early was beyond me but humanitarians that most cabbies are, I figured they were probably all out conducting a fund-raising drive for the mentally retarded and couldn't spare the time. Actually, we could've been ten minutes late instead of early for all it mattered because the first car didn't show up for a good twenty minutes and, then, you wouldn't believe what happened. Instead of welcoming it with open arms, a goddamn security guard with an oversized uniform and undersized brain gave the driver shit and told him to get the hell out of there. It turned out he didn't work for the company that had the taxi concession at the airport and even though that outfit was out to lunch and didn't give two hoots about all of us waiting there with our thumbs up our you-know-whats, he wasn't allowed to pick up a fare.

Finally, some acceptable cars showed up, screeching around the curved ramp leading to the loading zone. Great, I thought, these guys don't look like they're about to waste any time. Some joke! After burning rubber to get there, the drivers just lounged on the hoods of their cabs, looking bored and waiting for people to approach them. And if you weren't going where they wanted to go, forget it! Which meant if you were just going someplace close by like Mississauga, you could whistle. The prize catches were people going right downtown which was about a twelve-buck ride and some of the drivers even walked around bawling: "Who's going downtown?"

I put my hand up and before I knew it my suitcase was in the trunk of a cab that looked like it hadn't been

washed in a month and I was ready to go. Or so I thought.
The driver, a skinny little East Indian guy, figured why
settle for one fare when you can have three. So, instead of
taking off right away, he left me to cool my heels while he
hustled around and came up with another couple of guys.
Not bad. Instead of twelve dollars, he cut himself in for
thirty-six, because, believe me, he didn't so much as hint
that the fare could be split three ways. No fear of that. It
was strictly every man for himself and each one of us had
to cough up the full amount.

But, you know, in a way that's what I like about
Toronto and Montreal, too, for that matter. Everybody's
out chasing the buck and they make no bones about it. Of
course, it's the same rat race in Winnipeg except the rats
are smaller and slower. Yeah, there are a lot of high-rollers
in Toronto alright and that's probably why the pace is
faster than out West where people are still trying to kid
themselves that they're living in God's country where blue
sky and clean air are more important than money.

My car-pool buddies and I did get something for our
money besides a ride in a cab that smelled of stale booze.
On the way in, the cabbie kept up a running commentary
in a clipped, sing-song voice as though he was running a
tour bus or something, telling us what this road and that
valley was and where you could go if you wanted to get a
good view of the city. I think he spent about five minutes
on the CN Tower alone and to this day, I remember that
the damn thing's over 1800 feet high . . . for all the good it
does me.

This trip, I stayed at the Warwick Hotel (I think it was
on Dundas) because it was centrally located. I used to stay
at the Park Plaza but one morning I had a king-size hang-
over and looked out the window of my room which was on
the twelfth floor and overlooking the Royal Ontario
Museum. If you know the museum, you also know it once
had a courtyard where they recreated a Chinese burial
ground, complete with monuments and tomb. Well wak-
ing up that morning with a big head and looking down

and seeing that tomb gave me a kind of creepy feeling and I haven't stayed at the Park Plaza since.

Anyway, the next morning, I hit the streets, with my first stop Gail Barlow's last known address. It was one of those small, older, apartment buildings in the East End, down on Gerrard Street: a three-storey, red-brick walk-up in the process of being refurbished. Apartment thirty-two was right on the top floor and I was puffing a little by the time I reached it. Thank God, somebody finally smartened up and invented the elevator otherwise all of us middle-aged, overweight types would've kicked off from heart attacks long ago.

The paint smell was heavy in the air and I had to tip-toe through a minefield of paint cans in the hallway to get to the door. A sleepy-eyed kid was rolling some greenish colour onto the wall but took time out to watch me while I knocked. He sure didn't try to hide his interest either, just set the roller down on a paint can, wiped his hands on his overalls, and stood there looking at me.

"Can I help you?" I asked sarcastically, because I was a little pissed off at being stared at.

"Naw, it's O.K.," he deadpanned. "I get paid by the hour." A real wise-guy alright.

A couple of seconds later, the door opened and a middle-aged broad wearing a flannel robe which she held tight against her chest, stood there looking at me. It was after ten but she still had her hair up in curlers and her face, which was no hell in the first place, looked even worse because of some kind of cream she had smeared on it. By this time, the painter was just about looking over my shoulder. I tried to ignore him but it wasn't easy because I hate people who shove their faces into other people's business – especially long-haired punks like this one.

"Pardon me," I said in my best undertaker's voice, "is there a Gail Barlow at this address?"

She stared at me for a good thirty seconds before answering and I wondered if the question had been too complex for her to grasp.

"I live here."

"Yes . . . well, then I guess the party I'm looking for has moved." I could just about feel that painter punk's breath – not to mention his eyes – on the back of my neck and I had to fight the urge to tell him to take a hike.

I looked over her shoulder through the open door. "I wonder if we could go inside where it's a little more private."

Her mouth tightened and she clutched her robe more firmly against her sagging bosom. "My husband told me never to let strangers into the suite."

"Very wise man, your husband."

"Only got grade six education but does the crosswords just like a college graduate with one of your degrees."

I agreed that university diplomas weren't all they were cracked up to be and said I didn't have one either but was getting along alright. She softened a little then and, after making some more small talk, invited me inside. The last thing I saw before the door closed behind me was the big smirk on the face of that long-haired punk.

All I really wanted to find out from the broad was when she'd taken over the apartment and if she might've heard where the previous tenant had moved to. She helped me out with the first part anyway. She'd been in suite thirty-two for close to three months, having moved in the beginning of June. She'd never seen the previous occupant though.

"For all I know, Elvis Presley could've been living here." And she started laughing at what she figured was a pretty good line.

I said that wasn't who I was looking for and headed downstairs to the caretaker's suite. A friendly, heavyset old boy with a Slavic accent thick enough to spread on a piece of bread, he invited me in right away.

"A private detective!" His eyes widened when I gave him my card. "Joost like on da television."

"Something like that."

"O-o-o-o-h!" He kept nodding and smiling so much, I

thought he was going to piss himself from excitement. I guessed he was from some European police state or something because just the word "detective" seemed to carry a lot of weight with him and he was more than co-operative.

"Dat girl vit long blonde hair, nice looking, she move out three months already. I think she say one time where is she move but I no remember."

"She didn't leave any forwarding address?"

"For-vard . . . ?"

It turned out she hadn't so I was at a dead-end. But not quite. The caretaker remembered the name of the company that had moved her. And the reason why he remembered was that they'd been a little careless and had taken a chunk out of the wall when they were carrying something down the stairs. The caretaker had given them hell and they, in turn, had told him to piss up a rope. In response, the old man had taken down not only the name of the firm but the license number of the truck and had phoned in a complaint about the men. Nothing had come of it, he said. The company manager had said they'd have the damage repaired but in spite of repeated calls, nothing was ever done about it.

As soon as I saw the place, I could understand why. It was one of those small, fly-by-night outfits that charge a little less than reputable movers but consider the day a total loss unless they've busted up somebody's furniture. The manager wasn't such a bad guy though. As a matter of fact, after I told him the story, he became half-way human but he still wasn't about to show me the invoice for Gail's move. However, he did break down enough to say it was a local job which meant the girl was still in Toronto. That didn't help much though but I thought I knew something that would. I pulled out a twenty dollar bill and started fanning myself with it.

"Sure is humid in Toronto at this time of year," I smiled.

He looked at the twenty then at me, grinned and headed straight for a beat-up filing cabinet. Fishing out an invoice, he handed it to me and plucked the twenty all in one motion.

"Sure is," he said.

I jotted down Gail's new address, got some directions, and was on my way, thinking that I had it made and that it was only a matter of hours before I'd be talking to Gail Barlow and writing a happy ending to my assignment. But that isn't quite the way it turned out. Not even close. Because when I got to her new apartment, a trail that had seemed red-hot suddenly grew icicles. She'd moved again and not more than a couple of weeks before. One thing was sure: she certainly didn't believe in staying in one place too long. I checked with the tenants in the suites on either side but they didn't know anything. Or so they said. And this time, even the building's superintendent – a skinny Limey guy in his sixties – wasn't much help – at least not at first. Oh, he was co-operative alright. It's just that he couldn't for the life of him remember which outfit had moved her. I then asked him if it wasn't a bit unusual for someone to move out in the middle of the month after, presumably, being paid up 'til the end. And that was when I struck pay dirt.

"We refunded her last two weeks rent. It was worth it to be rid of her. When the coppers start coming around, well, that's the kind of tenants we can do without."

"The police came to see her?"

He shrugged. "I don't know if they came to see *her* but they flamin' well came to see *me*. Asked me all about her: if I knew who came to see her, if men were coming by at all hours. Things like that."

"Were they uniformed officers?"

"Naw, they wore suits. Plainclothes fellahs."

I guessed they must've been vice squad dicks although it was beyond me why they'd be inquiring about a girl who, according to her old man, was the next best thing to the Virgin Mary. I soon found out though. You see, private detectives, especially those who've been around as long as me, usually have a pretty good working relationship with the police. I've found that if you lay your cards on the table and are straight with them, they'll be more than co-operative because, after all, they're trying to do a service for the public the same as I am. And I say that even though I've spent some time in jail myself, but more about that later. I've only met a few cops who throw their weight around and play their roles and usually they're younger guys who are still wet behind the ears, same as some lawyers I could mention.

Anyway, I was put in touch with a vice squad officer who gave me quite an earful on Gail Barlow alias Barbi Fox because that's the name she happened to be using in her current profession which, according to the officer, was prostitution. In my business, you get used to surprises but I wasn't ready for that one. The Reverend Willis Barlow's fair-haired girl was a hooker! And that was why the vice dicks had been nosing around her apartment building, trying to see if she was plying her trade out of her own digs as well as in the massage parlour where she'd recently been arrested. The girl who never missed choir practice, it seemed, also never missed the opportunity to turn a trick. The vice cop shook his head ruefully when I filled him in on her background but he didn't seem anywhere near as surprised as I expected.

"That's par for the course. You'd be surprised at the kind of girls we bust. Some of them are no more than thirteen or fourteen and they're already veterans. Some of them come from good homes too. I dunno, maybe it's the dope that does it to them, melts their brains or their morals or whatever. I know kids are sure a helluva lot different from what they were in my day."

Well, in one way, I agreed with him but in another, I didn't. Kids are different from what they were in my day but so are parents. And as for dope, well, I've worked on some drug cases myself, like the time I was hired by a guy to find out who was pushing dope on the kids in his town and, in particular, his son. And I hate drug pushers as much as anyone but I've found there's usually a lot more to it than just smoking a joint or popping a pill. The kids who get really messed up get that way from more than just dope. It's what makes them take it that's usually the cause of a lot of screwed-up lives but, whatever it is, is usually a damn-sight less visible than the dope itself. I didn't know what Gail/Barbi's problem was though and the officer couldn't help me.

"She's not an addict," he said, glancing over the girl's arrest report. "We checked her for tracks and couldn't find a thing. Of course, she's still pretty new to the business. So far, we've only hauled her in once." He smiled wryly. "But she'll turn up again. They always do."

"Where can I find her?"

"That shouldn't be any problem. She's working for a guy who runs four massage joints on Yonge Street. Chances are she'll be in one of them." While he recited the names, I jotted them down and then headed back to my hotel to do some phoning. I struck out on "Sultan's Harem" and "Salon Exotica" but number three paid off.

"Good afternoon, the Kitten Club. May I help you?" The voice was throaty, professionally sexy.

"I'd like to speak to Barbi Fox, please."

"I'm sorry, Barbi's off today. Could anybody else help you?" she purred suggestively.

"No, I'm afraid not. I really wanted to get in touch with Barbi. Could you give me her home number?"

"I'm afraid we're not allowed to do that but we do have some other girls here at the Club that I'm sure could look after you. They're all very . . . versatile."

She sure didn't give up easily but then I guess with all the competition around they had to use the hard-sell.

"I'm sure they are," I said, "but I'd still like to talk to Barbi."

The put-on sexiness gave way to resignation. "O.K., Barbi'll be in at four tomorrow." Then she added sarcastically, "If you can wait that long."

I assured her I could and tried to make arrangements for an outcall. There were two reasons for that. One, I had absolutely no desire to wander into a sleazy joint on the Strip and, two, considering the nature of our business, I thought it'd be more private at the hotel. But it was no go.

"I'm sorry, Barbi's not doing outcalls this week. This is her week in the studio."

"Studio." That was a new word for it. Anyway, I thanked her, hung up, and thought about how I could kill some time since there was really nothing I could do until the next afternoon. Nothing in a business sense, anyway. A couple of my old war buddies were living in Toronto and I figured this would be a good chance to have a few drinks with them and shoot the shit about the old days. I hadn't seen them in a couple of years but guessed they still must be around – at least, I hadn't heard they'd passed away although a fair number of my old buddies had by then.

The number I had for Dan O'Leary, who'd been in my outfit in Holland, didn't pan out and I later learned he'd moved to the States where he was running his own business. I didn't have any luck reaching Harry Pelz either. Harry was an inspector of detectives with the Ontario Provincial Police and a helluva good guy. He was a corporal in my unit when I was a Regimental Sergeant Major in the Provost Corps or military police.

As a matter of fact, the two of us almost got blown up by a V-2 one time when we were reconnoitering canals in Antwerp. The bomb hit just on the next block and Harry and I were deaf for almost twenty-four hours. And I remember another time, we went to a firing range to interview a guy (I think it was in Belgium) and we made the mistake of approaching from the wrong side. Before we knew it, there were bullets flying all around us and we were both hugging the floorboards of the jeep which, by then, was driving itself. After we made it to safety and climbed out of the jeep, our hands were shaking so much neither one of us could light a cigarette which was something we needed very badly right about then but not as much as a good stiff shot of whiskey.

Anyway, I couldn't reach Harry either – I think he was away on holidays – so I was on my own. I didn't think I'd have too much trouble killing time because Toronto has always been one of my favourite cities; besides Montreal, it's the only place in Canada that has that big-city feel, like New York or Chicago. I really believe the pace is faster in Toronto than, say, in Winnipeg, because there's more competition and pressure, but a Toronto friend tells me I'm wrong. He says Torontonians move at a good clip because they don't want anyone to think they're from the Prairies or Newfoundland which most of them are anyway.

Westerners also sometimes accuse Torontonians of being unfriendly but I think that's a crock although I admit I've never been overwhelmed with outpourings of affection during my visits. I think what it boils down to is that people in Toronto don't really wish anyone bad luck but if it happens, they'd rather not know about it. On the other hand, in Winnipeg, Regina, and other prairie towns that are masquerading as cities, people *like* to hear about others' misfortunes – probably because there's so little else interesting going on. That probably accounts for the myth of western Canadian hospitality as well because if you're not friendly in places like Moose Jaw and Medicine Hat, nobody is going to give you the time of day and, considering the lack of entertainment alternatives, you're going to be in for a helluva boring existence. So when you come right down to it, friendliness in western Canada is really no more than a kind of self-defence.

Anyway, by the time I got through reading the newspaper, I was getting pretty hungry which made me decide against trying to find out if the old Victory Theatre was still in operation. In the old days, it was a going concern, with some pretty good burlesque acts but I couldn't see its ad in the entertainment section of the paper and figured it must've gone under. Years back though there'd be so many dirty old men in there, you'd wonder why they didn't have a raincoat concession.

If you've been to Toronto, you know there are a lot of good restaurants there but they aren't the kind of places you want to go to alone. So I thought I'd just hit some place convenient because I wanted to take a quick trip to the Kitten Club just to case the joint a little. You see, I still had no intention of going inside to see Gail Barlow. What I wanted to do was intercept her on her way in, sometime before four o'clock, and tell her about her old man and see what she had to say. I was pretty sure she wouldn't be too thrilled that I'd found her and knew her present profession wasn't something she'd trained for in Sunday school.

I'd also heard that the people running the massage parlours on the Yonge Street Strip were not the kind of guys whose feathers you'd want to ruffle and they might not take it kindly if I showed up at one of their places and started hassling one of their girls. So I thought it might be a good idea if I knew what the layout was and whether I could hang around the entrance and grab her before she got inside.

But, like I said before, I wanted to get something to eat first and, tired of hotel food, I thought I'd try some place different. I was right downtown and the scent of charcoal broiled steak was enough to sell me on a family-type restaurant on Bloor Street. I think it was called the Roy Rogers something or other. Yeah, really, a restaurant named for Roy Rogers right in the heart of Toronto, Canada. Leave it to a Torontonian to think that has-been cowboy star's name would bring in customers.

Funny thing is, it seemed to be working because there were quite a few people in there. I figured most of them were tourists since a few of them had sun-burned throats from walking around staring up at the tall buildings and, at one table, a middle-aged couple were arguing about whether the CN Tower was one of the Seven Wonders of the World. But even though the guy insisted that the Colossus of Rhodes had been displaced by the towering Toronto landmark, he couldn't sway his companion who declared: "Oh, I'm not saying the CN Tower's not awe-inspiring but it's certainly no historic monument."

"Historic, shmistoric," fires back the guy. "It's sure as hell put Toronto on the map. Can you imagine all the investment money it's brought in and all the jobs it created."

Well, he had her there alright. She just shook her head and dove back into her salad. By that time, I was already working on mine and eagerly anticipating the steak to follow. All in all, it was a pretty good meal and the Dale Evans clone who attended to me was an excellent waitress in spite of the silly get-up she was forced to wear. In a way, I felt kind of sorry for her because she looked pretty ridiculous in that ten-gallon hat and buckskin skirt and I think she knew it. That's probably why I left her a good-sized tip since I guess in a way I could empathize with her because, in my business, sometimes I'm caught in some pretty ridiculous situations and outfits too, although I hoped that wouldn't be the case in the Barlow matter.

Yonge Street. I remember it just after the war when it was a thriving commercial area. Clothing stores, jewellery shops, real high-class places selling the best merchandise, but by the mid-seventies, it was an entirely different story and the merchandise was a helluva lot different as well. The main commodity was sex – the raunchiest, rawest, and kinkiest money could buy – and in all forms, from the vicarious in dirty pocketbooks and magazines to the real goods, in hookers (male and female) ranging in age from twelve to whatever could still turn a trick. During the war, I'd seen my share of redlight districts in Holland and France but, believe me, Yonge Street didn't have to take a back seat to any of them although on Toronto's "Sin Strip," the free enterprisers who ran the "massage" joints weren't as frank as the European cathouse owners. Over there, they called them what they were: whorehouses. In Canada, and particularly along the Yonge Street Strip, they call them anything but that.

"Encounter studios," "sensitivity awareness salons,"

"body painting parlours," "sex therapy clinics." You name it, it was there, on the signs hovering above doorways leading to second-floor walkups, sandwiched next to each other in dingy buildings that had long since lost both their looks and their innocence.

I noticed another difference between Yonge Street and European redlight districts. At least as recently as 1976, there were still some pockets of legitimate commerce, like bookstores that sold honest-to-goodness literature: books you could read without getting an erection and weren't afraid to have lying around where non-perverts could see them. There were also a few other commercial misfits, like clothing stores and places that sold pottery or art supplies. Last, but not least, were the Karate schools and dance studios where lonely people go to meet other lonely people so they can be lonely together.

Even the smells on the Strip were cheap and tawdry. When the doors opened to the massage joints, the sweet smell of incense wafted out; and the dirty bookstores gave off the sour odor of cigarette smoke mixed with heavy, unsanitary mustiness. You could just about smell the roaches in the walls. There was only one smell that wasn't offensive. Somewhere, in the area there was a Hungarian restaurant and you could smell the food cooking – the goulash and chicken paprika with all the spices.

By the time I started my trek to the Kitten Club which, as I recall was just north of Wellesley, it was just approaching dusk and the only shops open were those selling sex or a reasonable facsimile thereof. The street was a sad circus with rock music blaring from the open doors of pinball arcades and brightly-lit windows displaying all kinds of sex gadgets and skin mags in plastic doggie-bags. It was the middle of the week and there weren't too many people on the street, just a few who through kinkiness or curiosity were drawn to the bright windows like moths.

I even went inside a couple of the stores myself and, let me tell you, just the titles of some of those pocketbooks were enough to get you excited. Now, I'm not big on censorship, but it makes you wonder what effect books like that could have on guys who've already got a screw loose. Sado-masochism, bondage, homosexuality, and God-knows-what-else. You know, I've often thought that if people took as much interest in science as they do in sex, we'd have discovered a cure for cancer long ago. But those porno shops, as seedy as they were, didn't really bother anybody when you come right down to it. Nobody was forcing anyone to go in if they didn't want to and the operators weren't standing outside yelling: "Step right in! Get your pussy pictures, vibrators, and inflatable dolls here!" Compared to the broads working the Strip, the dirty bookstores and peepshow joints were shrinking violets. But those girls, they were something else again. You didn't even have to look horny for them to accost you, just reasonably male and old enough to go to the john by yourself. I even saw broads try to hustle kids who couldn't have been more than fifteen or sixteen. I could just see the kid asking his old man for his allowance, saying: "Aw, Dad, can't you give me a few bucks more? I want to go down to Yonge Street and get a piece of ass."

The whores, lurking in every doorway and on every street corner, sure weren't shy about soliciting although they never did come right out and say they'd bang me for a price. Instead they'd say things like: "Would you like to have a good time, handsome?" and "Are you looking for some company tonight?" Of course, you didn't have to be a mental giant to know what they meant, considering the suggestive way they said it and the knowing winks. And the way they were dressed, there was no danger of anyone mistaking them for nuns, that's for sure.

At the time, hotpants were still big, at least on the Strip, and the tighter the better – so tight you wondered how they got them off at the moment of truth. Some of them looked like they were painted on but there hadn't been enough paint to finish the job because half their ass cheeks were sticking out.

And I don't know what they had against brassieres but it sure wasn't their breasts. Ninety percent of those rub-shop queens must've been braless, with their nipples sticking right out against their sweaters or seethrough blouses. Some of those tits weren't bad either: nice and firm and inviting. Of course, there wasn't any reason why they shouldn't have been firm since a lot of them belonged to girls who, in spite of some heavy makeup, looked no more than sixteen. And there were a couple who looked even younger. They were standing together trying to look hard-eyed and sophisticated when their figures hadn't even filled out yet. They reminded me of kids playing dress-up, with their flashy lipstick smeared on too heavily and false eyelashes that looked like perched spiders. There was something pretty sad about it alright. I mean, a kid younger than my daughter – if I'd had one – asking me if I wanted to go upstairs for a reverse massage on a waterbed. The thing is, after I walked away, a guy older than me took her up on it, which is even sadder. For him as well as her.

But I don't want to get into stuff like that because I didn't go down to the Yonge Street Strip to research a sociology term paper. All I wanted to do was check out the front of the Kitten Club to see how I could stake it out the next day and grab Gail Barlow before she got inside.

It didn't look too bad. The operation was on the second floor and the door at street level was locked, with a buzzer beside it that you had to press to get it opened. That meant Gail would have to stand on the sidewalk for – if I was lucky – ten or fifteen seconds which would give me enough time to confront her and make my pitch on behalf of her father.

That was all I needed to know, but it was a nice night and I kept walking, going as far as the new Eaton's shopping centre which was then under construction. Looked like it was going to be some building though. Then I turned around and headed back on the opposite side of the street, passing a small group of people in a little huddle on the sidewalk in front of a good-sized non-porno-graphic bookstore. A couple of guys – an old fellow with a full beard and a young man with shoulder-length hair – were playing chess by the light of the store-window while a half-dozen spectators watched silently. The bearded player wasn't silent though. Between kibitzing his opponent, he offered to take on all comers in a loud, heavily-accented voice. The board was set up on a small folding table and they had a timing clock and everything. Quite a sight. A couple of the onlookers nodded pleasantly at me when I paused for a quick look. It was nice to see something like that. I don't know why. It was just. . . . Well, it was nice. But a few minutes later, I was back running the gauntlet of hookers and trying to banter with cold-eyed broads who, when they looked at me, saw only a cock with a giant dollar sign stamped on it.

Anyway, that was the Yonge Street Strip in 1976. I haven't been back since but I hear it's pretty much the same in spite of the fact that there was a big stink a few years back when a little shoe-shine boy was sexually assaulted and murdered by some faggots who worked for one of the rub joints. I hear the hookers are a little less aggressive these days though, and are a little more discreet when they approach johns in the street. But the more things change the more they remain the same, particularly as far as making money goes, and that's probably why nothing much has been done about cleaning up Yonge Street even though the Toronto police would like nothing better than to run in every pimp and hooker on the Strip. Like they say: money talks. And, on that mild August night in 1976, I had the feeling that it had spoken to Gail Barlow and talked her into opting for a life of play-for-pay.

Figuring she might show up early I began staking out the Kitten Club at about three-thirty and passed the time looking in the windows of the stores on either side of the massage parlour's entrance, positioning myself so I'd be able to see her reflection. I didn't stand in any one spot for

too long because I didn't want to call attention to myself.
One good thing, I am nothing if not average-looking and I
don't have much trouble blending into my surroundings
but some people have also told me I look like a cop so I
had to be careful not to get too close to the Kitten Club
for fear of scaring off the subject. After twenty minutes or
so, I started to get bored which is a no-no when you're on
a stakeout because if your attention wanders, so can your
subject. Luckily, I snapped out of it in time because that
was exactly when Gail Barlow showed up. I caught her
out of the corner of my eye at the very instant she pressed
the buzzer. By the time I reached her, the lock had
released and she'd started to push the door open.

"Miss Barlow?"

She was wearing a form-fitting pair of slacks, spike
heels, and a lowcut sweater that revealed some well-tanned
cleavage. She was heavily made up but her blue eyes still
had the same clear innocence as in the photos and the
long, blonde hair still looked like prairie cornsilk.
Although she looked at me warily without saying anything, there was no doubt in my mind it was her.

"I'd like to talk to you, Miss Barlow."

"What do you want? Are you a cop?"

"No I'm a private investigator working for your father.
He retained me to locate you."

I noticed some people staring at us and I guess that
wasn't surprising considering the way she looked and the
fact we were standing on a busy sidewalk directly in front
of a massage parlour. Maybe they thought we were hag-
gling over the price or something because a couple of guys
were exchanging smirks and making no attempt to hide
their interest.

"Maybe we could go somewhere for a coffee," I
suggested.

"I don't want to go anywhere with you and I don't care
who sent you," she snapped and started to enter the building. I had to shove out my hand to keep her from shutting
the door on me.

"Please, Miss Barlow. It's very important that I speak to you. Ten minutes, that's all it'll take."

"I don't have the time. I'm late as it is." Her high heels clicked on the stairs with me following right behind.

At the top of the stairs, there was a kind of reception area with a couple of couches along the walls and a coffee table with some magazines on it in the centre. The lamps all had red shades and cast a pinkish hue that covered a multitude of interior decorating sins. The piped-in music was low and the air heavily spiced with incense. In one corner, there was a little desk with another painted-up broad sitting behind it, chewing gum and reading some kind of gossip rag. She looked up and said hi to Gail and gave me a mildly curious look. Behind her was a doorway covered by a floor-length curtain of a heavy material that looked something like velvet. Just as I was about to start my pitch to Gail again, the curtain was pulled aside by a big, mean-looking sonuvabitch wearing a muscle shirt and levis. He looked like he could've been a biker.

"Barbi baby!" he boomed at Gail. "What's happenin'?" Then he noticed me. "Who's this?" he asked, jerking his thumb in my direction.

"I just wanted to talk to this young lady. . . ." I began.

He winked at me. "Sure fellah, you can talk all you want but it's gonna cost you."

I thought fast. There was no way I was going to leave without completing my assignment but there was also no way I wanted to get the shit kicked out of me.

"Oh, of course," I said. "I'll be happy to pay. No problem."

Gail started to say something about not wanting to talk to me but the guy shut her up with a look.

"You heard what the man said. Look after him. And if he gives you any trouble. . . ."

"Trouble?" I said. "Don't worry about that. I just want to tell her something important."

"Sure you do," he snorted. "Sure you do." And he sat down on the edge of the desk and whispered something to the painted-up receptionist. As Gail led me through the curtained doorway, I heard them laughing and I had a pretty good idea at what. We walked down a hallway with doors on either side. Stopping in front of one at the far end, she opened it and ushered me into a small cubicle that was no more than about ten feet wide. Just enough room for the waterbed that dominated it. The lighting, sound, and scent were identical to those in the reception area. There was nothing else to sit on so I plunked myself down on the corner of the waterbed. It gurgled and swayed under me for a couple of seconds during which Gail Barlow stood there with her hands on her hips, not saying a word. Finally, she spoke.

"That'll be twenty-five dollars for half an hour."

I gave it to her and she left the room, coming back a minute or so later. I guessed she'd given the dough to her biker boss.

"You wanted to talk," she said. "So talk."

"Like I said before, I'm a private detective and I'm working for your father. He's been trying to locate you for some time now, a couple of months at least."

"Well you did your job. You found me. Now you can go back and tell him what a success I've made of myself. I'm sure it'll reinforce his opinion of me when you give him all the dirt. I'll bet you get off on that, don't you? You must really be proud of the way you make your living."

I fought back the temptation to say: "Look who's talking." Instead I replied: "Your father didn't send me to spy on you. He wants to see you. He wants you to come home."

She laughed bitterly. "Home?" She looked around the room. "This is the only home I've got. Didn't he tell you he kicked me out and told me never to come back?"

Well the Reverend Willis Barlow hadn't told me any such thing and I found out that he'd neglected to tell me some other significant facts as well, in spite of my urging him to be completely open with me. You see, a private detective has absolutely no interest in judging his clients' morals or motives but, like a lawyer, he has to know the whole story from day one otherwise it makes the job a helluva lot more difficult and sometimes results in surprises like the one I got from Gail Barlow.

According to her, she hadn't taken off without telling her old man but had been tossed out on her ear by that very person. And why had he shown her the door? She'd been pregnant and after keeping it to herself and the farm boy who'd banged her, for a few months, she'd broken down and laid the bad news on her father. To hear her tell it, his reaction was immediate and harsh. He said she'd brought shame on him as the minister of the town and that if the story got out, he'd be a laughing stock. So, as it turned out, she hadn't jumped. She'd been pushed. And that was a lot different from the version given to me by Willis Barlow.

The rest of the story was far from unique. After arriving in Toronto she'd gotten in touch with a counselling service for pregnant women in distress and through it, eventually got an abortion. One problem seemed to have given birth to another. The experience had really messed her up psychologically and probably led to her being in her present situation. It had most certainly left her with an intense hatred of her father.

"It was because of him that I had to kill the thing that was growing inside me! He made me kill my baby!"

I had no interest in arguing the pros and cons of the situation. I waited until she lit up a cigarette and composed herself.

"Regardless of what happened in the past, your father wants to see you now. And he doesn't have much time."

"He's ill?"

"Very. It's cancer and he's got a couple of weeks, maybe a month at the outside."

"And he thinks I'm going to rush back to be at his bedside?"

I shrugged. "He wanted me to tell you that he had something very important to say to you."

She laughed humourlessly. "I once had something very important to tell *him* and look what it got me. Well, you can tell that dear old father of mine that his whore of a daughter isn't coming back now or ever! His church and his flock were always more important to him than I was anyhow. I was nothing more than a prisoner of his piety, someone to sing in the choir and serve as an example to the other kids."

She must've noticed me staring at her because she suddenly lashed out. "Well, what're you looking at? Haven't you seen a Yonge Street whore before? You've done your job now get out! Go back to my father and tell him what I told you. And tell him I hope he burns in hell for what he did to me and my baby!"

I got up and started for the door, telling her: "I'll leave a ticket for you at the airport in case you change –"

"Don't bother."

"– your mind."

I thought about it a lot on the flight back to Winnipeg; the way Gail Barlow had undergone a complete change of character, and since, in my profession, you get to be a bit of an amateur psychiatrist, I tried to put the pieces together. The best I could come up with was that she was on some kind of combination guilt and vengeance trip and that by degrading herself in a rub joint, she was punishing both herself and her father. But then, maybe I'm way off base because, like I said, I'm strictly an amateur when it comes to figuring out what makes people tick. The hardest part of the Barlow case though was reporting back to my client. He didn't look any worse than the last time I saw him but then that wasn't really saying much. It was obvious that it wouldn't be long before another terminal case put a claim in on his bed.

"You found her?" It was the first time I'd seen him smile.

"Yes." I had a hard time meeting his eyes. "It's all here in the reports."

And it was. I'd debated whether I should maybe shade

the facts a little and not be too explicit about his daughter's current profession, her arrest, the comments she'd made about leaving home, and her feelings about her father. But professional ethics demanded that my reports be as accurate as I could possibly make them. That's what he was paying me for and that's what he got. I handed him the two typed daily reports covering my investigative activities in Toronto. Nothing was left out, not even his daughter's comments which I quoted almost verbatim. He squinted at the print.

"The words are just a blur to me," he said. "I think it's the medication I'm taking. Do you think you could read them for me?"

I did as he asked but not without a little selective censorship. It was one thing to write things down but another to have to read them to someone. I couldn't censor Gail's reaction to her father's plea though.

"Subject indicated she is unwilling to return home," I read. "She expressed considerable hostility toward her father. When advised that her father was terminally ill, she exhibited a total lack of concern, saying: 'I hope he burns in hell for what he did to me and my baby.'"

He looked at me in shocked disbelief. "An abortion! I never knew. . . . I never thought. . . ."

There was nothing I could say or do so I got up and walked out of the room without looking back. I didn't want to see him crying. It was bad enough just to hear it.

A couple of weeks later, the Reverend Willis Barlow made an honest man of his doctor and died on schedule. I read about it in the obituaries and, on the spur of the moment, I decided to go to his funeral even though it was being held in his hometown which was close to fifty miles from the city.

Why did I go? Well, it was a slow day at the office and it was a beautiful fall morning, just right for a drive in the country where the leaves were starting to turn and the air was crisp. You know, it wasn't until I reached the cemetery that I knew why I'd really come. I hadn't been there more than a few minutes when I started checking out the mourners congregated around the graveside. When I saw her, I went a little weak in the knees and the weakness grew when our eyes met. She gave me a little smile that I'm sure no one else saw and dabbed at her eyes. Gail Barlow had come home. And without all the makeup and wearing a plain black dress that came well below the knee, she looked just like a girl who'd never missed choir practice.

FOUR

Partners

O NE THING about this business, I get to meet a lot of people. So many that sometimes it seems like my life is one big revolving door shooting a bunch of faces through without me getting to know what's behind them. Then there are other times when you get behind the face and you're sorry you did because what's in the head isn't always so pretty.

The thing is, what with coming into contact with so many people, one thing a private eye should have if he wants to stay healthy is a good memory, especially for faces. Why for faces? Well, let's say you blow the whistle on some guy who's been screwing around on his old lady. His wife ends up getting a divorce, custody of the kids, and fat alimony payments and the guy ends up hating your guts because you got the goods on him. Of course, ninety-nine times out of a hundred, you never see the guy again but that hundredth time. . . . Well, you never know what can happen, so it's a good idea if you know what's what and who's who.

Still, I've gotta admit that I'm not always on top of things myself. Like this one time, a couple of years ago. I was heading back to my office after a ptomaine special at the diner across the street when I spotted this guy heading toward me. I picked him out immediately even though the sidewalk was crowded because there was something familiar about him and right away, I tried to place him. He spotted me at about the same time and stuck on a big smile so thinking that I either owed him money or he was a satisfied customer, I slapped on one of my own.

A couple of seconds later, we were standing in the middle of the sidewalk, beaming at each other and reaching out to shake hands like long-lost buddies. But our hands never met because all of a sudden, we both realize that we were not long-lost buddies or anything even close to it. The guy's face went through more changes than a baby with the runs and, somewhere in between, his Liberace smile became as extinct as the dodo bird. But his temper sure as hell didn't and he started in shaking his fist at me which was pretty appropriate, I guess, since at the same time, he was calling me a low-life bastard and a rotten sonuvabitch who'd sell out his own grandmother for a ten-spot.

And that was when I finally remembered where I knew him from because he'd used those same terms of endearment – along with a lot of others that were even less complimentary – the first time I'd met him a year or so earlier. Since it wasn't all that long ago, I wondered why I hadn't recognized him. And then it hit me. It reminded me of that line that the wise-guys used years ago when they cracked off to some chick. You know the one: "Take off your clothes and I'll see if I know you."

In a way, it was kind of like that with this guy because if he'd've had his clothes off I probably would have recognized him. Wait a minute now! It's not what you think. The only time I walk funny is when I've had a couple too many. The thing is, the last time I saw this guy, he was bare-assed naked which would have been alright if he was standing in a shower stall or playing volleyball at a nudist camp. But he wasn't doing either. He was standing in a closet in a seventeen-year-old chick's bedroom.

But how he got there and how I got there to flush him out is still only part of the story. There's another part, one that hasn't been told yet and probably never will be. One that I can only guess at even though I'd say my guess is pretty educated. But first things first. First, I have to lead up to my bare-assed buddy in the closet, whose trail goes back something like . . . well, let's say, twenty-five years even though that's not completely right.

You see, the guy I'm talking about is still around. Even now, I run into him once in a while and he still gives me a look like he believes in live and let live, only I should be the exception. So I don't want to make this too true-to-life, if you know what I mean.

O.K., anyway, this case started out like a lot of others with a guy phoning for an appointment and then showing up all fidgety and embarrassed because he figures he's not man enough to keep his wife happy in the sack and that's why she's shopping around. Only this guy wasn't as ill-at-ease as most of my clients. As a matter of fact, after the first couple of minutes, he started to take charge which, I later found out, was the way he usually operated. You see, he was one of those hard-driving, self-made men. But even though he'd been a wheeler and dealer in the business world for fifteen or twenty years, he still had the manner and appearance of the miner and lumberjack that he once was. With that bull-neck and those broad shoulders, he still looked like he could do a good day's work with a drill or axe.

There was something else different about him too besides the way he handles himself, so crisp and business-like. You see, most of the people I work for are Joe or Jane Nobodies – people you've never heard of before – but with this guy, it was different because as soon as he mentioned his name, I knew I wasn't talking to some nine-to-five type who carries his lunch in a brown paper bag. Nossir, I knew who he was alright and so would a lot of other people if I used his real name which I don't intend to do for reasons which will become obvious.

So anyway, this guy – I'll call him Eric Neilsen – showed up at my office and filled me in on the story. He didn't need much prompting and, in spite of the fact that he spoke with a slight Scandinavian accent and fractured a couple of phrases, I soon got the picture.

"My wife, Mr. Manweiler, is, I am quite positive, having an affair with another man. . . ." He hesitated for a second and put on this twisted little smile. "Or men."

"Have you got any idea who he, er, they, are?"

The look in his pale blue eyes was murderous.

"If I knew, I think I would be capable of handling this matter without your help."

I didn't argue with him. He was pushing fifty but looked like he could take care of himself in a scrap and this kind of set me to thinking because I wasn't particularly thrilled about tracking down his old lady's bed-partner just so Neilsen could beat him to a pulp. Thank Christ this sudden attack of conscience went away before it did any damage. Like I told myself then: "If I don't do it, somebody else will."

So I took down all the particulars as he spieled them out in this really bored tone of voice like he was dictating a laundry or grocery list or something.

"On many occasions, she has taken trips around the country – to visit friends or relatives, she *says*."

"And you have reason to doubt her story?"

"I have reason." He scowled up at the ceiling for a couple of seconds before going on. "You see, one time – last spring it was – she told me that she was going to visit her sister in Toronto for a few days."

"And she doesn't have a sister in Toronto?"

"Oh yes, it is true that she has a sister there. And when she returned from Toronto, she told me all about the wonderful visit they had together, the places they went for dinner and so on."

"So, what's the problem?"

"The problem is that I later discovered that her sister was in Vancouver at that particular time."

That punch-line was enough to convince me that I had a pretty clear-cut case of adultery on my hands and that it wouldn't take that much to get the goods on Mrs. Mar-

garet Neilsen. There was one drawback though. The fact
that she took her act on the road meant I'd have to farm
the assignment out to an operative in whichever city she
took it into her head to visit. At least, that's what I
thought. But as it turned out, I didn't have to sub-contract
because Neilsen insisted that I carry the ball from beginning to end. And he didn't even blink when I told him it
would be a two-man job and that expenses would be
pretty high.

Anyway, we had it set up that Neilsen would let me
know as soon as his wife was getting ready to take off on
another of her jaunts and sure enough, a couple of weeks
later, I got the word that Mrs. Neilsen was preparing to fly
to Toronto for a few days. I had to hustle my ass but I
managed to book space on her flight for my operative,
Ralph, and myself. Not only that, I also made reservations
for us at the hotel she'd be staying at which was the Royal
York. By now, I was kind of looking forward to the trip
because I knew we'd be going first-class all the way.

So, a couple of days later, there we were: Ralph, myself,
and Mrs. Neilsen, in the lobby of the Royal York waiting
to fill out our registration cards. Nothing suspicious had
occurred so far. Nobody had met her at the airport or the
hotel.

The first thing I did was edge in close enough to see
what room she'd been assigned then I took off and
checked the layout of the hotel. What I wanted to do was
to find out which room would give us the best view of her
door. Believe me, it wasn't as easy as it sounds because the
Royal York is one helluva huge hotel. Throw a couple of
sentries in front with those big bushy hats and the place
could pass for Buckingham Palace. Except Buckingham
Palace doesn't have the Union Station in its backyard.

And the lobby! Christ, the ceiling's so high, it's like
being in a cathedral or something which is probably why
everybody in there was whispering. Or at least that's the
way it seemed to me.

Anyway, by the time I got back to the desk, I knew

which room I wanted. Mrs. Neilsen was going to be in 907 so, ideally, we should be in 910 which is across and a little way down the hall. That way, we could have our door open just a sliver and keep an eye on her at all times. As it turned out, 910 was occupied but I managed to get 912 which was just about as good for our purposes. After all, peepers can't be choosers. Which is why I had to grease the desk clerk to the tune of a ten-spot because even though 912 was vacant, he said he'd already promised it to somebody which was probably a bunch of bullshit. But the main thing is we got set up like I wanted and that's why I always say that money is just as good as a search warrant. A legal document may give you the right but money gives you the privilege and that boils down to the same thing as far as I'm concerned.

After we'd settled into our room, the first thing I did was to call Mrs. Neilsen, making out as though I was with the hotel and was just checking up to see that everything was satisfactory. That let us know she was in her room and after Ralph listened outside her door for a couple of seconds, we also had a pretty good idea she was alone. Now all we had to do was to see if she stayed that way.

Man, you want to talk about boring! Compared to this, a snail race would have been exciting. From about ten-thirty that night until three the next morning, all we did was take turns peering out through a crack in the door. The only visitor she had turned out to be a kid with a room-service trolley stacked up with a couple of bottles of booze and some mix and ice. This was about eleven o'clock and from then on nobody so much as even looked at her door. By three o'clock, it looked like no one was going to show so we decided to call it a night but before turning in, I took an added precaution.

Most private detectives have their own pet way of finding out if someone has entered or left a room. It's really pretty simple although some guys make a big production out of it. All you do is stick a match or a bobbypin – something that nobody'd spot – between the door and the jamb. If the door is opened, whatever it is that you've stuck in there falls to the floor and you know that someone probably either went in or came out.

This time, my partner, Ralph, came up with a new twist. I figured he must've been reading detective stories or something because all of a sudden he gets this brainstorm and strings a long strand of hair across the edge of the door and the frame. Since he had his hair slicked down with about half a tube of Brylcreem, there was no problem about it staying there. I had to admit it was even less visible than a bobby pin so I went along with it. But I almost wished I hadn't because that goddamn Ralph was so smug you'd have thought he invented screwing.

Anyway, we got up at seven the next morning and checked out Mrs. Neilsen's door. The hair was still there which told me two things: one, no one had entered or left her room; and, two, Ralph's hair cream was the next best thing to liquid cement. Now it was boredom time again as we took turns peering out into the hall.

It was a real nothing morning with no callers for Mrs. Neilsen. Lunch time came and with it, room service for our subject. A covered tray of food and a couple of bottles of booze and some ice. When the kid wheeled out the trolley, it was sporting a couple of whiskey bottles that I recognized from the night before. Only now they were empty. Whatever the old dame was doing in there, she must've worked up a powerful thirst or. . . . Right then I started to wonder if we'd slipped up and someone had gotten in there without our knowing because two bottles of booze is a lot of juice for one little, middle-aged lady. And now, two more! But Ralph pressed his ear against her door again and still couldn't hear any voices so either she was alone or she was shacked up with a deaf mute, which I thought was pretty unlikely.

All that afternoon, nothing happened. At about five p.m., I called her room again to confirm that she was still there. A couple of hours later, room service showed up again with more booze and left with a couple of empty bottles and the luncheon dishes. By then, it was almost twenty-four hours since she'd checked in and she hadn't even set foot out of her room. Not that Ralph and I had exactly taken a tour of the city either.

That night – or, to be exact, morning – we stayed up until two a.m. and again nobody so much as looked at her door. By then, I'd begun to worry that my eyes were taking on the shape of the crack that we were peeping through and might stay that way.

Anyway, nothing happened that night either and the next morning, she – and we – checked out and flew back to Winnipeg and all we'd proved was that she'd spent a couple of days in Toronto on a bender. So it looked like a boring end to a boring case. Or at least it would've been if that had been the end of it. But it wasn't. Not by a longshot.

About a month later, there was Eric Neilsen again in my office telling me that this time he was sure his wife was playing around and that he even knew the name of the stud. Well, by now I'd started to think that maybe he wasn't playing with a full deck. But, what the hell! He was paying the shot so his wish was my command and there we were off to the races again.

"You say you suspect someone in particular. Do you know his name?"

"I should. He's my business partner."

He told me the guy's name was Dave Stenberg and rattled off a bunch of particulars like he'd been rehearsing for a week.

"Five-eleven, average build, dark brown, wavy hair, dark complexion, drives a new Lincoln, cream-coloured."

"My God, I don't know why you need me. Looks like you know just about everything about him already."

"Not everything," he said and gave me a smile that was no more than lip-deep. "I want to know why a good-looking young guy like him would want to jump in the sack with that old lady of mine because believe you me, she's far from the best piece of tail I've ever had."

I couldn't figure it either because according to what Neilsen told me this Stenberg was a real ladies' man. So much so that he'd even had a vasectomy so he wouldn't knock up all the chicks he was going horizontal with.

So it was stake-out time again but this time, we were watching both Mrs. Neilsen and this Stenberg character just to be on the safe side because if we lost one of them we'd still have the other. Days went by, then weeks but we still couldn't turn up anything to indicate they were doing the dirty deed together.

And every time I checked in with Neilsen and told him that we'd come up dry, he'd say: "Are you sure?" And his voice was all suspicious like he figured I was pulling a fast one or something and had sold him out. But anyway, after three or four weeks, he pulled us off the case and settled up his account. But not before giving me a long, accusing look and asking me one more time:

"Are you sure they aren't playing around?"

By this time he was getting to be such a pain in the ass that I was glad to be rid of him even though it meant kissing his money goodbye too. But those are the breaks and, if I was going to end up in the poor-house, at least I'd be halfway sane when I got there if I could keep away from loonies like Eric Neilsen.

But, like I said before, this business has more surprises than a guy who marries a transvestite because a couple of months later. . . . You guessed it. There he was again. And this time, his story was even wilder. It was as though he'd always been a little nutty and had finally graduated into big-league insanity. This time he was positive there was some hanky-panky going on. In fact, he'd swear to it.

"O.K.," I said, humouring him. "What is it this time? Is your wife carrying on in Toronto again or are she and your partner going at it hot and heavy here in the city?"

He glared at me disgustedly as though I'd added two and two and come up with five.

"It is not my wife who is involved in this illicit affair."

"Not . . . your . . . wife," I replied, wondering what the

hell he was going to come up with next. I didn't have to wait long.

"No. It's my daughter."

Well, if that didn't beat everything, his next comment sure as hell did, because he put the icing on the whole screwy cake by telling me that now he was convinced that his partner wasn't screwing his wife as he'd first suspected but instead was throwing it into his daughter who was seventeen-year-old jailbait and not something some forty-plus casanova should be fooling around with. Not that I thought that at the time because I figured here was another of Neilsen's wild goose chases and that his paranoia, or whatever you want to call it, when some guy figures all the chicks in his family are sneaking some nookie, was getting the best of him.

Christ, by this time I wouldn't have been surprised if he'd told me that his son was getting some Greek culture instruction from his scoutmaster or his priest or somebody. But Eric Neilsen seemed to have more bucks than brains and, since I needed the former more than the latter, I went along with him and set up a stakeout on his daughter, Connie, and my old quarry, David Stenberg.

One thing about being the boss, you get the cushier assignments. I gave myself the far from unpleasant task of keeping my corneas on Connie Neilsen who was one sexy looking piece and let me tell you, the way she dressed and pranced around, you could tell that she knew it too. Tight sweaters and short skirts. They were like a uniform to her. If it wasn't for the fact that her hair was long and dark, she could've passed for a junior Marilyn Monroe the way she switched her buns from side to side when she walked and put on this little half-smile when she knew guys were looking at her, which was most of the time.

And the way they looked at her! It sure wasn't the way they'd look at their kid sisters . . . unless they were a little on the kinky side, that is. Which reminds me of another case, but that'll keep.

Anyway, on the first day of the stakeout, I stayed with

her from the time she left for business school in the morning until she went home at about five p.m. All I got for my trouble was a lot of fresh air because it was one of those nice, crisp fall days. But as far as anything suspicious was concerned, it was a total wipe-out. As a matter of fact, the only thing that did happen convinced me that her old man was out to lunch.

At noon, Connie met a guy in front of her school and they went off together to a nearby restaurant, all lovey-dovey. But the guy was not Neilsen's partner but a boy about her own age. Nice looking kid, well-dressed, tall and slim, and wearing one of those team jackets that high-school jocks use to advertise their virility. That started me thinking that it was pretty unlikely Connie would want to fool around with some middle-aged guy when she had a boyfriend who looked at her like she was a T-bone steak and he hadn't eaten in a week.

The second day of surveillance was just about a re-run of the first. I followed her to school then spent the rest of the day hanging around outside. At noon, she met a girl-friend in front and they headed off to the same restaurant she'd frequented the day before. At one p.m., she was back in school and didn't leave until four-thirty when she headed straight home. And it was like that for the next few days as well. By then, it was Thursday. Eric and his Frau had just gone out of town for a few days and I figured it was now or never because now cute little Connie had the apartment all to herself.

By this time, I was getting to be a fixture on the street where Connie's school was located which happens to be one of the main drags in Winnipeg so I thought it was time to put on one of the half-assed disguises I use from time to time. Nothing elaborate. Just a pair of fake glasses – the kind with non-prescription lenses – and a security guard's uniform, which was easy to get since security guarding is another facet of my operation.

O.K., so now at least I looked as though I had some reason to be in the area as I patrolled the block, making sure I kept the entrance to the business college in sight at all times. Now I didn't have to worry about getting dirty looks from the merchants in the area or being rousted by some eager-beaver cop. Yeah, I figured everything was smooth sailing now. But that only shows you how wrong you can be. It was that damn uniform, I guess. I wanted something for my guys that looked kind of official, not one of those Mickey Mouse deals with a lot of braid like a Shriner's outfit. The trouble was, it looked too official, too close to the kind of uniform that commissionaires wear, which in itself, shouldn't have been a disadvantage. But it sure as hell was that particular afternoon.

You see, as most people know, in a lot of Canadian cities, commissionaires are kind of para-policemen and they're given the job of ticketing over-parked cars. O.K., you're saying, but what the hell does that have to do with a private eye who's staking out a seventeen-year-old chick who's supposed to be doing it with her father's business partner? Well, just this.

As I was strolling along, minding my own business, this lard-assed old broad with about a half-dozen chins rolled up in front of me like a Sherman tank and just stood there blocking my way. I took a step to my left and *she* took a step to her right. For a minute, I felt like we were doing an old-fashioned waltz. But the look on her battle-axe face told me that the last thing she wanted to do with me was dance. Her map was beet-red and the veins in her neck were bugging out like pieces of knotted string. Then she began to let loose with that big yap of hers and her voice seemed even madder than the rest of her if that was possible.

"What's the matter with you anyway?" she yelled.

"I beg your pardon –"

"Is that how you get your kicks, taking money from poor people?"

"Taking mo –"

"You oughta be ashamed of yourself. Who do you think

you are? Some kind of Gestapo? Why don't you go to Germany or Russia or someplace?"

"Madam, I don't –"

"You don't think! That's what you don't!" she bellowed like a foghorn.

By that time, there was a real crowd gathered around us and I could feel my face get red-hot as I heard the snickering and saw people nudge each other and point as though they were watching some kind of circus sideshow.

"That's all you goddamn Gestapo can do. Just slap tickets on cars when they're no more than a minute or two over, without even caring that it's money out of people's pockets that they can't afford what with prices and taxes and God knows what-all."

She cocked her head and looked at me accusingly. "Do you know how much a quart of milk costs these days?"

I told her that I didn't and started to edge away but she took a quick step and blocked my path.

"Too damn much that's what! And now you go and slap a ticket on my car when that meter must be out by a good ten minutes and is so crooked that it's highway robbery to expect me to pay it!"

"Listen, lady," I pleaded. "You're making a mistake. I –"

"You're the one who's making the mistake if you think I'm gonna let you get away with those . . . those Gestapo tactics."

And with that, she took this pale yellow parking citation and ripped it into a hundred confetti-sized pieces. She was standing so close that some of the shreds floated down inside my jacket where I found them some time later. Then she stuck this self-righteous smirk on her kisser, turned on her heel, and marched off to the accompaniment of a round of applause from a circle of busybody onlookers who were glaring at me like they figured I was the commandant of Auschwitz.

All that was left for me to do was slink back to my post and keep an eye out for Connie Neilsen but, believe me, my mind sure wasn't on my work after that run-in with that hatchet-faced old bat. The only consolation I had was thinking about the summons she'd have to face when she didn't show up to pay the ticket. Let her try her yelling and bitching routine on some judge and see how far it got her.

Four-thirty. It was the same routine all over again. Connie got into her car and I followed her to her apartment building in the west-end of town. Still no sign of Stenberg. I hung around until eight, at which time my operative spelled me off and I was finally able to go home after a long and – as far as my client was concerned – uneventful day.

And, if that wasn't bad enough, Connie's father called me from up north and refused to believe that I hadn't turned anything up. Like before, it was as though he figured I'd sold him out or something. Man, you could just about feel the distrust seeping through the receiver. But I guess he didn't completely believe that I'd double-crossed him because he told me to keep on the case which meant that first thing in the morning, I was back in front of the apartment building getting ready for another routine day. But as it turned out, it was anything but that. But not at first.

At first, I followed her to school as usual and saw her enter the building. After that, since I was fed up with hanging around that block, I had Carl Miller, one of my operatives, come over and take my place. Then, for the rest of the day, I just stayed put in my office, fielding calls and catching up on some paperwork.

Well, about four-thirty, Carl reported in and told me that Connie had broken her routine. She'd left school at four and headed for home. I told him to keep an eye on her apartment and headed over to the lot where Stenberg usually parked that big Lincoln of his. Somehow I wasn't too surprised to see it gone. Playing a hunch, I headed for the west-end and cruised the blocks around the Neilsens' apartment building. And what did I turn up? Just Dave

Stenberg's cream-coloured Lincoln, that's all. It was parked on a sidestreet a block and a half away.

"Aha," I said to myself, "maybe her father isn't such a kook after all."

And I hustled right over to pass the word to Carl who was parked in the back lane watching the windows of the Neilsen apartment which were now lit up since it was late fall and got dark quite early. Before I could break it to him, he turned to me and said:

"He's inside. Came walking down the lane just after I called you. After he went in, I went up and listened outside her door. There were two voices: a man's and a woman's. He's in there alright."

"Just two voices?"

"Just two."

And we smiled at each other as though we were a couple of cats who'd just been invited to a canary smorgasbord.

I got into his car and we kept an eye on the windows of the Neilsen apartment. The curtains were drawn and the lights were on in the living room and Connie's bedroom which I knew from studying the floor plan of the apartment that Eric Neilsen had given me.

Six-twenty: the light in the living room went out.

Six-twenty-five: ditto for the light in Connie's bedroom. We waited a couple of minutes and the lights in apartment 310 remained out. It was time to move.

Stationing Carl outside the door to the Neilsens' apartment, I went off in search of the caretaker. It took only a couple of minutes to run her down. A small, wiry woman in her mid-fifties, she seemed unimpressed when I showed her my card and said Eric Neilsen had hired me to look after his daughter.

But it was a different story when I told her that Connie had been receiving threats and that, though I knew she was in her suite, there was no answer when I knocked on the door. Well, that lit a stick of dynamite under her and she jingled out a ring of pass keys and we headed toward the elevator at a gallop.

When we reached the apartment, I introduced her to my partner then let her go ahead and knock on the door. Just as I figured, nobody answered. With a little urging, I got her to use her pass key but just as she inserted it, the door swung open and there stood Connie Neilsen – Miss Sweet Innocence – holding her robe clutched tight around her breasts, yawning, and pretending to wipe sleep from her eyes. Just the hall light was on but I could see that her lipstick was smeared.

When she saw Carl and me standing behind the care-taker, her eyelids shot up like they were on springs. That was when I thanked the caretaker for her assistance and told her we could look after things from there on in.

After she'd padded away down the hall, I told Connie who we were and that we were working for her father. Well, at that, she almost collapsed. She had to lean against the wall for support, she was so shook up. Before she could compose herself, I asked:

"Where's Dave?"

While I waited for an answer, I looked her over more closely. The way the robe outlined her curves, I was pretty damn sure she didn't have anything on under it.

"He's not here."

She didn't even ask, "Dave who?"

I had my guy stand at the door while I started to look around.

"You'd better tell him to come out."

"There's nobody here." By now her voice was quavering.

I flicked the light on in the living room. There was a whiskey bottle on the coffee table and a couple of glasses.

"Do you usually drink out of two glasses?" I asked.

She didn't answer. At least not with words. Her face told the whole story though. It reminded me of one of those detergent commercials because, believe me, it was whiter than white.

I started up the hallway toward her bedroom, telling

her: "You might as well tell him to come out. We know he's in here and we know what he was doing here."

She just bit her lip and didn't say a word so I stepped into her bedroom and switched on the light. The bed was unmade with only a sheet for covering. A couple of blankets were in a tangle on the floor. I stepped over to the closet door, turned the knob and yanked. And there, sandwiched in amongst a forest of coats and dresses was Mr. David Stenberg in all his naked glory, looking as meek and shamefaced as a kid caught with his hand in the cookie jar. I looked over to the cookie jar, alias Connie Neilsen, and she looked so desperate that I made a quick check to see if there were any windows handy that she could jump out of. Then I turned back to Stenberg and the things that Eric Neilsen had told me about him flashed into my mind. Maybe Neilsen was right. Maybe Stenberg was some kind of shit-hot ladies' man. But let me tell you, that night he was just another aging lecher with a fear-shrivelled prick. When he finally came out of the closet, he had one of Connie's dresses wrapped around his middle like a sarong. I gave him a chance to get dressed and then we joined Connie and Carl in the living room. The first thing Stenberg said to me before we left the bedroom was:

"Don't I know you?"

I figured he might have seen me somewhere because his office was located near mine but I said "No, you don't know me."

Then he said: "I guess you'll have to make a report of this."

"That's right."

"How long have you known Eric Neilsen?"

"A couple of months."

"Then you probably don't really know him; know what kind of man he is and what he's capable of."

I shrugged. It was none of my business. He was paying the shot and that was good enough for me.

"It's not the way you think," he began.

"It's not what *I* think that counts," I said. "That's up to Connie's father. It's just a job to me."

We were in the living room by now.

"But you've got no real proof we were doing anything . . . well, improper." It was a bluff and a half-hearted one at that because he knew we had him by the bags.

I pointed to the whiskey bottle and the two glasses.

"The girl is seventeen years old, Mr. Stenberg. I guess you know that. And somebody gave her some whiskey and that same somebody was hiding in her closet in the raw. If that's not proof, it'll have to do until something better comes along. Let her father decide if it's proof or not."

Now he really started to panic and his hands shook like hell as he poured himself a good stiff shot. And, in the background, Connie was moaning away and saying that she couldn't stay there because her old man'd kill her when he got back to town and found out what she'd been up to.

By then, what with Connie whimpering and Stenberg shaking, it was quite a scene and I figured that Carl and I might as well take off before it got any hairier. And that was when Stenberg played his last card.

"Suppose you fellows were working for me this evening. What would it be worth?"

"No chance," I said.

"C'mon, how much? Name it. I'll give you ten times what Eric's paying you. Twenty times."

"That's not the way I do business," I said and started for the door, gesturing for Carl to follow.

"Well, what do you know?" Stenberg sneered. "A goddamn window-peeper with scruples!"

"Look who's talking," I shot back. "At least I'm not shagging my best friend's daughter!"

It could've developed into some heavy mud-slinging but just then there was a knock on the door and Connie Neilsen gave a little strangled cry.

"That must be my boyfriend!"

Her boyfriend! Now if that didn't beat the shit out of

everything! And, you know, she was right. When I opened the door, there was the kid she'd been so lovey-dovey with a couple of days earlier, the boy she'd gone for lunch with.

"Come right in," I smiled as Carl and I brushed past him. "I think you're expected."

You know, I often wondered what kind of story Connie fed him but, knowing her, I guess she handled it alright and had him eating out of her hand . . . or whatever.

Anyway, when Eric Neilsen got back to town and read my report, his reaction was a damn sight different than I'd expected, believe me. Instead of being hopping mad and threatening to cut the balls off the guy who'd been messing around with his daughter, he chuckled to himself, saying over and over again: "Wonderful. Wonderful."

He was so elated that he took me out to Rae and Jerry's which is one of the best eateries in the city and bought me the biggest steak in the place. And that was one of the few times that I got a bonus for my work which really surprised me because I thought it might be one of those cases where the bearer of bad tidings gets it in the neck. After all, hadn't I just told him that his friend and business partner was porking his underaged daughter? And what did he do? Just carried on like he'd won the Irish Sweepstakes, that's all.

So it was a strange ending to a strange case. Or at least it would've been even if it had stopped right there. But it didn't end either when, or how, you would've expected. You see, after Neilsen paid me off, I figured if I ever saw him again, it would be by accident so you can imagine my surprise when about ten days later, he showed up at my office.

"I have just one other thing to ask of you," he said.

"Oh boy. What is it now?" I thought to myself but I didn't say anything because even though he said "ask," I could tell from his manner that it was more of a command than a request.

"Well, if I can be of any help. . . ."

"I'll pay you for your time of course," he said which

made me feel a lot better. Then he told me what he had in mind.

"I'd like you to come with me to my lawyer's – he's just down the block – and witness a document for me."

"Is that all? Sure, I'll be glad to."

And I climbed into my coat and off we went. Only we didn't go to his regular lawyer and this struck me as kind of strange. But only until I saw the document he wanted me to witness. As a matter of fact, I've still got a copy of it and it looks like this:

RELEASE

I, Eric Neilsen of the City of Winnipeg, in Manitoba, Manager, in consideration of the sum of one dollar and other good and valuable consideration, hereby release and forever discharge David M. Stenberg of 212 Barton Crescent, from all manners and cause of action which I now have against him arising out of an incident which occurred on Friday, the 1st day of November, 1959, between the said David M. Stenberg and my daughter Connie Neilsen at suite 310 - 1828 Palmer Avenue, in the said City of Winnipeg, absolutely and forever.

In Witness Whereof I have hereunto set my hand and seal this 12th day of November, A.D. 1959.

(SIGNED AND SEALED

in the presence of)   ((Sgd.) E. M. Neilsen)

(A. Manweiler (Sgd.))   Eric Neilsen

Even while I was scribbling my signature, I had this uneasy feeling and if it wasn't for the fact that the release had been drawn up by one of Winnipeg's better-known lawyers – a guy who's pretty prominent in the city even now – I might have backed off. But I went along with it because I figured, what the hell, a lawyer's an officer of the court so he must know what's legal and ethical and all that stuff that's supposed to mean so much to the legal profession.

But later, when I got back to my office, I went over that

release again and I knew there was only one word for an agreement like that: blackmail. Here was my client agreeing to let Stenberg off the hook for messing around with Connie for "one dollar and other good and valuable consideration." "Good and valuable consideration." You didn't have to be a genius to figure out what that meant. His share of the business. What else? And if Stenberg hadn't come across, he would've been facing a charge for contributing to juvenile delinquency and probably some kind of civil action as well. If that's not coercion, I don't know the meaning of the word.

I began to wonder if such a document was enforceable since in my business you have to be kind of a half-assed lawyer and I knew that unconscionable agreements aren't binding. But then, I guessed it didn't really matter because there was sure as hell no way that Stenberg was going to take it to court considering what it would do to his reputation in the business community, not to mention the fact that he was married and had a couple of kids about Connie's age who probably wouldn't think much of their old man's cradle robbing.

Anyway, like I said before, I felt pretty uneasy about the whole deal right about then but as the days passed, I began to forget all about it. After all, it was all in the past, right? Wrong!

A month later, just before Christmas, it was back in my present again. And, off and on, it's stayed there ever since. I can remember it like it was yesterday. I had this place staked out and I was listening to some Christmas carols over my car radio when, all of a sudden, the programme was interrupted by a news flash. A plane had gone missing up north somewhere and there was a search being conducted. I thought to myself that it was sure a lousy time of year for something like that and then I froze as I heard the name of the missing pilot: Eric Neilsen.

That was all there was on the news that night. Search planes were out but there was no sign of Neilsen and his twin-engine Cessna. But the next day, that all changed. A search pilot spotted the remains of the aircraft and, later on, a corps of searchers on snowmobiles found what was left of Eric Neilsen. And guess who supplied the identification for both plane and pilot? David Stenberg who, as it turned out was a co-owner of the aircraft.

Well, maybe it's my suspicious nature, but every time I added up two and two, I came up with a very disturbing four. Fact: flying weather was ideal at the time of the crash. Fact: Neilsen had made radio contact with a nearby airstrip just prior to the crash and gave no indication that anything was wrong. Fact: there was evidence that the craft had been damaged by a minor explosion before it had slammed into the snow-covered terrain. So what happened? I wish I knew but I do know that Neilsen had just gotten through blackmailing his partner and had suddenly ended up dead. Coincidence? Sure it could've been but if it was, it was a helluva convenient one for David Stenberg who, aside from Neilsen, was the only other person who flew that plane.

But, as suspicious as I was, it still took me a long time to do anything about it and, even then, it wasn't very much. During my dealings with Neilsen, he'd dropped the name of his long-time lawyer, Barry Gold. I knew Barry as a straight-shooter and figured that was why Eric hadn't used him on the blackmail caper with Stenberg. I don't really know what the hell I thought I could accomplish but I called on Barry and laid out some dirty linen.

Maybe I shouldn't have. After all, there was the matter of client-investigator confidentiality, but since Neilsen was six feet under and Barry was the kind of guy who could keep his trap shut, I figured there was nothing to lose. When I finished feeding him the story, the veteran lawyer shook his head in amazement.

"I didn't know anything about this. Not a damn thing."

"I know," I said. "I guess Eric didn't think you'd go along with it."

"He was right about that." He stroked his chin, thinking. "So that's why. . . ."

"Why what?"

"Maybe I shouldn't tell you this. . . ." He paused then added quickly: "Oh, what the hell. What harm can it do now? Looks like it's already been done." He went over to a filing cabinet, pulled out a folder and waved it at me. "See this? These are the papers I drew up for Eric a week or so before he died. He was in the process of having Stenberg's share of the business signed over to him. He was going to get the whole shooting match for next to nothing. I couldn't figure why Dave would go along with it. Now, I know."

"It's pretty hard to bargain when you've got your nuts in a vise," I said.

"Ouch," he winced. "Yeah, you're right. Dave was supposed to sign the papers when Eric got back from up north."

"You mean *if* Eric got back."

He threw the file onto his desk. "Well, that's all ancient history now. Stenberg said he changed his mind and wants to hang onto his share."

"I'm not surprised," I said. "Eric got the business alright but not the way he expected."

Barry nosed around and talked to the R.C.M.P. and a crown attorney he knew. They said they smelled something too but without any hard evidence, there was nowhere they could go. So that was where it stood. And stands.

As far as I'm concerned, it's a closed file. Still, it's awfully hard to think of it that way when one of the subjects in the case keeps popping up from time to time. Because, like I said earlier, I still bump into Stenberg on the street every now and then and when I do, everything comes back to me like it was yesterday: the betrayal, the illicit sex, the blackmail, and finally, the violent death of a guy who always seemed so sure of himself you'd have thought he figured he was going to live forever.

But no one does. And neither will I. But until the day I cash in, I'll probably keep wondering about David Stenberg and whether he pulled off the "perfect crime." Of course, I won't be the only one. Because, judging from the look on Stenberg's face when we run into each other, it's a safe bet that he's doing a helluva lot of wondering too.

FIVE

Six Days on the Road

Like I said before, I think this stuff about people in the West being more friendly than those in the big, bad East is nothing more than a load of crap. And I should know since I was brought up in a place called Southey, Saskatchewan, which if not in the heart of the West is at least in the vicinity of the liver or kidneys. Mind you, Southey, which is about forty miles north of Regina, was a pretty nice place to grow up in and in spite of the fact that we lacked a lot of the amenities that kids take for granted today, we did O.K. For example, just because we didn't have fancy indoor rinks didn't mean we couldn't play hockey. Nossir, we'd just flood somebody's backyard and away we'd go even if it was twenty or thirty below. And the fact that we didn't have uniforms or proper equipment didn't mean a thing. Christ, I was almost fourteen before I found out the N.H.L. used rubber pucks. Before that, I'd figured they used horse-buns just like we did but probably got them from some higher-class type of animal.

Even after some forty years, I still like to go back to Saskatchewan because I still have some friends there. But as for westerners being the salt of the earth, well, don't make book on it. Of course, I have to admit I didn't always feel that way. At one time, I was just as much a victim of prairie propaganda as anyone else. Yeah, I think I really believed that hearts automatically became purer and smiles wider as soon as you got west of the Ontario-

Manitoba border. But all that changed over the years. I can't say exactly why or when but I've got an idea an incident in 1975 had at least something to do with it.

I'd had a divorce case in Saskatoon and after wrapping it up, I decided to stop off in Regina for a couple of days before heading back to Winnipeg. There were a couple of business possibilities I wanted to look into plus I thought I'd look up an old buddy of mine whom I played baseball with in the thirties with the old Regina Redsox. Playing ball in Regina was one of my more pleasant experiences but the city also held less happy memories such as the time I tried to get into the Mounties when I was about seventeen and a sergeant told me to come back when I started to shave. I would've too but the war got in the way.

Anyway, I'd managed to locate my old teammate and we had a nice lunch at Frank's Cafe which is a downtown landmark in Regina. Nothing fancy about it. Just a family restaurant that advertised home cooking. And not the kind you get in homes where some broad thinks she's Julia Child if she manages to keep from burning a TV dinner. No, Frank's was a real nice place. Housed in a single-storey building on 11th Avenue, the place had little to set it apart from your average neighbourhood restaurant. Except for one thing. You see, aside from the fact that Frank's was larger and busier than most cafes, it also had the distinction of being about the best-known meeting place in the city. In the Queen City when people said: "See you at Frank's," nobody ever had to ask: "Frank who?"

But, like I was saying, after we had lunch and my friend had to go back to work, I still had some time to kill so I walked around for a while, finally ending up at the Kings Hotel down on Scarth. I understand it's been torn down but back then it was a pretty nice place with a lot of atmosphere and local colour, so I thought I'd stop in for a quick one – a drink, that is.

It's amazing how when you push open the door of a

beer joint, you're slammed with a giant wave of sound but after you're in it for a while, you only notice the noise when it stops. Even though it was the middle of a weekday afternoon, there was a pretty good crowd although you couldn't see that much of it through the haze of cigarette smoke. And everybody was trying to make themselves heard so that meant they had to outshout the people at surrounding tables. Not expecting to see anyone I knew, I started to look for an empty table when I heard someone close behind me yell.

"Hey, Manweiler!"

As I turned, I saw some movement out of the corner of my eye but before I could make out what it was, a fist crashed into the side of my head. If it hadn't been for the wall, I would've ended up on my ass which would've been big trouble because even through blurred vision, I could see that the guy who suckered me looked mad enough to give me the boots. I had another break too because the blow caught me high on the cheek instead of on the temple and, while my eyes watered and a numbing pain spread over the side of my face, I wasn't really dazed so I was able to ward off the clumsy, roundhouse shots that followed. After missing with a windmill right, the crazy bastard lowered his head and bulled into me, catching me in the ribs. It knocked some of the breath out of me but I managed to get him in a headlock, holding on for dear life while he thrashed about and tried to knee me in the balls.

Like I said, at first I was a little stunned, more from surprise than anything else, but now I was starting to see about twenty shades of red. I mean, there I was minding my own business and this lunatic comes from left field and belts me in the mush.

We tussled around for another minute or so, both of us puffing and him swearing and threatening to kill me if I didn't let him go. Finally, I'd had my fill of the crazy sonuvabitch. Since he wouldn't listen to reason and the bouncer, if there was one, was playing hide-and-seek, I figured I had to take matters into my own hands. By this time, we'd attracted quite an audience and I felt like a real idiot waltzing around with this maniac. Lining up his head with an open spot on the wall to my left, I lunged forward, taking full advantage of the fact I outweighed him by about fifty pounds. It must have been quite a sight with me lumbering down an aisle between the tables and picking up speed with every step.

There was a sharp crack when his head hit the wall and I hoped it was the wallboard and not his skull. He gave a delayed-reaction spasm of energy then he was all deadweight. I released my hold and he sank to the floor as limp as a rag doll.

And, wouldn't you know it, the Invisible Man, the pub's beer-bellied bouncer, picked that moment to find his balls and come blustering onto the scene.

"C'mon, take it outside. We don't want no goddamn brawls in here. Next one starts anything is gonna answer to me!"

I gave him a disgusted look as I straightened my tie which somehow had got flipped up over my left shoulder. My chest was still heaving from exertion when – whattaya know – the guy who'd jumped me started getting to his feet, with the help of a couple of fellows who, from the way they were glaring at me, must've been his buddies. For the first time, I got a good look at him but, in spite of the fact he looked familiar, I couldn't place him. He had some kind of uniform on – dark green with a company crest on the shirt pocket. Looked like he might've been a truckdriver. Truckdriver. It was as if a projector had started up in my head, re-running a scene from a five-year-old movie because that was how long it had been since I'd seen him last. It was the truckdriver thing that did it. That's how I made the connection and that's also how I connected up his name – Myron Tomlik. His eyes still weren't focusing properly and he seemed to be looking beyond me when he sneered: "This ain't the end of it. Not by a longshot. You're gonna get yours, ya goddamn Judas. Alex and the rest of the guys, all it'll take is one phone call to get 'em down here and then we'll see what a big fuckin' hero you are."

Now that I knew who he was, I also knew he'd like nothing better than to kick the shit out of me but I guess his booze-courage had dissipated because he contented himself with calling me every name he could think of and allowed himself to be led away by his pals.

As his buddies hustled him out the door, with the bouncer following close behind to make himself look important, Tomlik jerked his head around and spat towards me. Either he was still groggy or just naturally a poor shot but anyway, the gob of saliva was wide of the mark – so wide, in fact, that it hit the bouncer on the side of his beefy and now reddening neck.

Well, that bouncer probably didn't have much of a sense of humour – at least not as much as some of the bystanders who were busting their guts laughing. He just roared like a wounded bear and charged after Myron who, by this time, had miraculously sobered up and was hotfooting it through the lobby with the bouncer in close pursuit. I didn't stick around to see what happened. I was thinking about what Myron had said about some other guys having a bone to pick with me and I guessed he was right. I also thought about him calling me a Judas. And, you know, I guess he was right about that too.

The whole thing – the sequence of events that ended with me getting that smack in the head – began in the summer of 1970, when I got a call from the manager of a Winnipeg trucking company called Prairie Freightlines (not the actual name of the company). Actually, the outfit wasn't just a local operation. Although the head office was in Winnipeg, the firm also had freight terminals in Saskatchewan and Alberta. From these terminals, trucks – mostly tractor-trailer rigs – were dispatched locally, provincially, and on a prairie-wide basis. Anyway, the manager, whom I'll call Ted Stevens, wasn't too happy with the way things were going in their Regina branch and he thought that the main problem was with the drivers. He told me the work-injury and absentee rates were a lot higher than those at their other terminals and that the Regina management hadn't been able to come up with a satisfactory explanation.

That was just the tip of the iceberg though. There were other problems, large and small, like drivers failing to meet delivery schedules which meant customers didn't get their shipments when they needed them. Other matters of concern ranged from an alarming number of damaged consignments to a rash of equipment breakdowns and pilferage. Stevens had also gotten reports from Saskatchewan sources that some of the drivers had been drinking on the job and had, on occasion, become abusive with both customers and the public.

According to the Winnipeg manager, he'd gotten all kinds of stories from the Regina brass but none of them had either explained or resolved the problems. And that was where I came in. He wanted me to go to Regina and find out just what the hell was going on. Of course, it wouldn't be as easy as it sounded because if I just waltzed in there and started nosing around, no one, including the management who were probably protecting their own asses, would give me the time of day. I needed a good cover. And before I left for Regina near the end of June, I hit on one that was a stroke of genius if I do say so myself.

My brainstorm was that I'd pose as an inspector for White Trucks, having first found out that Prairie Freight-lines' Regina fleet was largely comprised of this particular make. My cover was that White Trucks wanted to check on the performance of these vehicles under everyday conditions, which gave me a perfect excuse to hang around the terminal and – better still – accompany the drivers on their hauls. Ted Stevens set the whole thing up with the Regina brass who promised me total co-operation and, to make my act more convincing, I got hold of every manual I could find on White Trucks and took a crash course on everything from fifth wheels and tachometers to split-shifts and air brakes.

And, finally, to put the icing on the cake, I got a printer to run off some fake checklists for me with headings covering various performance areas, for example, electrical, powertrain, brakes, and the suspension system. They had the White logo in bold letters across the top and looked so official they almost fooled *me*. The best part of the deal though was that no one in Regina, from the manager down, had any idea what my real mission was, which meant I didn't have to worry about anyone letting the cat out of the bag.

I'd had my cover blown on other occasions and once a whole month's work had gone into the toilet just because one guy whose mouth was too large for his brain shot off his mouth.

Anyway, when I showed up at the Regina terminal, the manager welcomed me with open arms. You see they'd been having a little trouble with that year's model – the clutch was slipping on a couple of the tractors – and I guess he figured if he got on my good side, I might get "my" company to reimburse him for the repairs. Of course, there was as much chance of that as of Bo Derek fixing me breakfast in bed. But, naturally, I didn't tell him that because, what the hell, it was no skin off my nose if he thought he was chalking up brownie points with White Trucks. The guy's name was Art – Art McCrea – and he had one of those red faces with a little network of purplish veins near the surface. It was a real whiskey-drinker's kisser and, having seen him knock the stuff back, I knew it was honestly come by. A big, bluff guy, he seemed well-liked by those who worked under him, all of whom – including the drivers – called him by his first name.

You could tell he didn't throw his weight around because when he showed up in the warehouse unexpectedly, the men didn't suddenly come up with academy-award-winning performances to make it look like they were busting their asses when there really wasn't anything for them to do except maybe push a broom.

I didn't deal with Art all that much though. My main

contact was Ken Staller, the dispatcher. A middle-aged, wiry little guy with sharp features, he reminded me of one of the less trustworthy members of the rodent family. Actually, it wasn't his looks that turned me off so much as his handshake. He had one of those limp, fairy numbers that made you think you'd grabbed onto a couple of stalks of month-old celery by mistake.

He was co-operative though, I'll say that for him because he was the one who lined me up with the drivers I travelled with while I ran my so-called performance checks on their tractors. For those who don't know, when I use the term "tractor," I'm not talking about your John Deere or Massey Harris farm type but a regular truck with a cab and frame that slides under the trailer and hooks it up to a locking mechanism that's commonly called the "fifth wheel."

Anyway, the whole thing went pretty smoothly for the first couple of weeks, when I'd be on the road two, maybe three, days at a crack. The routes varied but most of the time, we'd head north up to Prince Albert and North Battleford and once I even got as far as Lloydminster which is right on the Alberta-Saskatchewan border. But the trips I liked the best were the short hauls to Melville or Yorkton because they took us on the scenic route through the Qu'Appelle Valley which has always been one of my favourite spots. Now, it might not seem like much to someone from B.C. or Ontario but when you live in Saskatchewan and are used to seeing nothing but flat, treeless land and the only hills are those made by gophers when they scoop out their holes, the Qu'Appelle Valley is like an oasis in a desert of wheat. And the best time to see it is in the early morning when the sun begins to spread over Echo Lake, turning every ripple into a jewel, and the hills that sweep right down to the water's edge start to come in out of the dark and turn a rich green.

But even the most dyed-in-the-wool Saskatchewan booster would have to admit that places like this are few and far between unless you go 'way up north. The rest of the province is pretty well what raced past us on the hauls to North Battleford which were the first ones I went on and which, at first, were pretty uneventful. The drivers were friendly enough but, initially, they didn't feel at ease with me sitting beside them busily making notes on my phony checklists and trying to look as though I knew what I was doing. Later on though, after I'd been on some good piss-ups with them, the word must have gotten around that I was an O.K. guy because they started to loosen up and treat me like one of the boys.

The first breakthrough came on a haul to Prince Albert and North Battleford. I was riding with a guy by the name of Alex Androyko, a big farm boy from somewhere around Estevan. He was in his late twenties and although he'd only been on the road for about five years, he figured he was the King of the Road himself.

We'd just pulled out of the terminal when he slid a tape into the player below a dash that had more dials and gauges than some planes I've been in. Hanging from the rectangular rear-view mirror was an air-freshener with a picture of a naked broad on it. It had a pine scent and I thought that was kind of inappropriate since none of the girls I ever went with smelled like a tree, although, come to think of it, some of them didn't smell like women either.

Alex turned up the volume and the music blasted out so loud you'd have thought Merle Haggard was right there in the cab with us. It wasn't a bad song but I might have missed something because even after hearing it a half-dozen times, I'll be damned if I knew why he was proud to be an Okie from Muskogee. Anyway, it was better than listening to the roar of a White Freightliner which, when you get it revved up, sounds like a cross between a B-29 and a Sherman tank.

A lot of drivers installed tape-decks in their rigs because when you get a little way out of town, the reception is no hell from some of those Mickey Mouse stations with fifty watt transmitters and sometimes you get nothing but static. A couple of guys also had CB's but Alex said they weren't worth the money and that if he got one it'd only be so he could give and receive tips about radar traps.

By the time we reached the outskirts of Regina, I'd lost about fifty percent of my hearing and the music had become bearable. As loud as it was, it still didn't blot out the diesel whine as Alex shifted and accelerated through about a dozen gears. I could tell by his expression that he got a big charge out of piloting that rig and feeling the surge of power that it took to lug a fifty-foot trailer and twenty-five tons of freight. He was like a kid with a fifty-thousand-dollar toy because, you may not believe it, but that's about what the company had shelled out for his tractor.

A couple of miles down the road, he reached behind him into the sleeper and fished a couple of bottles out of a case that had been covered with a blanket. Driving with one hand, he shoved the neck of one of the bottles into the side of his mouth and bit down on the cap. In one motion, he twisted his head and the bottle, and the cap popped off. When he smiled at his accomplishment, I half-expected to see a gap where some teeth had snapped off but they were all there. He handed the beer to me and repeated the stunt with a second bottle. He took a big slug and jerked his thumb over his right shoulder.

"There's more back there when you want one. Anyway, it's your turn to open the next round."

I shook my head. "No way. At least not without an opener. I've still got most of my teeth and I want to keep it that way."

He laughed and took another gulp of beer. I did the same in spite of the fact it wasn't the kind of breakfast I was used to. But even though it was only six-thirty in the morning, the stuff didn't taste half-bad.

"A little early for this, isn't it?" I asked, holding up my bottle.

"Never too early," he chuckled. "Never too early for cold beer and warm pussy."

"Yeah, I guess you're right but beer usually makes me sleepy, especially when I'm driving. How about you?"

"Hell no. It don't bother me at all besides if it does, I got something that can keep everything but my cock up for twenty-four hours." He dug around in his shirt pocket and came up with a small tin-foil-wrapped bundle. He handed it to me with a sly smile.

"Go ahead, take a look."

I opened the package. There were about a dozen tablets in it. They looked a lot like aspirins except that they were pink rather than white. I didn't have to be told what they really were, but Alex filled me in anyway.

"Bennies, pardner. The real shit. Suck up one of them babies and you won't have to worry about renting no hotel room tonight because, brother, you ain't gonna be doing any sleeping. Just gonna be doing a lot of this."

And he widened his eyes and stared out the windshield like some kind of crazed owl. I started to bundle them up again.

"Shit, don't do that, Manny!" Like most of the other drivers, Alex called me by the nickname I'd gotten tagged with as a kid. The funny thing was, I hadn't even mentioned I had one. It just seemed that if you had a name like "Manweiler," people just naturally figured that your nickname had to be "Manny." He reached over, grabbed one of the pills, and popped it into his mouth, chasing it with a draught of beer.

"Christ," I thought to myself, "and here it is barely sun up. This is going to be some day."

Next, Alex started coaxing me to take one too and, finally, to get him off my back, I made like I was taking one but I actually palmed it and shoved it into my pocket when he wasn't looking. Later on, I began to wish I'd taken it just for self-defence because the sonuvabitch did nothing but talk for the next two hours, telling me his whole life story, including the more intimate details of his sex life which was something I could get along without.

"Manny, I'll tell you," he said, "a lot of guys like to do

it the same way all the time, y'know, just climb on and pump away until you blow your load. Not me. I'm more – whatayacallit – adventurous. I like to keep the broads guessing. And they really go for it too, you know what I mean?"

And he gave me this giant wink as though I'd been let in on one of the great secrets of our time. Now, his blowing off was bad enough but what really cheesed me off was the thought that he might really be getting as much pussy as he wanted me to believe, because even though he was about as bright as a fifteen-watt bulb, I had to admit he wasn't bad looking and he had a mop of blond curly hair that gave him a boyish look that some broads seem to go for. And do you think I could shut him up? No way. What with the booze and the benny, he was a one-man talka-thon. After helping himself to another beer, he was off and running again.

"You know," he said seriously, "I think if I ever get off the road, I'll become one of those – whatayacallit – studs. You know, those guys who get paid for screwing horny broads so they don't have to play with themselves."

That was too much. By now, I was totally fed up with his non-stop blabbing but there wasn't much I could do about it because I wanted to keep on his good side so, humouring him, I said: "Your wife is sure lucky to have a guy like you around." He didn't seem to notice the sarcasm.

"Yeah, you better believe it," he crowed, dropping his hand to his crotch and giving his plumbing a little heft. "I put the meat to her every morning whether she wants it or not just to keep her from getting too hungry when I'm away. And it don't matter what time it is neither. Like, take this morning. Got up at quarter to five, had to be at work by six, but I still took the time to throw a length into her." He grabbed his crotch again. "Yessir, all I gotta do is wave this here magic wand of mine and she spreads her legs like a goddamn wishbone. Man, talk about moanin' and groanin'! And when I get her all oiled up and humping like she wants to shove her old honeypot right through me, well, sometimes I pull out and let her look at it for a while just so she can appreciate what she's gettin'."

And that's the way it went until we got to Prince Albert. When we pulled into the terminal yard, Alex jumped down and went into the dispatch office. Then, a short time later, he came out and backed the trailer into one of the loading bays and, after cranking down the dolly wheels, unhooked his tractor. He then drove over to another trailer spotted next to the high chainlink fence surrounding the yard and hooked on. While he connected the air hoses and the cables for the trailer lights, I started to crank up the dolly wheels.

"Hey, you do that pretty good," he shouted down from the back of the cab. "I should hire you full time."

We left for North Battleford that afternoon carrying a load of beer – cases and cases of the stuff stacked on wooden pallets right up to the back doors. After grabbing some lunch at a truckstop a couple of miles out of town, we went a little further before Alex pulled over onto the shoulder, hopped down from the cab and went around to the back of the trailer. A couple of minutes later, he was back behind the wheel, grinning and smelling of beer. He wiped his hands on his shirt and turned to me.

"Well, buddy, we just got ourselves a couple of cases of beer for the trip home."

"Yeah? Just how did we do that?"

"Simple. There's a couple of cases back there that got damaged somehow. Nothing much, just one bottle in each case."

"Which means?"

"Which means the consignee won't accept them."

"So how does that get us any beer?"

He checked the sideview mirror then gunned the rig back onto the highway.

"Well, what happens then is that they put in a claim for the damaged goods and the hauler gets to keep whatever can be salvaged."

"Yeah," I said, "but won't the company want to see the damage before paying the claim?"

"Naw, Art don't worry about chickenshit stuff like that. What the hell, it's not coming out of *his* pocket."

All along, I'd been drafting a mental history of the trip, in particular, the things I thought would be of interest to the company's head office. And then, later, I planned to follow the format of previous trips and write out a detailed report of the day's happenings and mail it to a post office box in Winnipeg where my secretary would pick it up and relay it to Ted Stevens. The reason I sent them to a post office box rather than to my office or Prairie Freightlines itself was that there was a chance – albeit a slim one – that someone might catch a glimpse of the envelope before I managed to post it and I didn't want a little thing like an address to trip me up. In my business, it's better to err on the side of caution than to take a chance and see a month's work shot down in flames. And that's also why on under-cover assignments the only notes I make are those that are shipped off immediately.

Now, some people may call that paranoid but not me because there've been times when if someone had got wise to my act, my health would've taken a sudden and painful turn for the worse.

As I said earlier, for the first couple of weeks, although I kept sending out my reports like a good little boy, there wasn't really all that much to write home about. Sure, there were incidents of boozing and screwing around when the drivers should've been on the road and these alone would've been enough to get some guys their walk-ing papers but, until Alex pulled the stunt with the beer shipment, I hadn't witnessed any actual rip-offs. And, in spite of the fact he probably considered me his partner-in-crime, that caper had been duly noted and reported to Winnipeg. But it wasn't 'til the next day that I had some-thing juicy to forward to my client.

We'd partied it up in North Battleford 'til about three in the morning and what with sleeping in and being hung-over, we were late getting away for the trip back to Regina. On the way, we were supposed to drop the trailer at Prince Albert and pick up another one for the last leg of the haul. Since we were a couple of hours behind schedule, Alex laid a heavy foot on the gas pedal.

"How do you like the way this motherfucker moves, Manny?" he smiled, taking a slug from one of the bottles he'd salvaged from the damaged cases.

"Great, Alex," I said, hoping I didn't look as sick as I felt. "Just great."

He was sure making up time, I'll say that for him – at least until we were just east of a little place called Radisson, where he jammed on the brakes so hard the trailer jack-knifed a little. And it was all because of a broad, a little hippie chick who was hitch-hiking at the side of the highway. She was wearing grubby coveralls, a lumberjack shirt, and a pair of workboots and even with shoulder-length, straight, dark-brown hair, looked just like a guy, as far as I was concerned. But not to Alex. I don't know what it was with that guy but it was like he had radar when it came to broads. Maybe it was because he was horny all the time. He reminded me of someone who hasn't had a square meal in a week and can smell food cooking from ten miles away.

"Give her a hand with her shit," he ordered, "and let her in first." He winked. "I know how you like to sit next to the window."

The fact that there was a sign in the cab saying "No Riders" didn't mean a damn thing to him when broads were concerned. He was a real pussyhound alright. But I have to admit the girl didn't look all that bad even decked out in those Sally Ann rejects. Her hair seemed clean enough and even though she wasn't wearing any make-up, she didn't have that washed-out look like a lot of hippie broads whose idea of outdoor activity is smoking marijuana in the backyard of some commune.

I helped her with her luggage which consisted of a scruffy duffle bag and a battered suitcase held together

with a piece of rope. Then I gave her a hand-up into the
cab where Alex was mentally rubbing his hands with
anticipation just at the thought of getting so close to some
pussy. He didn't waste any time in putting the make on
her either. I didn't pay much attention to the crap he was
handing her because I'd heard it all before but it went
something like this.

"Been on the road long?"

"A while."

"Must get lonely being by yourself and all."

"Sometimes."

"Got a boyfriend?"

She hesitated a little before answering. "No."

"Not butch, are ya?"

Alex was a lot of things but subtle was not one of them.
And, as it turned out, neither was she. She burst out
laughing and when she stopped, said as cool as anything:
"Christ, if you want to ball me, why don't you come right
out and say so instead of going through all this bourgeois
bullshit?"

Alex affected a hurt look. "Who said anything about
balling? I was just trying to make conversation. Geez,
what kinda guy do you take me for, anyway?"

She looked at him appraisingly. "The kind who thinks
women exist just so you can have something to stick your
dick into besides your hand."

He flushed with anger. Braking sharply, he cut the
wheel, and brought the rig to a shuddering halt on the
gravel shoulder. "Get the hell out of my goddamn truck
you lousy dyke," he bellowed.

She was already grabbing her bags out of the sleeper. I
started to help her but Alex stopped me.

"Let her get her own shit. She don't need any help from
a man, anyway. She's probably one of them – whataya-
callem – women's libbers who don't need nothin' from a
man, least of all, his plumbing. She probably gets her
kicks by playing 'hide the salami.'" He leaned over and
leered at her. "Or maybe you got a German shepherd

that's trained to do tricks with you. Is that how you get fixed up?"

I jumped down to let her out of the cab and, in spite of what Alex had said, helped her down with her luggage. Too embarrassed to look her in the face, I mumbled a good-bye. When I got back in the tractor, Alex leaned across me and shouted down at her.

"Maybe next time, you'll get lucky and get picked up by some butch queer like yourself. That's the only way you'll ever get your rocks off anyway, because no real man would ever have anything to do with any ugly douchebag like you!"

The girl looked up at him, smiled sweetly, and said: "You know, if I ever do turn into a lesbian, I'll bet some psychiatrist will trace it back to my meeting up with you because you're enough to turn anyone off of men."

And she gave him an old-fashioned single-finger salute and squatted down beside her bags, looking as if she hadn't a worry in the world. Alex looked anything but that. He was fuming so much he took it out on the truck, grinding the gears as we roared away. Not that he admitted it though.

"Make a note of that, Manny," he bawled. "See the way that fuckin' clutch is slipping?" Then he changed the subject if not his mood. "Y'know, Manny, it's a goddamn good thing we got rid of that bitch. She's probably a guy – one of those Transylvanians – y'know those guys that dress up like broads."

Since the girl had been dressed in men's clothing, I couldn't see the logic in his argument but I kept my mouth shut because I didn't want to get him any madder. I figured about the best thing I could do was humour him.

"Could be," I said. "I hear there's plenty of them around these days. Anyway, whatever she or he was, she didn't look that shit-hot to me anyhow."

"Yeah," he sneered, "like something you'd run into on Halloween night. What a douchebag!"

We rode along in silence for a while. Alex had this

thoughtful expression on his face and was drumming the steering-wheel with his fingers. Finally, he turned to me and frowned.

"D'ya think if I'd offered her twenty bucks, she woulda dropped her strides?" Without waiting for me to answer, he shook his head. "Naw, the bitch is probably so dumb, she still thinks it's to piss with."

I later learned that my report on this episode was one of Ted Stevens' favourites. But there were others that also held his interest and one of them had to do with a run I made with Myron Tomlik who – to refresh your memory – is the guy who hit me with the sucker punch in the Kings.

I'd been on a few short hauls with Myron a couple of weeks earlier and he'd kept his nose reasonably clean aside from getting kickbacks at a couple of service stations that bumped his gas bills and charged him for imaginary tow-jobs and tire repairs. He, of course, didn't know I'd forwarded a blow-by-blow account of these capers to Winnipeg. No, like the rest of them, he considered me one of the boys – someone who got a kick out of seeing the company take it in the ass. He even threw a few bucks my way, calling it my "share." Anyway, on the next trip I took with him which, I believe, was to Melfort, he showed me just how much he trusted me. And I showed him – although not until later – just how misplaced that trust was.

We'd left the terminal shortly after six a.m. and were shooting the breeze the way we usually did when out of the clear blue sky, Myron hit me with: "Y'know, Manny, I'll tell you the truth, when you first showed up, me and some of the guys, we had you figured for a stoolie – a company spy."

My hands started to sweat. I wondered if he'd gotten wise to me and was playing some kind of cat-and-mouse game.

"But not any more. Now we know you're an alright guy," he smiled. "At first there, we tested you a little, y'know, to see if you'd shoot your mouth off about this or that, but you didn't and that's a good thing. For us. . ." his mouth tightened, ". . . and for you too."

It took me a little while to convince myself he hadn't been on a fishing expedition but, a couple of minutes later, something happened that satisfied me I was home-free. We were just leaving the outskirts of Regina when Myron grinned and said we were going to make a slight detour. He then swung the rig onto a dirt road heading east. Up ahead, the sun had painted the wheatfields gold. It was really something to see. I was so wrapped up in it, I didn't notice the car until we were almost on top of it. But then I made up for lost time, repeating the license number to myself over and over again until I committed it to memory. You see, I had a hunch the driver of that vehicle was out there to do more than just admire the view and, as it turned out, I was right. Myron slowed, passed the car which was a ten-year-old Chevy sedan, then pulled over and stopped. Shoving his door open, he started to climb down, saying: "I'll be back in a minute."

I followed his progress in the sideview mirror but lost him when he went behind the trailer. Then one of the rear doors swung open and, a couple of minutes later, closed again. By the time Myron hoisted himself behind the wheel, I was slouched down on my side, pretending to doze. Although, as I said earlier, I don't usually write things down, I'd taken the opportunity of jotting down the license number of the car, thinking it was too important to trust to memory.

We circled down a series of backroads and came out at the highway. Myron gunned the machine onto the asphalt and we were back on our route having lost about twenty minutes and who-knows-what from the trailer. He ran through the gears then turned toward me. "Not gonna ask what that was about?"

"If you don't want to tell me, I don't want to know."

"I like that," he laughed. "That's a good way to think." He winked broadly then volunteered the information that he was "just shifting the load a little."

I shrugged. "What the hell, it's a big company."

"That's what I always say. They can take the loss. Besides, if those fatcat bastards at the top would pay us a living wage, we wouldn't have to steal."

It was always the same. Basically honest guys who ripped off the company they worked for always had the same rationale for their dishonesty. The company could stand the loss and the workers were being mistreated. Two of the biggest copouts for thievery in the books. But at least guys like Myron had some kind of excuse, half-assed as it was. In my business, I also run into professional types, like lawyers and businessmen, who also have sticky fingers but they don't even try to justify their larceny. I guess they figure, what with their money and position, they have a right to rook anyone they can. They also have the opportunity of grabbing with both hands whereas guys like Myron have to make do with chickenfeed and are lucky if they can score a hundred bucks worth of loot at a time.

It was my guess that Myron had made a pretty good haul on this early morning caper though. I'd gotten to the terminal a little early and watched them finish loading the trailer. Right at the back were pallets stacked high with cartons of cigarettes. Nice and light and nice and expensive. There'd be a shortage at the other end – that is, if the load was checked off properly which, more often than not, wasn't the case. And even if the receiver did catch the shortage, it could be passed off as a foul-up at origin because shortages and overages were both common in the freight business and it wasn't anything new for consignees to have too much or too little of whatever it was they'd ordered.

On our way back to Regina that afternoon, Myron's needle was stuck on the same sad song he'd given me earlier about it being impossible to have a decent standard of living on a truckdriver's wage.

"Believe me, you're lucky you haven't got a family to support. Christ, you gotta be a millionaire to feed and

clothe them proper. There's no way I could do it if I didn't
pick up the odd buck here and there. It's not really stealing either when you consider the dough the bosses make
off the sweat of guys like us."

Guys like us. He thought of me as someone like himself
– a working stiff who had no choice but to go through life
taking orders from a privileged class of higher-ups who'd
throw you a crumb every now and then if you managed to
catch them in a good mood.

"It's not gonna be that way with my kids," he continued. "Nossir. They're gonna get good educations and call
their own shots. None of this kissing ass and begging for a
two-bit raise. Nossir, not my kids. They're gonna have a
helluva lot more than I did. That's why I went in hock up
to my ass and bought a new house last year. The payments
are killing me but at least they got a nice place to live. Me,
when I grew up we had a tar-paper shack with an outdoor
shithouse. In the winter, it was so cold it was like sitting on
a fucking skating rink.

"None of that shit for my kids. They got a place they
can bring their friends without being embarrassed."

I didn't think he was bullshitting me. He was only in his
early thirties and already saddled with a wife and three
kids. It couldn't have been easy for him because two of the
kids were under five and there was no way his wife could
take a job. He seemed like a good family man alright and I
knew for a fact he was a hard worker who'd jump at the
chance for some overtime and the extra money it meant.
Yeah, it wasn't easy for him. Nor would it be any easier
after I sent in a report on the stunt he'd pulled that
morning.

When we got back to the terminal, he parked the rig
and we started toward the warehouse. I'd intended to head
for my hotel, grab something to eat, and write up my
report but Myron stopped me.

"Wait until I punch out. Then I'll take you to my place
for supper. I'll barbecue a couple of steaks and you can
get some homecooking for a change. We can stop off and

grab a bottle on the way and make a party of it. Whattaya say?"

I couldn't think of a good excuse so I accepted the invitation and we arrived at his split-level bungalow a little before seven. While he got the coals ready, I chatted with his wife, Bertha, tried to break the ice with the two younger kids who stole peeks at me from behind their mother's wide-hipped frame, and sipped on a rye and water.

Bertha was friendly, the kids were reasonably well-behaved, and the steaks were great so, all in all, it was a very pleasant evening – a lot different from what I'd been used to over the last five weeks when I'd just about hit every greasy spoon within ten miles of my hotel.

When we finally called it a day, it was almost midnight and Myron and I had just polished off the last of the booze. He offered to drive me back to my hotel and as I got into his stationwagon which was parked in the driveway, I noticed another vehicle in the garage. It was a navy-blue, 1965 Chevy sedan and I didn't have to look at the plate to know it was the same one I'd seen that morning. But I did anyway. It was the one alright and since Myron's oldest kid was twelve, it was pretty obvious who'd been driving it. His partner-in-crime had been his wife or at least that's the way it looked to me.

When Myron dropped me off, I thanked him for a very pleasant evening and went upstairs to write my report. As far as I was concerned, that pretty well wrapped up my assignment but Ted Stevens wanted me to stay in Regina for another week just to make sure that everyone who should've been nailed was. I didn't turn up anything big on that final week – just more of the same boozing, pill-popping, and petty thievery – but it was memorable just the same because a couple of days before I went back to Winnipeg I went to one of the weirdest piss-ups I'd ever seen, one that ended up with a skinny-dipping session right in the heart of Canada's Queen City. And this is how it happened.

On paydays, it had become a regular thing for a bunch of us to get together at the Drake or Kings for some heavy-duty drinking and this one was no exception. I always tried to take it easy and stay half-way sober so I could pick up bits and pieces of conversation that might be of interest but sometimes it wasn't easy what with all the free rounds floating around. Alex, Myron, and a bunch of other guys were there, drinking and hustling the beer-parlour queens that always seem to be around on the drivers' paydays. We pulled a couple of tables together and there were about a dozen of us boozing it up, talking shop, and trying to keep the water buffaloes, which is what the guys called female freeloaders, from ordering drinks on our tab. We did buy a couple of rounds for three broads sitting at the next table though because they weren't bad looking and were well-known for their talents which didn't include either cooking or sewing.

Anyway, by the time we closed the bar, the crowd at our tables had thinned out and there were just the three girls, Alex, Myron, myself and an out-of-town driver called Red who had a room in the hotel and agreed to play host to a little party to mark the first anniversary of Myron's hemorrhoid operation. With each of us lugging a case of beer, we stumbled upstairs, shooshing each other with such conviction that a number of doors along the hall opened up and the occupants stuck their heads out to see what the hell was going on.

Once inside, I started to case the broads to see how much more I'd have to drink before they started looking good enough to take a run at. Amy, a sandy-haired babe with a flat Mick face and a ton of freckles, had the best build. Nice full upthrust breasts under a clinging sweater, although she probably owed it all to a steel-reinforced brassiere, and a curvaceous caboose that moved when she walked as though it had a life of its own. She was starting to get a little thick in the waist but that wasn't surprising considering she was in her late thirties and was known to drink the occasional beer . . . or case.

The other two looked like they had some Indian blood in them. Not a hell of a lot, just enough to give them dark eyes and hair and high cheekbones. Marie, about thirty, had the nicest face of the three – fine features and large almond eyes. The only thing that detracted from it was a scar above her right eye that looked like a second eyebrow. Her figure was no hell though. Non-existent tits and a gaunt frame with a perpetual slump.

Lucy, the third one, was to put it bluntly, a dog. She weighed in at about one-seventy and when she laughed, her eyes almost disappeared into the folds in her fat face. She also smelled of b.o. mingled with cheap perfume. Unless somebody got drunk as a skunk, I didn't think there was much chance of her seeing any action that night.

As it turned out, I was wrong because the whole crew saw quite a bit of action although it wasn't the kind we'd anticipated. It all began with Alex Androyko – who else? – suggesting a game of strip poker. The broads were game and so was Red but taking my clothes off in front of a crowd never appealed to me, so I begged off. Myron did the same. Not out of any sense of modesty but because he thought it might interfere with some serious drinking. So while the cardplayers sat on the floor in a circle, Myron and I drank beer and kibitzed. After a while, what with all the stripping and drinking, it looked like a bunch of Doukhobors at a beer garden. The girls, in particular, were lousy poker players and, before long, they were down to bras and panties (Amy's had a nice touch: a red heart stamped right on the crotch).

Alex still had most of his clothes on and Red had only shucked his shoes, socks, and shirt. It was funny to see the difference in attitudes among those broads. Marie and Lucy sat hunched over, trying to cover their breasts with their arms but not Amy. What she had is what you got. Her jugs overflowed her brassiere and nipples the size of silver dollars showed right through the cups. Every once in a while, Alex gave her the eye, flicking out his tongue like a boa constrictor. Once, even though it was pretty obvious she was getting a charge out of turning him on, Amy put on a pained expression and said to Alex: "At least you got something that moves. If you could teach it to play poker, maybe we'd get somewhere."

"It can do something better than that," he smiled, doing the snake bit again.

"Oh yeah, I'll bet," she said, taking two cards.

"Lose another couple of hands and you'll find out."

"Don't make me laugh."

Alex looked at his cards and said smugly, "One more hand after this ought to do it."

Marie was dealing and she asked Red how many cards he wanted but he had his head down and seemed to be studying his hand. At least that's what we thought. After a minute or so went by without him answering, we realized why the game was being held up. You see, Red wasn't deliberating. He'd passed out, although how he'd managed to remain in a sitting position was beyond me. Not that it lasted long, because as soon as Marie shook him to try and wake him up, he started to topple over. Pissed off that Red was holding up the game which, in turn, kept the girls from dropping the last of their laundry, Alex grabbed hold of our unconscious host and tried to hoist him onto the bed but Red weighed about two-fifty so, after some futile straining, he gave up and shoved him underneath instead which all of us got a kick out of.

Now, while the others were playing, Myron and I hadn't exactly been idle either. We'd been putting the booze away pretty good – especially Myron who, by this time, was feeling no pain. He did feel something else though. As Amy passed him on her way to the can, Myron reached over and shoved his hand down the front of her briefs, copping a healthy handful of snatch.

Ever the lady, Amy responded with a slap on the ear and a colourful suggestion as to what he could do with his hand. Well, that plus the fact that the rest of us started laughing didn't sit too well with Myron. I could tell he was burned up and I watched him when the others went back to their cardplaying. Instead of the good-natured ribbing he was dishing out before, he started tossing insults at Alex and the girls, telling them what shitty poker players they were and how they thought a royal flush was what Queen Elizabeth did when she went to the john.

They ignored him, even when he staggered to his feet. Weaving from side to side as if being rocked by a stiff breeze, he unzipped his fly and pulled out his cock. The game was going hot and heavy and, except for me, nobody gave him so much as a look. So, not getting a rise out of them, he went further – a lot further.

Wobbling up beside Alex who was sitting cross-legged and showing off by shuffling the deck with one hand, Myron aimed his dick like a Bengal lancer and stuck the end right into Alex's ear. Christ, I almost fell of my chair! And the craziest thing about the whole deal was that Alex still didn't get wise. He was so wrapped up in the game, plus being pretty juiced, that he probably figured he was being pestered by a fly or something because he slapped at it without even looking up.

And that goddamn Myron, not having enough brains to quit while he was ahead, decided to try it again. Alex had just won the hand with a straight flush, Queen high and was telling Amy that when she had nothing left to take off, she'd have to shave her box, when Myron took aim and this time gave it a good thrust into his buddy's right ear. Well, if he was looking for a rise from Alex, he sure as hell got it. Alex whirled around, saw what Myron was up to, and just about hit the ceiling.

"You fucking pervert!" he roared, lunging at Myron and tackling him around the waist. The force of his rush carried both of them across the room where they went sprawling onto the bed which promptly collapsed beneath them and on top of Red who was still sleeping it off under it.

Well, that was some scene alright. Alex and Myron were wrestling on top of a mattress that was listing at a forty-five degree angle and Red, who was pinned beneath it, was thrashing around like a beached whale and shouting bloody murder. And if that wasn't enough, the broads got into the act and tried to break up the fight which, considering that the combatants were pissed, didn't amount to much. Let me tell you, you haven't seen anything until you've watched three almost-naked women on a caved-in bed trying to break up a tussle between two drunk truckdrivers while another lay squashed beneath them. Seeing Red's face turning the colour of his hair, I grabbed a corner of the spring and heaved and he squirted out like toothpaste from a tube.

Like most booze-induced brawls, the scuffle between Alex and Myron soon fizzled out, after which they got soppy and sentimental, apologizing to each other, shaking hands, and vowing to stand by each other until hell froze over or they got drunk again, whichever came first. Now, at that point, any sensible person would have called it a night – or morning, since it was about three a.m. But not us and that's how that skinny-dipping caper I mentioned came about. We were just finishing off the beer when someone suggested that we go down to Wascana Lake for a swim. By that time, I had almost drunk myself sober and didn't think much of the idea but I didn't want to be a wet blanket, so I said: "Sure, why not?"

And the seven of us piled into Alex's '69 Olds and screeched out of the hotel parking lot leaving a trail of rubber thick enough to trip over.

Wascana Lake. One of Regina's scenic wonders. There are probably others but I can't think of them right now. This lake, right in the heart of the city's a man-made body of water created by the damming of Wascana Creek. I don't know how much it cost to bring it off but it was worth every penny because without Wascana Lake, Regina would be about as picturesque as, say, Moose Jaw which looks about the way it sounds. Not that I'm saying Moose Jaw's a hick town or anything but up there, if you're not wearing a baseball cap with a John Deere emblem on it, you feel undressed. But don't get the idea

I'm knocking farmers because, if it wasn't for agriculture, you might as well put a sign on Manitoba and Saskatchewan, reading: "Closed Until Further Notice."

But back to the Wascana Lake caper. After taking a leisurely cruise around the legislative grounds, we parked near the shore, a couple of hundred yards from the docks. It was a cloudy, sultry night and the water was like ink. While the others peeled off their clothes, tossing them in scattered piles, I sat down and had a smoke, thinking that in a couple of days, this night and the people in it would be ancient history – just another closed file.

They were splashing around like kids and there was just enough moonlight to silhouette them. Their voices, shrieks, and curses sailed across the water.

"See how *you* like it!" Splash. Somebody getting a dunking or a faceful of water.

"You dirty bastard! Doesn't your old lady ever give you anything at home?"

Amy fending off one or all of the guys.

"Let's all piss in the lake at the same time and see how much we can make it rise."

Alex's booming bass. Saying it for shock effect but probably half-meaning it.

"Jesus Christ." Me. Wondering how the hell I ever got into this because it was really above and beyond the call of any private eye's duty.

It was quite a night alright and, as it turned out, it was the last I was to spend with Alex and Myron because the next day, Ted Stevens called me from Winnipeg and terminated the assignment.

Of course, the guys at the terminal all thought it was White Trucks that was calling me back East and they told me to make sure I told the company what the problems were with their respective tractors. I told them I would. They also wanted to throw a big blow-out for me but I said I had to get away that evening. When we shook hands, Myron and Alex told me I was a great guy and they wished I could stick around.

Now, you may think it was hard for me to look them in the eye, considering that over the past several weeks, I'd been stabbing them in the back on a daily basis. But it wasn't. I didn't feel in the least ashamed or guilty about exploiting their friendship to get the goods on them because that's my job. That's what I get paid for and that's what the private eye business is all about – getting information – and to be good at it, you have to do what it takes even if it's something you won't find in the Boy Scout Manual.

Of course, people are always saying: "Why nail the little guy to the cross? It's the higher-ups who're the biggest crooks." I don't totally disagree with that either because, like I said before, I've run into so-called upper-crust types who've been dipping into the till as well. But I can't pick and choose my clients. If someone hires me to go after someone at the top of the social register, I'll give it as good a shot as I can to nail them too.

I don't want to portray myself as some kind of investigative machine though. I have feelings. For example, I knew there was a good chance Myron, Alex, and some of the other guys who were playing games, would get in hot water when I made my reports to the company's head office. I also saw them as basically decent guys with families to support and dental bills, car payments, and mortgages to pay and knew that if they lost their jobs, they could kiss most of what they owned good-bye.

I recognize these things but I can't let them influence me; otherwise I might as well get out of the business because I wouldn't be doing myself or anyone else any good. And it would be just as bad if I turned someone in because I had something against them because another thing a private investigator should never do is to use an assignment to settle a grudge. That's as bad as letting someone off the hook because he's a friend.

There's also another slant to undercover work – one that I seldom discuss because it's difficult for someone on the outside to grasp. You see, when I'm on an undercover assignment, I don't think of myself as a real person. I'm a character – someone I dream up to achieve a particular purpose – so the relationships I get involved in relate only to that character and not myself. They're just extensions of whatever role I'm playing at the time.

Sure, the consequences for the people who get hurt are real enough but I can't get too shook up about that because the way I look at it, they're not really happening to people I've grown close to. They're happening to friends of a character I've created. If I had really been Manweiler the truck inspector instead of Manweiler the private eye, turning Alex and the others in would have been a pretty hard thing for me to do. But there was no Manweiler the truck inspector so there was no one to feel for the drivers who, having made their beds, were now forced to lie in them in spite of the fact they'd suddenly become very lumpy.

How lumpy? Well, within a couple of weeks of my returning to Winnipeg, I learned that Myron Tomlik, Alex Androyko, and three other drivers had been given their walking papers. But that wasn't all. Ted Stevens felt the problems occurred because the Regina management had been too lax and he gave the chop to Art McCrea and Ken Staller as well.

It was quite a casualty list alright and I guess the victims didn't have much trouble putting two and two together and coming up with Manweiler, which accounts for the rough reception I got at the Kings five years later. Well, it wasn't the first time and it probably won't be the last. Oh yeah, I didn't lay a charge against Myron. I figured, what the hell, what with his family and his mortgage payments and everything, the poor guy probably had enough troubles already.

SIX

If It Weren't for Sex I'd Have to Get a Job

YOU KNOW, if you went by everything you read in the newspapers and magazines and see on TV, you'd think the sex revolution has taken North America by storm and that it's the most natural thing in the world for everybody to be laying everybody else without anyone so much as batting an eye because it's the "in" thing and they're all having such a great time getting their rocks off. But, as far as I'm concerned, the sexual revolution is nothing more than a hyped-up catch-phrase dreamed up by some media type to sell whatever it is he's selling, because if a genuine, one-hundred percent sexual revolution really has taken place, it's sure as hell news to most of the people I deal with. The Permissive Society, open marriages, and free love make good copy but as far as the average person is concerned, it's still: "What's yours is mine," which is to say that most marriage partners still want to keep each other's sex organs under lock and key. Now, your average swinger might call that a hang-up. But not me: I call it my stock-in-trade.

You see, when you break it down, a private detective's work is pretty well divided into two basic categories: industrial crime and divorce work, with the latter making up the lion's share. Now, considering the liberalization of divorce laws over the past fifteen or twenty years, you wouldn't think adultery would play such a large role in today's divorce cases but, the truth is, it does. Of course, there's no denying grounds like mental cruelty and irreconcilable differences are becoming more popular but you can take it from me that good old-fashioned adultery is still as big as ever.

And although I don't pretend to be any kind of psychologist, experience has taught me there are a couple of reasons for that. One, a lot of husbands and wives still subscribe to the maxim that variety is the spice of life, with sex being no exception and, two, adultery is the best grounds for a quickie divorce. With adultery, there's no waiting around for any statutory separation period and no hassle about trying to prove something as hard to pin down as mental cruelty. So that's why adultery is still big business for a private eye and that's also why some so-called adultery cases are no more than staged mini-dramas with everything – including the cast of characters – set up like pins in a bowling alley. But I'll tell you more about that later on. Right now, I want to deal with the real thing – the nitty-gritty of what a private eye has to go through to get the goods on wandering spouses who are getting their oil changed in extra-marital garages.

A good example is this case I had involving a woman who thought her old man was catching a bit on the side – maybe he gave himself away by smiling too much or maybe he was pleading too many headaches when she groped for his plumbing. Anyway, she called me one day and right off I could tell it wasn't the easiest thing for her to do. Maybe she was embarrassed or nervous or something but she said something that reminded me of that comedian – I think his name's Norm Crosby – whose gimmick consists of butchering the English language, usually in a way that sounds dirty. For example, he might say "misconscrewed" instead of "misconstrued." Frankly, I don't see much in that kind of humour if that's what they call it, but I did get a laugh out of this woman who phoned me because after I confirmed that yes, she was speaking to Arnold Manweiler, she came out and hit me with: "Do you demonstrate adultery?"

Well, before I replied, two or three good comebacks flashed through my mind but I didn't have the nerve to use them. Like: "Give me the tools and I will do the job" or "That depends on what you look like." But instead, I settled for: "Unfortunately my license doesn't allow me to do that, ma'am, but I do conduct investigations into suspected adultery of others."

Again, it was probably her nervousness at calling a private detective about a very delicate matter but whatever it was, my comment went right over her head and she went on as though not a single conversational hair had been out of place. My answer seemed to suit her though because she made an appointment for the next day and, better still, kept it.

The lady, as it turned out, was a Mrs. Betty Randolph and it seemed her husband had lately taken to wandering off two or three times a week without offering any explanation for his absences.

When Mrs. Randolph would ask her husband, Herbert, where he'd been after coming home pretty late in the evening, he'd just say: "out" or "around." Well, that wasn't good enough for Betty. She wanted to know just what hubby Herb was up to and, if it was what she thought it was, she wanted to know who it was with. They'd only been married a little over two years and she was a nice-looking brunette – about twenty-five, tall and slim, with a nice tight little ass and long legs that I tried to see as much of as I could when she crossed them. I managed to see quite a bit because this was about fifteen years ago when mini-skirts were in and dirty old men got a new lease on life. Tight sweaters were in too and Betty showed hers off to pretty good advantage although her breasts were a little on the small side. All in all, she was pretty nice alright.

As a matter of fact, a lot of guys would probably wonder why a guy would want to cheat on her and maybe in the back of my mind I wondered the same thing. But in my business, if I've learned one thing it's that there's no accounting for taste when it comes to sex, because I've caught guys who had the prettiest wives you could imagine shagging broads you wouldn't want to be seen on the street with. So there's no easy answer when it comes to sex or, for that matter, maybe no answer at all.

Anyway, it's not up to me to explain why so many husbands feel it necessary to prove their manhood by shoving their meat between whatever receptive pair of thighs happens to come along. I'll leave that for the shrinks. My job is to catch them at it – to come up with enough proof for a divorce suit to stand up and, thank God, it isn't as hard as it used to be when you pretty well had to catch a couple in bed to establish adultery. These days, you can make a pretty good case if you can prove they've spent the night in the same room which is a step up as far as I'm concerned because in spite of what Joe Public thinks, private eyes aren't professional voyeurs who get their jollies by peeping through windows at some poor unsuspecting, but horny, twosome who are sawing off a piece or two.

The thing is, at the time I took the Randolph case, a private detective still had to have some pretty solid evidence of adultery to make it stick which meant that I had to do my homework. Now, in a case like this as in all surveillance jobs, I always try to get as much of a profile on the subject as I can – everything from his looks to his interests – as well as his day-to-day schedule or as close as I can come to one, from the moment he gets up to the time he goes to bed, wherever that might happen to be.

Betty was a big help there and she told me pretty well everything I needed to know as well as supplying me with a snapshot of her husband who, as it turned out was a big guy – well over six feet – with the build of a fullback. Not the kind of guy a private eye particularly likes to tail. He was twenty-nine, employed as a draftsman with the city's engineering department, and drove a 1962 Oldsmobile sedan to work getting there about nine a.m. I also learned that he sometimes took his lunch to work while on other occasions, he ate in his building's cafeteria. After working until five p.m., he returned to his suburban duplex by about five-forty-five. This information was just a matter of routine though. It was what he did those two or three nights a week after work that interested me but Betty wasn't much help there. He had few friends – at least few that called him at home – and no outside interests of which his wife was aware. No, that's not quite true. He did have one and I was hired to find out what it was.

It wasn't going to be easy though. You see there was no real pattern to the nights he took off. One week, it might be Monday and Wednesday, the next, Tuesday and Thursday, or Monday, Tuesday, and Friday. That made it a little more difficult, also much more expensive, because that meant I had to maintain surveillance every evening. But that wasn't the worst of it. The worst thing was that Betty Randolph couldn't give me any leads. If her husband was doing some extra-curricular wickdipping, she had no idea who it was with. And that was unfortunate because it's always a lot easier if you have some idea who the subject might be messing around with. That way you can just stake out her place and that saves a lot of wear and tear on your tires – not to mention your nerves – from trailing someone all around the city, trying to see without being seen.

And, believe me, it's not like it is in the movies where everything goes according to a script. In real life, anything can happen. If you get too close you can get spotted and blow the whole deal so you have to stay a good distance back which means that sometimes you lose the quarry and while you're sitting there with egg on your face trying to think up a good story for your client, the subject is home free and heading for a nice, undisturbed piece of ass. I hoped that wouldn't be the case with Herbert Randolph because his wife was a damn attractive woman and if I did a good job for her . . . well, you never know.

Anyway, at seven p.m., Monday, June 12th, there I was parked a few doors down from the Randolph place, waiting for Herb to make his move. The Olds was in the driveway but there was no sign of the subject until eight-fifteen when he came out of the house, got in the car and took off, heading west. I followed at a safe distance until he pulled over in front of a drugstore. He stayed inside for seven minutes, came back out to the car and returned home where he remained for the rest of the evening. Although paranoia is an occupational trait in my business, I didn't think he could've spotted me.

Tuesday was also uneventful. His sole trip was to a neighbourhood service station. The rest of the week was more of the same but I was making a half-decent buck so I had no reason to complain. Still, I didn't like to see someone blowing their money if they were on a wild goose chase which is what I told Mrs. Randolph when she dropped in at the office to pick up my reports.

"This type of service is pretty expensive and unless you're pretty sure your husband is involved in some sort of affair, unless you have some evidence, it might be best to discontinue surveillance for the time being."

She took nervous drags from a cigarette and looked everywhere but at me. "I have some evidence . . . at least, I think I have."

And with that, she reached into her purse, pulled out a pair of jockey shorts, and dropped them on my desk.

"In what way . . . what kind of evidence is this?"

She picked them up and showed me the front. "Those stains. There on the front. Is that the kind of evidence you were talking about?" Her voice was low with embarrassment.

I went through the motions of checking out what certainly looked like shot-spots and agreed that it could've been semen but suggested there might be more than one explanation for how it'd gotten there.

"It got there on one of his evenings out," she said. "I know because they were in the washing the next morning. I was going to show them to you before but I was embarrassed and, besides, I didn't know if it would be of any help." I admitted it was evidence of a sort but purely circumstantial and offered another explanation, trying to put it as delicately as possible.

"Well, maybe he masturbates. That could account for the stains as well."

She reddened a little. "Would he have to go out for three or four hours at a time to do that?"

Not being an expert on jerking off, I conceded that I didn't know and the interview concluded with her stuffing the shorts back into her purse and asking me to continue staking out her husband which I agreed to do. So for the second week in a row, it was the same old waiting game. But this time, it paid off. And on the first day at that.

It was about seven-thirty that Monday when Herb Randolph backed out of his driveway and headed off with me in not-too-close pursuit. One good thing, he wasn't one of those rubber-burning types, so it wasn't that much of a trick to keep him in sight. He didn't go that far before things started to happen either. As a matter of fact, he only went a couple of blocks before pulling over to the curb and picking up a short blonde chick who appeared to have been waiting for him. I let them get a good headstart before I began following again because before she got into the car, the woman seemed to be looking my way.

I managed to stay with them until they got to an open area next to the old Winnipeg Airport which used to be called Stevenson Field. At that point, they turned into a narrow, overgrown service road that was no longer in use and ended up in the middle of a stretch of prairie, a couple of hundred yards from where I was parked behind an abandoned hangar.

"Great," I grumbled. "There they are getting their rocks off and here I am with no way of getting close enough to see without being seen."

So I took out my field glasses and watched and waited. First, I saw two heads close together as they started necking. Then there was a lot of movement and I put two and two together because it's no easy trick to screw in the front seat of a car, but don't ask me how I know. Then they suddenly went horizontal and there were no heads. A minute or so later, just as I was getting ready to risk it and see if I could make it to the subject's car on foot before they got through humping, a head came up and I pulled back behind the hangar. Then, as I kept watching, a huge wad of crumpled tissue paper came sailing out the window on the driver's side. Then there was more movement and I lost sight of them again. Feeling it was now or never, I made my move. Calling upon my Second World War army training, I crouched down and loped across the field commando-style, realizing how foolish I looked and hoping nobody, particularly the subject and his broad, was watching me. Wonder of Wonders. I got right up to the passenger side without being spotted and heard a duet of heavy breathing coming from inside the Olds. Heavy enough that it covered my own, thank God, because by that time, I was pretty winded.

The breathing gave way to rustling noises and a moaning. "Oh, ho-n-n-n-e-e-e-e." By then, I was huddled down right against the door taking it all in and I won't try and tell you all that moaning and groaning didn't get to me a little although I tried to tell myself the sweat on my forehead came from my exertion. Anyway, slowly, I raised my head, glanced in the window, and saw a bare foot and ankle resting on the back of the seat on the driver's side. As I hoisted myself a little more, the ankle grew into a well-rounded calf, then a creamy, if somewhat fleshy, thigh.

I couldn't see where the thigh ended though, and I had Herbert Randolph to thank for that because that's where the dumb bugger had his head, chomping away on the broad's pussy while she quivered and moaned, "Oh God," as if she was thanking Him for her ecstasy. Her legs were spread just about as far apart as they could go and her right knee was jammed tight against the dash and Randolph's head was smack between them rolling from side to side and up and down. And all the while, he was making gurgling noises like he was playing a water-logged har-

monica. Maybe the broad got off on that particular tune
though because even though she looked pretty damn
uncomfortable she sure as hell wasn't complaining. And
neither was he in spite of the fact that he pretty well had to
scrunch himself into a pretzel to get into eating position.

All in all, you couldn't say there was very much romantic about the scene. He was bare-assed with his shorts and
pants bunched under him and her skirt had been pulled
up almost to her neck. But you had to give them credit.
They still seemed to be having a helluva good time. And I
guess, in a way, I was too although there was certainly
nothing particularly erotic about the scene. In a way, it
was like something out of a pornographic movie – something to laugh at rather than get turned on by. But then I
guess sex never was meant to be a spectator sport
although these days a lot of people seem to be making a
good buck out of it.

Anyway, I'd seen all I needed to and I straightened up
and started to leave when, all of a sudden, Herbert Randolph jerked his face out from between her legs and
looked directly up at me. For a moment, it was like we
were both frozen. He looked at me and I looked at him.
Then, finally, with his lips and chin glistening as though
he'd been eating a particularly juicy watermelon, he
cleared his throat and in a voice as cool as anything said:
"Do you have the time?"

Can you imagine that? Caught in the act of eating out a
chick and the guy has enough balls to come out with
something like that! My comeback couldn't come close to
matching it but I wasn't thinking about snappy replies at
the time. I just wanted to get out of there without tipping
him off so I put on my best officious tone and said curtly:
"Yeah, it's time you got the hell out of here. Don't you
know this is private property? C'mon, move it!"

He grumbled a little and the broad scrambled up to a
sitting position and by the time I'd covered a dozen yards,
the Olds was tossing up dirt as he made a mid-field U-turn
and headed back to the road. But that wasn't the end of it.

The last act of this little sex drama – at least as far as I was concerned – took place in my office when I handed Betty Randolph my final report. I watched her out of the corner of my eye while she read it but she didn't so much as lift an eyebrow. When she'd read through the whole thing, she just said: "He was really doing that?"

I nodded.

She paused and said kind of wistfully. "He's never done anything like that with me." Then she added hastily, "Not that I would have let him. That's . . . why it's positively perverted."

But she didn't look all that shocked to me. And that was all she said after paying me off and leaving. I never did see her again which didn't particularly surprise me because when it comes to the crunch, a lot of husbands and wives decide against going through with a divorce action. Usually they confront their straying partners and after a big scene or two, patch up their relationships – at least until next time. So, aside from the oral sex angle, there wasn't anything really different about this case. Still, the way they were getting their sexual jollies was significant to me at the time because, in a way it was my introduction to the world of kinky sex – at least that's what my generation calls it. People today look at it differently though. These days if you're not into whips and chains or whatever, you feel as out-of-date as an honest politician. But like I was saying, fifteen or twenty years ago whenever you caught someone going horizontal it was usually to get into the good old missionary position. The only thing that was missing was the Bible. But although this going down on a broad was something new – at least as far as my professional experience was concerned – there was still a lot of the more conventional variety of messing around going on too, and my involvement in these so-called "normal" cases sometimes turned out to have a strange twist or too as well.

I don't know why but during one period, almost all my clients were women who wanted to find out if their husbands had been sticking their hands into some other chicks' cookie jars. The week after the Randolph case, while visions of pussy-eating were still dancing in my head, another broad came up to my office and hired me to check up on her old man. Seems he had a full-time job during the day and drove a cab evenings to pick up a few extra bucks. I suggested this didn't leave him much time, or for that matter, energy, for fooling around.

"Saturday afternoons."

"Saturday afternoons?"

"Every Saturday afternoon, he takes off for God knows where. He says he goes drinking with his buddies but he never tells me where. And besides, he doesn't hold his liquor all that well and if he'd been drinking all afternoon, I'd certainly be able to tell."

The woman – I'll call her Jane Dough in honour of the retainer she gave me – was one of those mousey little types who are lucky to snag any kind of husband and don't want to take a chance on losing them. She told me her husband would show up at home late in the afternoon with liquor on his breath but cold sober and she thought she smelled a rat – a rat named Doug, which was her old man's name. Well, I told her I'd put a tail on hubby during one of his Saturday afternoon jaunts and see what turned up and that's when the case got a little complicated because she insisted on coming along for the ride.

Now, I usually try to discourage clients from going along on this kind of an operation because sometimes they're liable to lose control and do something they – and I – might be sorry for. After all, catching your mate fooling around with someone else can be enough to send even the most passive person over the brink. But Mrs. Dough wouldn't budge and, since her going along was a condition of my employment, I went along with it, against my better judgement.

So on a bright Saturday afternoon in June, there we were trailing her husband to a downtown hotel. Leaving Jane in the car, I followed Doug into the building and located him in the lounge where he was sharing a table with an exotic-looking brunette who, as far as looks were concerned, was a big step up from his wife. I wondered how he managed to latch onto something like that considering he was no more than average in the looks department himself but, like I said before, there's no accounting for tastes. Anyway, there they were all nice and cozy and looking into each other's eyes and the whole schmeer. Sitting at the bar, I watched them finish their drinks and leave. But they didn't go far. Trailing them at a safe distance, I saw them head down the hall all lovey-dovey and laughing. They were paying so much attention to each other, they wouldn't have noticed me if I'd been dressed like the A & W Rootbear. I tracked them up a flight of stairs and down another hall before they stopped in front of room 218 and the broad fished a key out of her purse. A couple of seconds later, they were inside the room and I was heading back outside to lay the bad news on my client.

Her mouth tightened and she just sat there for a couple of minutes without saying anything. Then she took a deep breath and said: "Well what are you waiting for? Let's go."

She was out of the car and heading for the hotel entrance before I'd gotten halfway through telling her why it wouldn't be a particularly great idea for us to bust in on her husband and his girlfriend. It didn't really matter though, because she was bound and determined to find out who her hubby was shagging and there wasn't a damn thing I could do to stop her. So there we were standing in front of Room 218 with Mrs. Dough as anxious as a kid on Christmas morning and me wondering what kind of hell was going to bust loose if and when Doug opened the door.

"Go ahead. Knock," she ordered.

"Maybe we should talk this over a little first."

"If you don't, I will!"

Listening outside the door, I heard the sound of bedsprings playing an old familiar tune. The grim look on Jane's face told me she'd heard it too.

"Go ahead," she hissed. "Knock!"

I did as I was told and the bedspring concerto stopped. But that was all that happened. There was no sound from within and nobody came to the door. Jane gave me a look that was more of a command and I pounded on the door again. Still no response. I shrugged and was ready to pack it in when she reached up and whispered in my ear.

"Yell 'fire.' He's terrified of fire. If that doesn't make him open up, nothing will."

I looked at her like she was nuts. I could just see it, me yelling "fire" and half the hotel stampeding out the door. That's all I needed to get nailed with a charge of giving a false alarm or maybe even manslaughter if someone got trampled or had a heart attack.

"No way," I whispered back. "It's too dangerous. It's –"

She pulled out a couple of twenties and waved them under my nose and, all of a sudden, I began to appreciate her logic. Making sure no one was around, I put my mouth almost up against the keyhole and bellowed:

"Fire! Everyone please leave your rooms immediately! There's a fire in the building!"

Well, like Jane said, they were the magic words alright – a helluva lot better than "Open Sesame." Before you could count to three, the door was yanked wide open and there stood Doug Dough, scared shitless and stark naked. But what surprised me even more, considering the fear in his eyes, was the fact that he still managed to keep one of the biggest and reddest hard-ons I'd ever seen. But that was only until he spotted his wife in the hall. Then, it pulled a pretty good disappearing act, as the blood drained from both his face and his prick as if someone had just pulled a plug.

All in all, it was an afternoon of surprises, for me as well as Doug, because Mrs. Dough's reaction to the whole situation was completely unexpected. Instead of screaming at her husband and calling him down for being a two-timing bastard, she just walked up to him and said in the sweetest voice you can imagine: "So this is how you spend your Saturday afternoons, dear."

And she even maintained the sweetness when she went over to the bed and gave the once-over to the brunette who had the sheet pulled right up to her chin. It still wasn't high enough though because Jane not only saw her face but recognized it as belonging to her sister.

"Why hello, Susan," she cooed. "I thought you always went shopping on Saturday. Or is Jack doing it today? You're so lucky to have such a good husband."

And she turned and looked daggers at her own who was struggling into his clothes and looking about as comfortable as a breakdancer with the runs. The funny thing about the whole case was that it never ended up in divorce court. Once again, the matter was settled between the parties themselves although, for the life of me, I couldn't see how because I know if I'd been in Jane Dough's shoes, the papers would've been full of reports of a double homicide. But people, like someone once said, are funny, and it seems that the funnier they are the more chance there is I'll run into them.

Maybe it's the whole sex thing that makes divorce cases the least predictable of any I've handled and in thirty-odd years, I've seen a helluva lot of clients come and go. Sex seems to do strange things to people. Guys – and broads too – will take any kind of chance when it comes to getting a good piece of ass and there's no way of telling how someone's going to react when they're caught with their pants down or off, as the case may be. Personally, I like to wait until they're through sawing off their chunk because some involuntary coitus interruptus can make a person pretty testy and I try to avoid being on the receiving end of someone's bad temper unless it's absolutely necessary. Like this one particular time when good luck rather than good sense kept me from ending up in the hospital. Again it involved sex. What else? And again it involved a woman who was trying to get the goods on her old man. This time though, I was pretty sure I'd end up testifying in court because the lady was referred to me by her lawyer who was already preparing the divorce papers.

The lady in question was a Mrs. Lillian Molette and she already had a pretty good idea who her husband was humping. All she needed was some evidence that would stand up in court and she'd be able to wave bye-bye to her philandering spouse. Lillian and her husband, Ken, were both in their late twenties and the alleged paramour in the case was a thirtyish widow named Harriet Lenz, who lived about half a dozen blocks from them. Friends of Lillian's had told her they'd seen Ken paying regular visits to the Lenz home and that was enough to send her in search of a lawyer. I was glad Lillian had such good friends who took an interest in her husband's business because a residential stakeout is a lot easier than trailing someone all around the city waiting for him to make an illicit connection. I knew where the honey was, now all I had to do was wait for the bee to come buzzing around.

So I had an operative stake out the Lenz place and settled back to wait for results. They weren't long in coming. On the second evening, my man, Ralph, phoned to say the subject had entered the Lenz bungalow at about nine p.m., and was still there. I told him to keep an eye on the place and I'd be right down.

Now, this was a good twenty years ago and, like I said before, you just about had to catch them actually screwing to make a case. Just finding a guy in the same house with a broad wasn't good enough. So when I met Ralph just up the street from the Lenz place, I told him we'd have to find out what was going on inside. Well, this didn't particularly thrill him because although he was a good enough worker, he was the kind of guy who tried to steer clear of anything resembling violence and the subject, Molette, was a big sonuvabitch who didn't look like he had much of a sense of humour.

According to Lillian, he was also pretty good with his

fists, having used them on her from time to time. That
made me want to nail him to the cross even more because
I've got no use for wife-beating creeps. So, after telling
Ralph to watch the front door, I went into the yard and
started to circle around to the back to try and get a look
inside. By this time, it had gotten pretty dark and I
thought it was safe enough to risk being taken for a peeping tom.

Creeping along the side of the single-storey house, I
heard voices coming through a partly open window.
Molette and the widow, and, if my suspicions were correct,
they were in the lady's bedroom. I also suspected they had
more in mind than checking out Mrs. Lenz' stamp collection. As the minutes passed, it grew darker and I grew
braver, and eventually, I was crouched down right under
the window. Thank God, there was a high fence on that
side that shielded me from the eyes of nosy neighbours.
Squatting there, trying to keep the cramps out of my legs,
I heard the usual sounds of fevered lovemaking – the rustling, the heavy breathing, and the murmured endear-
ments. Then came the main event – the rhythmic creak of
the bedsprings and the ecstatic grunts as he put the meat
to her. I waited until he'd mounted her and was getting a
good, steady stroke going before I chanced a peek inside.

It was like watching a skinflick because they hadn't even
turned off the light, which wouldn't have been so bad
except they hadn't pulled the shade all the way down. I
guessed they probably got turned on by seeing each other
in the raw or something. Actually, that's one phenomenon
that makes my job easier because it seems that people who
are cheating on their spouses like to screw with the lights
on. It's just married people who like to do it in the dark,
probably because they're sick and tired of each other and
are trying to pretend they're getting their rocks off with
someone else.

Anyway, the foot of the bed was no more than a yard or
so from the window and Ken Molette's thrusting bare ass
was no more than another yard beyond that so I had a

ring-side seat for the action. What I saw was plenty enough to make a divorce case and I could have taken off right then and there but like I said before, I hate wife-beaters so I wasn't just satisfied with having him by the bags. I wanted to squeeze them a little too. After all, what's a little salt in a wound anyway? So I went around to the front and knocked on the door while Ralph backed off a few paces and looked at me like I'd lost my marbles.

It was close to a minute before anyone answered and it wasn't who I'd expected. Since it was Mrs. Lenz' place, I'd assumed she'd be the one to answer the door but that isn't what happened. Standing there in the doorway was Ken Molette and I wondered if I hadn't made a mistake by not leaving sleeping dogs lie. He had his pants and an unbuttoned shirt on but no socks or shoes and he didn't look too happy at being interrupted.

"Yeah? What do you want?"

"Excuse me for bothering you but there's something I'd like to show you," I said.

"I don't want to see anything," he snapped. And, as he started to shut the door, I heard him mutter: "Goddamn salesmen."

"I'm not a salesman," I countered, adding with as much earnestness as I could summon up, "really, I think you'll want to see this. It's very important and I'm sure you'll find it interesting."

Maybe he figured he wouldn't get rid of me unless he humoured me but for whatever reason, he finally gave in and stepped outside. I beckoned him to follow me and started around the side of the house with him a couple of steps behind. It was pretty dark by that time but the light from the bedroom window let me see that he had a very confused look on his face when I pointed inside.

"Right there," I said. "Go ahead and look. I think you'll find it very interesting."

For some unknown reason, instead of belting me, he did as he was told and hunkered down in front of the open window. He stared through for a good thirty seconds, with me peering over his shoulder and seeing the same thing he did which was Mrs. Harriet Lenz, still spread-eagled on the bed with her pussy aimed straight in our direction. Yeah, really. That hairy triangle was primed and waiting and not more than six feet away and I think I would've gotten hornier than a dozen woodpeckers if that big bugger hadn't been standing right in front of me and I wasn't preoccupied with trying to think of what he might do next because even though it was pretty dark out there, I had a pretty good idea he wasn't smiling. As a matter of fact, he wasn't doing much of anything. He seemed stunned and turned around and looked at me as if in a daze.

"Who the hell –"

Before he could finish the sentence, I slipped my card into his hand, told him that no doubt I'd be seeing him in court, and headed out of there as fast as my chubby, little legs could take me.

Afterward, I thought that I'd taken too much of a chance by pulling that stunt but the look on his face had been worth it and, as it turned out, I did see him in court. Mrs. Molette went through with the divorce and got rid of the bum. She's married again now and I hope the union is a lot happier than her first. As for Mrs. Lenz, I don't know how she's making out but after seeing her in that candid pose that night, I've often been tempted to drop in. After all, even though a lot of water has gone under the bridge since then – who knows? – she just still might be leaving that damn shade up.

The foregoing cases are what you might call surprise parties. Now, most of the time, I'm on the delivering end of the surprise but there have also been times when I've been the surpris*ee* rather than the surpris*er*, which ties in with what I said earlier about some divorce cases being better rehearsed than a Broadway musical.

On one of them, I tailed the subject – an average-looking woman in her mid-thirties – to a rendezvous with her lover at a motel on the outskirts of Winnipeg. After waiting a couple of hours until the lights finally went out, I knocked on the door to give her the bad news but, before I could get a word out, she lit into me, bawling: "Christ! What kept you? Do you realize it's almost two in the morning?"

Her boyfriend, looking equally pissed-off, chimed in with: "Why the hell couldn't you phone if you knew you were going to be late?"

And the broad finished up by asking: "Do we have to take off our clothes and get into bed or is this good enough?"

What I said to them and later, to the shyster lawyer who masterminded this exercise in collusion would only lower the tone of this book and is probably better left unsaid.

SEVEN

Possession Is Nine-Tenths of the Law

THERE ARE a lot of sayings that've been repeated so often everybody considers them true even though they may not be all that well founded in either law or logic. One of them is the time-worn cliché that possession is nine-tenths of the law. Not that it's a complete load of crap, mind you. Just ask some hippie who's been busted for having a little weed in his jeans. He usually even gets hit with the last tenth for good measure and winds up being hauled in front of some judge who figures his day is wasted unless he gives somebody a criminal record. Of course, the fact that Hizzoner might smoke marijuana isn't a factor since when professional types do something it's fashionable but when Joe Citizen pulls the same stunt, all of a sudden he's treated like Public Enemy Number One.

This business about possession being nine-tenths of the law does hold true in some other cases as well though – the dirtiest and most heartbreaking kind that a private detective could ever hope to find himself saddled with. I'm talking about child custody cases. Or maybe cases isn't the right word because every one I've been involved with has been a battle from square one right down to the final acts of marital dramas that are always heavy on personal tragedy.

I went over some of them in my mind on the flight to

Vancouver, the way a battle-hardened veteran goes over a past campaign to prepare himself for the next.

The trip to the Coast was the good news. The bad news was that I still had to find one husband-and-father and one kid before I could get down to the nitty-gritty. Which was? To help kidnap the kid in question.

That's right: kidnap. Of course, I'd make sure I stayed within the law every step of the way but, in a moral sense, there's no other way to describe what I was planning to do because I was being paid to find a seven-year-old girl and help take her away from her father without his knowledge or consent. Pretty dicey business and I can't pretend that I liked it one little bit. Why did I take the assignment then? There was the challenge, of course. A job like this is always one helluva challenge, and it's particularly satisfying if you can bring it off, but there's more to it than that. There's always at least one other reason for getting yourself hip-deep in heartbreak: the other parent.

Diane Statten was quiet-spoken, intelligent, and on the verge of either suicide or a nervous breakdown. She'd been under a doctor's care ever since her husband, Bradley, had taken off with their only child, Stacey, a month or so earlier.

In their mid-twenties, the Stattens had gotten married shortly after Diane discovered she was pregnant. Even though they were little more than kids when they tied the knot, according to Diane, it had been a relatively happy union until the last year or so. She was doing well selling real estate but Bradley had a dead-end job in the shipping department of a large wholesale furniture firm. About a year earlier, he'd started to hit the bottle and this led to arguments which, in turn, led to him drinking even more and staying away from home for a couple of days at a time. Finally, he lost his job and his drinking hobby became a full-time vocation.

Diane had finally told him to hit the road unless he straightened himself out and he did just that. But he didn't go alone. While his wife was out showing homes to pro-

spective buyers, Brad Statten threw some of his and Stacey's stuff into a couple of suitcases, picked up the girl at a
nearby day-care centre, and took off for parts unknown.

They weren't unknown, at least not totally, by mid-
May of 1972. And that's why I was winging my way to the
West Coast and checking out the engines on my side of the
DC-9 to make sure they were still intact.

The warning sign went on and I extinguished a cigarette
that I hadn't yet lit. It's not that I'm a nervous flyer. It's
more like I've got this thing about obeying orders. It probably goes back to my service days because when you were
in the army during wartime, you were only told to do
something once and if anyone ever said please, you could
be pretty sure they were being sarcastic.

I've done quite a bit of flying in my time but I have to
admit I still get a little tightness in my chest and my palms
start to sweat just before the plane takes off or lands.
When it roars down the runway, I find myself uncon-
sciously trying to help it lift off by tugging on the arm-
rests. And when it touches down, I automatically push on
the floor with my feet, jamming on some imaginary brakes
so the damn thing won't slam into the terminal.

There's another thing. Have you ever noticed how
everybody on a plane can be shooting the breeze and
joking and then, in that critical ten seconds before taking
off or touching down, it's as though someone has thrown a
switch cutting the power to everyone's vocal chords? It's
like we all know the whole bundle's on the line – the dice
have been cast and within seconds we'll know whether we
hit a lucky seven or crapped out. The worst part for me is
when the plane lowers its landing gear and it sounds like
half the fuselage has jumped ship. That's when I paste on
a big smile because if we crash and someone finds my lips,
they'll at least know that I cashed in like a man.

I wasn't smiling this time though. I was still on the
threshold of the Statten case but it already had a pretty
good hold on me. I'd helped regain custody of children
who'd been spirited away by a husband or wife before but

that was usually with the aid of court documents and the cooperation of the Winnipeg Police Department. This one was different. Diane and Bradley Statten were neither divorced nor legally separated and the court order granting custody to Diane – coming after the fact – was too little and much too late.

What Bradley had pulled off might've been spiteful and vicious but it wasn't illegal. Diane had a lawyer working on the case and he'd obtained a restraining order prohibiting Bradley Statten from taking the child out of the province but it wouldn't be in effect until Statten was served with the document and no one had any idea where he was. All they had to go on were guesses and one clue – a letter sent to Diane by her husband a couple of weeks after he and Stacey had disappeared.

I was called into the picture a couple of days afterward when it seemed apparent that Bradley was no longer in the province and, consequently, no longer subject to a Manitoba court order. It was the letter that convinced Diane Statten that the case required some extra-judicial attention. On my first visit to her home, I checked out both the letter and the envelope which carried a Montreal postmark.

"Does your husband have friends or relatives in Montreal?" I asked.

Diane Statten toyed nervously with a slim, silver, charm bracelet, working it back and forth across her wrist. Her eyes flicked toward me then away.

"No, at least none that I know of." She had a pale, washed-out look and a voice to match. I attributed it to the tranquilizers I knew she was taking.

Sitting in the living room of her modest bungalow, I tried to piece the story together while Diane's mother fluttered around, alternating between consoling her daughter and asking me if I wanted more coffee. It was obvious that Martha Lanham was worried sick about her daughter and she expressed her concern by being overly-solicitous. I could see the irritation growing in Diane but she managed to keep it in check – at least most of the time.

"Mother, would you please sit down," she said finally. "You make me nervous, hanging over my shoulder and running around like a chicken with its head cut off."

The plump, middle-aged woman gave an apologetic smile and sat down in an upholstered rocker. But no sooner had she touched down than she was up again, cooing: "You'll have another cup of coffee, won't you, Mr. Manweiler? There's plenty more in the pot. It's one of those large ones – I think they call them the party size." She turned to her daughter. "That *is* what they call them, isn't it, dear?"

"Mother!" I could almost hear Diane gritting her teeth.

Mrs. Lanham looked totally bewildered. "Yes, dear?"

"Why don't you go and lie down for a while. You must be tired and you know you're not well."

The older woman looked hurt. "There's nothing wrong with me. I feel fine. Doctor Grainger said that if I just keep taking my pills, I'll hardly know that I have arthritis."

Diane Statten spoke slowly, softly, like a teacher instructing a slow learner.

"Mother, I know you mean well and you've been a big help to me but. . . ." She paused, searching her mother's face to see what effect her words were having. ". . . I'd like to speak to Mr. Manweiler alone."

"But . . . but, I'm your mother," replied Mrs. Lanham, as though that covered everything. Her eyes blinked in confusion behind her horn-rimmed glasses and her hands, needing something to do, patted her freshly-sculpted hair-style, a bouffant number that was popular among middle-aged matrons with forty bucks to blow.

In spite of the fact that everything she did irritated Diane, me, or both of us, I thought she was probably one helluva nice woman and it was obvious she was hurting as much as her daughter. That was why she was racing around, trying to find new ways of doing things that didn't have to be done. She was afraid to stop doing and start thinking. I felt sorry for her and, even though the stuff was lousy, I complimented her on the coffee and suggested I could do with another cup. She beamed as though I'd just made her day and bustled off in the direction of the kitchen.

"I should've come down to your office, I guess," Diane said, smiling ruefully, "but with this medication I'm taking, I don't like to drive." She waved her hand toward the kitchen. "She means well but. . . ." She let the sentence trail off.

"I know," I said. "My mother's the same way. She still thinks I'm twelve years old. I think she would've gone overseas with me during the war if she could've, just to make sure I dressed warmly."

She smiled, showing small, even teeth that looked as though they belonged to a little girl. There was a lot of the little girl in her appearance in other ways too and maybe that's why her mother was so protective. She had a slim build and her small breasts, coupled with long, coltish legs, gave her a tomboyish look. To top it off, her auburn hair was cut really short and with her fine features and a sprinkle of freckles, she reminded me of Peter Pan. Except for her eyes. They were large, feline, green, and all woman – the kind a guy could get lost in. She was a cute little thing alright and I wondered why a guy would want to take off on her without so much as a good-bye. But then, I discovered long ago that there are a lot of strange people in this world and I think, by now, I've met at least half of them.

While Mrs. Lanham was busying herself in the kitchen, I got the rest of the story from her daughter and re-read the letter that had been posted from Montreal. It was a rambling, obscenity-laden attack on Diane and her family and concluded by saying: "Don't try and find us. If you do, you'll face the consequences and so will Stacey. She's better off without you and so am I. You're no mother and you sure as hell were never a wife."

That business about facing the consequences was bad enough but what really threw me was his sign off. "See you in Hell." I looked toward Diane but she was consciously trying to evade my eyes.

"Has your husband ever been under a doctor's care?" I asked.

She looked at me blankly. "A doctor. . . ?"

I decided to come right to the point. "To oe more specific, a psychiatrist. Does he have any history of mental problems?"

She paused then said in a voice that was little more than a whisper. "He . . . he had a problem with his nerves a couple of years ago and has been taking medication on and off ever since. Or at least he was until he began drinking heavily."

It's always that way. No matter how many times I tell clients that they have to level with me and be just as open as they would be in a confessional, they always hold things back. Usually because they're embarrassed, but some times, it's because they're hiding something from themselves – something frightening or painful that they just don't want to face.

Before I could probe any further, Mrs. Lanham returned and Diane pointedly changed the subject. It wasn't until she walked me to my car that I got the whole lowdown or about as much of it as she was ready to give me. It was low and it was down, that's for sure.

Bradley Statten, if his wife could be believed, was one very troubled human being. He'd had more than a "problem with his nerves." He'd had a breakdown. The story about their living a life of domestic bliss was just that: a story. His history over the past year had included a suicide attempt after which a psychiatrist had diagnosed him as a borderline schizophrenic. That was bad enough and it shook me up to think that he had the girl with him but the worst was still to come. I was behind the wheel and getting ready to take off when Diane turned back to me and said as an afterthought:

"I think there's something else you should know."

"What's that?" I asked, shifting into drive.

"My husband took his gun with him."

It turned out that the gun in question was an unregistered thirty-eight that Brad Statten had said he'd bought for "protection" although he never said against what. I shut the car off and looked at Diane, shaking my head.

"I think this is a job for the police, Mrs. Statten. Your husband sounds like a sick man to me. Also a dangerous one."

She leaned down, looking right into my eyes. "That's why you have to help me. You're my only hope. I've been to the police but they just keep telling me they can't do a damn thing, that my husband hasn't broken any law." Her voice started to break and her eyes glistened. "They say they can't interfere in family disputes." Hysteria was reaching out to grab her by the throat but she fought it off. "My daughter is stolen from me and they call it a family dispute," she said bitterly.

I nodded sympathetically. She was right. But it wasn't entirely the fault of the police. A lot of the time, they couldn't do anything because the law didn't allow them to. Of course, there are other cases where the cops can do something but don't just on general principles.

For example, I've seen a lot of cases where big, brave, macho men were slapping their old ladies around and the cops just told these wife-beaters to keep the noise down because the neighbours were complaining.

Of course, on the other side of the coin, sometimes police officers go to a lot of time and trouble to haul some wife-beater into the station and book him and, before his fingerprints are even dry, there's dear little wifey popping in to say that her big daddy was just playing and didn't mean any harm when he broke her nose and blackened her eyes. And she winds up by pleading with the Crown and/or judge to turn the bum loose so he can go home and take up where he left off. It's a two-way street alright and whichever way you look down it, you see nothing but crap.

Anyway, these were the kinds of thoughts in a holding pattern in my mind while my plane circled Vancouver International Airport looking for an opening in the drizzle and fog hanging over the lower mainland. Trickles of rain spattered and whipped across my window. Wisps of vapour streamed past the blinking red light on the wing and the motors accelerated into a high-pitched whine as we came in for another pass. Geometric patterns of street lights and neon signs grew larger and brighter. Did you ever notice how at night, from the air, every city looks like a gigantic Disneyland?

Another minute or so of tensed muscles and we were on the ground and I was teaching myself to breathe again. "That's it. Breathe in. Hold it. Now, breathe out. No, no, dummy! You breathe *in* first!"

It was the first time I'd been to Vancouver in May and I wondered if there was any truth to the rumour that the city had a six-month monsoon season. I later found out that it was just so much eastern propaganda though. It was the middle of the month when I made this particular trip and there was a bit of a downpour for the first day or two but after that, it was strictly blue skies and sunshine and I'm not getting greased by the Vancouver Tourist Bureau to say that either.

I've got a pretty good idea where all that b.s. about Vancouver being located in the middle of a tropical rainforest started too. Right in the heart of the Prairies, in places like Regina and Winnipeg, where people are still scraping icicles from their eyelids at Easter.

"Well, it may be cold but at least it's not damp." That's about all you hear during five months of Manitoba winter as we prairie types keep trying to convince each other that thirty below zero is the best thing for your health since Vitamin C. Of course it's not damp. How the hell could it be? It never gets warm enough for anything to thaw. So, out of envy or whatever, we spread the myth that all

Vancouverites have webbed feet from slogging through puddles three hundred and sixty-four days a year and the two main industries on the Coast are umbrella manufacturing and selling drugs. Come to think of it, the second part of that probably isn't so far off the mark but that's another story.

Another thing that isn't so far off the mark is the accusation that some car rental agencies aren't averse to ripping off unsuspecting customers. While waiting for my suitcases to show up on the carousel, I checked in with the agency from which I'd arranged to rent a car. The dark, heavily-made-up chick behind the counter was doing her nails and, for a while, I thought I was going to have to wait until they dried before she'd give me some attention. It wasn't until I started drumming my fingers on the counter that she looked up, giving me a smile that looked as brittle as her makeup. I gave her my name and she fished a sheet out of a drawer beneath the counter and asked: "You wanted a Camaro, is that right?"

"No," I said with as much patience as I could muster after being aboard a plane for about four hours. "I made arrangements to rent a Chevy sedan, in dark blue or green, if possible."

She frowned and tossed her mane of thick, brown hair. "Well, it says Camaro, right here."

"I don't care what it says there, miss," I said, feeling my control starting to slip away and fighting against it. "When I phoned in my reservation, I specifically requested a Chevy sedan – just a plain family car in a plain, conservative colour. What I *didn't* request. . ." – and I ticked them off on my fingers – ". . . was a polka-dotted Porsche, a plaid Cadillac, a yellow jeep, or a Camaro in any colour."

For all the good it did me, I could've been speaking Swahili. The same practised smile stayed right there on those lush, painted lips as she chirped brightly: "You'll like the Camaro. It's a lovely shade of red." She jingled a set of keys at me and turned the smile up another notch.

"I will *not* like the Camaro," I gritted, "because I am not taking the Camaro. I want the car I contracted for."

It was the old game about sticking a customer with a different car than the one he ordered – one that commanded a higher rental fee and meant more profit for the company. A Chevy went for about a hundred-and-a-quarter a week while a Camaro would run close to one-seventy-five.

Her smile wavered but held. By this time, a number of other customers had gathered in front of the counter and Miss Fingernails must've figured she couldn't waste any more time with me because she finally conceded defeat, saying: "We just might have one Chevrolet sedan left . . . if it's been returned. . . ." She studied the rows of keys hanging on a pegboard then feigned surprise. "Yes, it's back. You're in luck, sir."

The reason I needed a nondescript car was obvious. It was my intention to stake out Bradley Statten, get a make on his movements, and establish a pattern. I wanted to know where he went and when and where the girl was when they weren't together. I could just see myself bird-dogging him in a red Camaro. I'd stick out like a sex maniac in a nudist camp and it would take him all of ten minutes to get wise to me. The car I ended up with was a new Chevy four-door sedan. Dark green, it was the kind of car you could pass a dozen times a day without noticing.

On the drive into the city from Richmond, I started making plans. I already had a general strategy outlined but now it was time to start inserting some specifics – the whens and wheres, as opposed to the hows. I've always been one for setting things up so that as little as possible is left to chance. Sure, you always hope for a break but you can't sit around waiting for it. You've got to cover every angle and cover it for as long as it takes to pay off.

There's something else too though. After you've been in the business for as long as I have, you develop a kind of special sense – I guess you could call it investigative intuition. Sometimes, I can tell right off when something isn't kosher even when there's nothing tangible I can put my finger on. Yeah, this sixth sense of mine has paid off enough in the past that when it was triggered during the first stage of my investigation of Brad and Stacey's disappearance, I paid attention to it. And that's how I got onto a scent that eventually landed me in a seaport city a couple of thousand miles from where I first picked up the trail.

The way it happened was this: after getting as much information as I could from Diane Statten, I tracked down all of her husband's known relatives and acquaintances, using every technique in the book to try and pry some information loose. It was strictly no soap. His parents were living in Winnipeg but I couldn't get a thing out of them except a door which slammed in my face and a telephone receiver that did likewise to my ear. Harry Statten told me to quit harassing them while his wife, Janet, chimed in that she'd call the police. It was plain to see that they thought their dear little Bradley could do no wrong and that there was no love lost between them and their daughter-in-law, Janet Statten telling me that I must be "some kind of pimp to work for a whore like her." A real barracuda, that one.

I also managed to trace Brad's older brother, a long-distance driver for a furniture-moving outfit. Fred Statten wouldn't talk either but then I hadn't expected him to. A visit to his company's office did pay off to a certain extent though, when the dispatcher told me that Fred had been on a run out east a couple of weeks back and had been in Montreal on April 23rd which – perhaps not so coincidentally – was the same date on the letter Diane got from her husband. Right away, I smelled a red herring and figured that wherever Brad and Stacey were, it sure as hell wasn't in Montreal. But several more days went by before I got my first real lead. It came about like a lot of them do, through someone getting a little careless.

The phone call came early in the afternoon on Tuesday, May 16th. I'd been on the job for over a week with little more to show for it than some mileage on my shoe-leather when I picked up the receiver and heard Diane Statten talking a mile-a-minute. It was a while before I could get her to calm down and the first thing I could understand was:

"Her clothes are gone." While she struggled to catch her breath, I jumped right in.

"Whose clothes are gone? Settle down, take a deep breath, and give me the whole story."

Irritation competed with mounting hysteria. "Stacey's," she shrieked. "Whose do you think?"

It took a little more soothing before she was calm enough to communicate. The upshot was that she'd come home for lunch and discovered that some of her daughter's clothes were missing. Brad had taken some when he'd split with the kid but most of Stacey's things had been left behind in the rush. Now, all of a sudden, her closet was stripped bare and Diane was frantic.

"He must be in the city. Stacey must be here too." Her voice was a mixture of joy and terror.

"How do you know it was him?"

"He was the only one beside myself who had a key."

I suggested he could easily have given it to someone else and that a third party might have entered the house and made off with Stacey's things.

"How about his family? Do you think any of them would pull a stunt like this?"

"His mother sure would," she snapped. "As far as that old witch is concerned, Brad is an angel who can do no wrong. She even tried to blame me when he started drinking."

She wanted to call the police then and there but I dissuaded her. I had a hunch that if we let out enough rope, somebody just might manage to hang themselves. By then it was almost two and I knew I'd have to move quickly. I jumped in my car and hustled down to Brad's parents' place. I didn't get there any too soon. Within ten minutes, Janet Statten came out, carrying a large carton which she stashed in the back seat of her car. I tailed her for a dozen blocks or so before it became obvious where she was heading. We were already half-way to the main post office and I dropped back, knowing that if she spotted me, the whole deal would go up in smoke.

I parked on a sidestreet and watched her lug the box into the post office. A couple of minutes later, she came out empty-handed, got into her car, and drove away. That was when I made my move. Hurrying to the parcel-post wicket, I pushed in at the head of the line and buttonholed a clerk.

"Excuse me," I wheedled. "My wife just brought a parcel in and now she's afraid that she may not have put the correct name and address on it."

The balding, middle-aged clerk looked noncommittal.

"It's that one right there," I said, pointing to the carton Janet Statten had left. It was on top of some smaller ones that'd been piled on a low, four-wheeled cart.

"That one?" he asked, tapping the box.

I nodded. He peered at the label, then at me, and frowned. "Well, it's addressed to B. Statten, General Delivery, Vancouver, B.C. Does that sound alright to you."

"Yes, it sounds just fine to me," I smiled. "Sorry to trouble you but the wife's a real worrier, you know."

He nodded and grinned knowingly then turned toward a fat broad who was tapping the counter with a coin, trying to get his attention. I was grinning like a jack-o-lantern all the way to my car. It could've been better. The package could've had a street address. But it was better – a helluva lot better – than what I had before. At least now my search had been narrowed down by nine provinces. My smile disappeared pretty quick though when I spotted a commissionaire placing a parking ticket on my windshield. In my rush to get into the post office, I'd forgotten to put a coin in the meter.

"Jeez, I was just inside for a couple of minutes," I protested.

"And you didn't pay for them," he retorted. "That's the trouble with you young people. You all want something for nothing."

Young people. Yeah, that's really what he said. Imagine that! And there I was on the shady side of fifty. Of course, the fact that the old bugger must've been pushing seventy might have had something to do with his perception.

Anyway, by six that evening, I was on a plane bound for Vancouver and the rest you already know except for what happened after I bedded down at a downtown motor hotel and staked out the Vancouver post office the next morning. To keep from looking too conspicuous, I kept on the move, roaming from one side of the reception area to the other but always making sure I had the General Delivery wicket in sight. By noon, my feet were sore as hell and I had a crick in my neck from swivelling my head at a three-hundred-and-sixty degree angle. But by twelve-thirty, all of my pain and patience paid off. It was him: Brad Statten. Just to be on the safe side, I checked the photo Diane had given me. Where he was clean-shaven before, he now sported a droopy moustache and his hair, which had once been medium length, now came almost to his shoulders. He sure wasn't any fashion plate either, decked out in a pullover sweater and a pair of scruffy jeans. His appearance wasn't what bothered me though. It was something else.

Stacey. She wasn't with him. Where was she? My mind flew to his letter – to the "consequences" he'd threatened if his wife tried to find them. Chances were his mother had already tipped him off that I was on the case. Could that have been enough to set him off? Had he just been blowing smoke in that letter or was he really twisted enough to snuff his own kid just to punish her mother? I tried to blot that thought from my mind, arguing that if the girl wasn't alive why would he go to the trouble of getting her clothes sent out? I think I only half-convinced myself though, and while I watched Bradley Statten claim his parcel, I felt a chill that had nothing to do with the temperature.

He certainly didn't look skittish and, actually, there was no reason why he had anything to fear. Even if he knew someone was on his case, he'd certainly have no way of knowing that I'd tracked him to the coast. There was no reason for him to get edgy or irrational and I had no intention of giving him one.

I knew I'd have to be more careful than I'd ever been before. If I blew it, there could be a lot of consequences that no one, least of all a private eye who's just trying to do a job, should have to face. I didn't want to wind up looking at my conscience for the rest of my life and not liking what I saw.

Cradling the package in his arms, Statten headed for the door, with me trailing some distance behind. I waited until he crossed the street and opened the door of an old, cream-coloured Ford. The picture of innocence, I strolled past the vehicle, giving it a casual glance and committing the license plate number to memory. When I was far enough down the street, I broke into a trot, hotfooting it to the lot where my own car was parked. Tossing some money at the attendant, I screeched into the street just ahead of a surge of traffic. I was in luck. Statten was stopped at a light. I slowed down, letting a van get between me and him. The light changed and the chase was on. Some chase. He was one of the easiest people I've ever had to tail – so easy, in fact, that I began to wonder whether he'd caught on to me. He crept along at about fifteen or twenty miles an hour which, for Vancouver, is like standing still.

Heading east on Hastings, which is one of the main drags in Vancouver, I lost him at one light but caught up with him at the next. By this time, we were heading into the seedier part of the business district. Where before there were office buildings and department stores, now the street was lined with pawnshops, greasy spoons, flophouses, and skid row hotels. We'd just crossed Carrall Street when, without signalling, he cut over to the curb and pulled into a parking space. I was too close to him to risk trying to find a spot of my own so, instead, I drove by and quickly circled the block. He was out of the car by then, plugging some coins into a meter. I pulled into the first spot I could find – a half-dozen car-lengths behind him – and waited. Dodging traffic, he crossed the street and headed into one of the more notorious skid row pubs. I'd spent quite a bit of time in Vancouver and knew the place as a hangout for hookers and dope-pushers and the sad smorgasbord of losers they preyed on.

From what I knew of Brad Statten, I wasn't surprised at his choice of watering holes. Not knowing how long I might have to wait, I shoved some coins into the meter, then strolled down the block to a news-stand that was almost directly opposite Statten's beat-up Ford.

Ducking inside, I took a quick look out the window just to play it safe but there was no sign of him. I turned back and ran smack into the stony gaze of the shop's proprietor, a middle-aged, stocky, Chinese guy. He was standing on a raised platform behind the cash register and from his elevated position, he could take in every inch of the cavernous establishment which looked a lot more like a warehouse than a smoke and news store.

His thick, oily hair was carefully combed and meticulously parted. He looked like a sallow-skinned Buddha. His arms were crossed against his chest and he was completely motionless except for his eyes which flicked from side to side like a snake's tongue, catching every play by everyone in the place.

There sure as hell was enough for him to watch over. There were shallow bins containing newspapers from all over the world, in all sizes and languages. The place smelled strongly of new paper and old wood. I checked for a Winnipeg paper but the most recent issue I could find was three days old. I fished a *Vancouver Sun* out of a wire stand at the front and forked over some change. He dropped it in the register without giving it or me a glance. Those hard, slitted eyes just kept darting from side to side, making sure that no goddamn round-eyed shoplifter was going to get away with shoving a *London Times* or *Washington Post* under his coat and dishonouring the proprietor and his ancestors by beating them out of fifty cents or a buck.

I was glad to get out of the place and into some reasonably fresh air. The joint smelled of smoke and decay and was so clammy you figured you were in a basement. Dimly-lit too but maybe that was no accident. The owner probably figured that if he kept the place dark enough, the health inspectors wouldn't get wise to what a dump it was and condemn it. A real dive alright and yet there was that Chinese guy standing there acting like it was Buckingham Palace and he'd been entrusted with the Crown Jewels.

While I slouched behind the wheel, shifting my glance between the paper and the street, a fortyish hooker in white, vinyl boots, with half her jello-ass hanging out of a pair of red hotpants, gave me the eye. I smiled and shook my head, wondering what kind of guy would pay money for something like that. Then I remembered some of the broads we used to get next to in France and Holland during the last war, and I knew.

Brad Statten came out of the hotel about a half-hour later but that was just to stuff some more loot into his meter. The second time he came out it was a different story. He was carrying a case of beer and I figured he had to be heading for home now. Equally obvious was the fact that he sure as hell hadn't joined A.A. In one way that was an advantage for me because with him getting into the booze, there'd be less chance of him spotting me and more chance of him making a mistake that could open the door to my getting Stacey back for Diane.

I don't know if he was flying high on booze-courage or what but he was driving a lot faster now and cutting in and out of traffic. I tramped on the gas and kept him in view as he turned right on Main Street. As I rounded the corner, I saw him hang another right and head into Chinatown which, in Vancouver, consists of about half a dozen blocks. There was quite a bit of traffic on Pender and he was right in the middle of the flow. It was a one-way street and I pulled out to pass, hoping to get a little closer but it was no dice. Both lanes were plugged. When the light changed up ahead, Statten made it through but when it turned red again, I was on the wrong side of the intersection and cursing myself for letting him get away. All wasn't lost though. I still had the license number of his car.

Ordinarily, I wouldn't have even bothered tailing a guy in a car just to find out his address when a quick trip to the Motor Vehicle Branch would've done the trick. But the vehicle Statten was driving might not have belonged to him so tracking down the license number might not have done me any good. But, once I lost him in the downtown traffic, I had no other choice. Just as I feared, the car wasn't registered in his name. The owner was a George Kaves who lived in a high-rise near the foot of Stanley Park in the city's West End.

I now had two choices. I could stake out Kaves' place and pick up Statten's tail again when he returned the car or I could do something a little sneakier but easier. I opted for the latter and placed a call to the car's owner. Like I said before, I've always believed that to be a good private eye, you have to be part actor and part con-man and this gave me a chance to test my theory.

"Mr. Kaves?"

"Y-e-e-e-a-h." The voice was tentative and suspicious.

"My name is Brewster – Frank Brewster. I'm an insurance adjuster for Universal Assurance Corporation."

"Oh, yeah?"

"Yes. One of our clients was just involved in an accident downtown and we're trying to locate anyone who might have witnessed it."

"Can't help you there, man," he said, sounding relieved. "I've been home all afternoon."

"Well, our client reported there were a number of cars around at the time of the collision and he took down the license number of one – BLT 621 – which I believe is registered in your name."

"That's my car, but I wasn't in it. I loaned it to my buddy this morning. He had to go and pick something up at the post office."

"Well, that's just about where the accident took place," I said cheerily. "Maybe your buddy's just the guy we're looking for. Perhaps you could give me his name and phone number and we could get in touch with him."

Kaves did more than that, giving me his pal's address as well. I thanked him, hung up, and immediately dialed Statten's number. I didn't really have to since I already knew where he lived but if his buddy told him about giving me his name and number and I didn't follow through, it might make him suspicious. When Brad Statten answered, I gave him the same spiel I'd laid on his pal and he bought it hook, line, and sinker.

"Sorry, Mr. Brewster. If there was an accident on Cambie today, it's news to me. I didn't hear or see a thing."

"Well, I guess I'll have to keep looking then, Mr. Statten. Sorry to trouble you."

I'd have to keep looking alright, I told myself, but at least now I knew where. I cruised by his place early that evening. Statten was holed up in an old, three-storey home on Burnaby Street in the city's West End. It was a tumbledown frame building in an advanced state of decay and if it'd been a horse, someone would've shot it a long time ago.

Most of the block, in fact, most of the West End, seemed to be made up of apartment buildings of varying sizes but there were some houses, by themselves or in small clusters, that'd escaped the wrecker's ball. Some of them were single-family dwellings while others, like the one Brad Statten was living in, had been subdivided into suites or furnished rooms.

I was amazed at how much the West End had changed since I'd last been in Vancouver some five years earlier. Not just physically, either. The whole feel and smell of the place. In the sixties, it was pretty well a quiet residential area inhabited by nine-to-fivers and a smattering of hippies but by the seventies, the picture had become a whole lot meaner, uglier, and louder. Soft drugs turned hard and gravitated to the West End with both users and sellers. The office girls who bartered sex for drinks, dinners, and a chance to escape from a typewriter or keypunch soon found themselves competing with broads whose favours were strictly C.O.D. Yeah, you just had to wander down Davie or Denman to see that the district had gotten quite a bit raunchier and a damn sight kinkier.

Fifteen or twenty years ago, you'd have to go down to Granville or Hastings if you wanted to find a hooker, but, by the early seventies, you could see them on Davie at just about any time of the day or night, their faces painted with professional lust and their bodies squeezed into clothes two sizes too small. Broads weren't the only ones on the prowl either. At any given time, you were just as likely to be accosted by a woman, man, or anything in between. And it was those in-betweens that really stole the show. Talk about drag queens! One night, I took a stroll down Davie and the whole street looked like a stage for an unrehearsed gay revue. Unrehearsed because some of the things that happened sure as hell couldn't have been planned. I saw three transvestites – one was a spitting image of Elizabeth Taylor – get a hose turned on them by the caretaker of an apartment building who wasn't too thrilled about having his front lawn decorated by a trio who wanted to be queen for more than just a day.

Yeah, it was quite a street alright and it probably still is in spite of the best efforts of residents to clean it up because if what I've been hearing is true, some Vancouver judges aren't above savouring the delights of the ladies of the night themselves and it's probably more convenient for them to latch onto their nookie right downtown, like near the Hotel Vancouver, or in the nearby West End.

Not that Davie was one big hooker haven. Oh no, there

were a lot of other commercial operations going on there. Everything from a Love Shop and strip club to a twenty-four-hour pancake house where people hung around all night, staring into their coffee cups and seeing themselves. The only thing I really liked about the area – and you can probably tell by looking at me – was the different food scents spicing the air, especially at night. The perfume of fish-and-chips, mingling with pizza, Chinese food, and fried chicken was enough to drag the most devout food-aholic off the wagon and if I hadn't been so busy on this caper, chances were I'd have put on a good ten pounds.

But I didn't have too much time to kill in restaurants, or anywhere else. You never do when you're on a stakeout and one big stakeout was pretty well what this case amounted to, at least until that final, climactic day. But that day was till a long way off when I registered at an apartment hotel almost directly across the street from Statten's place. It was early Wednesday evening, and for once, luck was in my corner as I managed to get a one-bedroom suite overlooking the street. It was on the eighth floor and I would've preferred something closer to ground level, but I knew I could've done a whole lot worse.

Both the living room and bedroom faced onto Burnaby Street and, to keep an eye on Statten's place, I could either park myself in front of the sliding glass door leading to the balcony or look through the small window in the bedroom. The window in the bedroom was so high I would've had to stand to see out, so I opted for the former and pulled up a chair – not an upholstered one but a hardbacked kitchen variety, because it doesn't pay to get too comfortable when you're on a stakeout.

By this time, the car Brad had borrowed from his buddy was no longer in sight and I guessed he'd returned it. I had my binoculars at my side but I was close enough that I wouldn't really need them to pick out Statten. But when he and the girl came out of the house at about 8:30 p.m., I grabbed for them in a hurry. As soon as I saw

Stacey, the tightness that'd been in my chest all day started to seep away. She was alright. She had a wooden expression but although her lips were pressed in a tight line and she looked far from happy, at least she didn't look as though she'd been mistreated – at least, physically.

Sure, her long, straw-coloured hair was in tangles and her complexion was pale but she looked like she was eating regularly anyway. She was a far cry from the way she looked in the photo Diane Statten had given me though. In the picture, Stacey's birthday smile lit up her face with bubbly energy. Now it was blank and downcast and her movements listless. No wonder, what with her being snatched from her mother and friends and hauled to a strange city by a guy who could charitably be described as "mentally unstable."

I wondered what he'd told her to get her to go with him. Not that it mattered. Whether he conned her or took her by force, it was all the same. He had her now and I knew it wasn't going to be easy to get her back.

She was wearing a white blouse, red sweater, and a pair of brown corduroy bib overalls. I wondered if they'd been in the package he'd picked up that afternoon. That afternoon. It already seemed so long ago.

Wherever Stacey and her dad were going, she didn't seem too enthused about it. As they crossed the street and headed west, the girl fell behind – at least, until her old man turned and grabbed her roughly by the arm. She winced with pain and began to half-trot to keep up with her father's long strides. When they stopped at the corner to let a car go by, she stood staring fixedly at the sidewalk. I didn't know what to make of it. Sure, she could've just been in a sulky mood and trying to needle her dad or then again, she might've been genuinely terrified of him. One thing I knew, he sure as hell wasn't treating her the way a loving father would be expected to.

Maybe Diane Statten was right. Maybe she hadn't

coloured the facts as I'd suspected. Maybe he *had* taken Stacey just to spite her. Maybe he *was* using the kid as a weapon to inflict pain on her. Maybe. I had a lot of time for maybe's as I sat behind that balcony door, waiting for them to return.

EIGHT

A Waiting Game

CALLING Diane Statten that night was like playing Santa Claus because what I told her was probably the best present she ever got.

"You found her? You mean, you actually saw her? Thank God." She rattled on like a machine-gun. "How was she? How did she look? I mean, did she look alright? She didn't look sick or anything? She didn't look thin like she wasn't eating properly?"

I calmed her down and told her Stacey looked O.K. and that I had her husband's place under surveillance.

"But you can't watch it twenty-four hours a day," she countered. "Suppose he moves. Suppose he just packs up and takes off in the middle of the night? Where does that leave you then? How would you ever find him again?"

"He's not going anywhere. He's got no reason to. As far as he's concerned, he's home free."

I could tell her that with some confidence for two reasons. First, when Brad and the girl were away, I shot over to his building and called on the caretaker, pretending I was looking for an apartment. The guy told me there weren't any available right then but said there might be a vacancy in a couple of months. This gave me the opportunity to find out that rents were paid on a monthly basis at the beginning of each month which meant that Brad Statten was paid up until the end of May which was still two weeks off. And, second, when I spotted Brad and Stacey returning a half hour or so later, Statten was carrying a couple of bags of groceries, which meant they had a suite where he could do some cooking as opposed to a light housekeeping room. All in all, it looked like he and Stacey had achieved some degree of permanence and I wasn't too worried about them checking out on a moment's notice. After I laid this information on Diane, I tried to ease her worries about Stacey.

"She looks a 100 per cent," I lied. "Through the binoculars, it was like she was sitting on my lap and she looked well-fed and clean and she was reasonably well-dressed. But remember," I cautioned, "this is only square one. Now comes the hard part."

I could feel her excitement coming through the telephone wire. I understood it but it worried me. I knew I had to defuse it, otherwise the whole caper stood a good chance of going down the drain.

"I want you to grab the first plane down here. I'll pick you up at the airport and we'll take it from there. But remember, you're going to have to do everything I say. One mistake and . . . ."

Neither one of us wanted me to finish the sentence.

"I will. I promise," she said huskily.

Her plane was due in at 9:30 Thursday morning and I got to the airport about half an hour early. It was a beautiful day. Clear blue sky and the sun hadn't yet burned away the crispness in the air. I hoped it was an omen and that something besides the sun was smiling down on us. It's not as though I'm superstitious but I've found that although preparation is the key, sometimes the door still manages to stick a little without some luck to grease the hinges.

What a sight she was. For the first time since I'd met her, Diane Statten had some colour in her cheeks and sparkle in her eyes. I latched onto the two suitcases she pointed out and started for the car but she checked me.

"Wait. That's not all."

The news didn't thrill me since I'd told her to travel

light in case we had to move fast. And I was even less enthused when I saw the rest of her baggage which consisted of a huge brown teddy bear. Its large glassy eyes stared up at the ceiling as it lay on its back on the steadily rotating baggage carousel. Diane put the grab on it.

"I just had to bring it," she said apologetically. "It's Stacey's favourite. I don't think she'll ever outgrow it." Then with mock formality, she shoved out one of the bear's paws. "Mr. Manweiler, I'd like you to meet Theodore Bear."

I went along with the gag but told myself: Christ, that's all I need – to lug an overgrown toy bear around. But I kept my trap shut. She was floating on happiness and I didn't want to burst the bubble, at least not until I had to. There'd be time enough for that later when I laid out the nuts and bolts of my plan.

I smuggled Diane into the apartment through the underground parkade in back. There was no way I wanted to take a chance on her husband spotting her until we were ready which meant outfitting her with a disguise. According to my instructions, she'd purchased a black, shoulder-length wig. She modeled it for me and it gave her a kind of Cleopatra look that made her seem more feminine and sexier than before. I didn't dwell on that too much though because we were going to be sharing the same apartment and I didn't want to be preoccupied with anything but business.

"Here try these on." I handed her a pair of lightly-tinted sunglasses. They were the modern kind – the ones with lenses the size of saucers, and, together with the wig, they gave her a completely new image. She checked her reflection in the hall mirror.

"Do you think it'll work?" She sounded doubtful.

"Can't miss," I said, adding. "As long as we don't take any chances."

She nodded absently and started fussing with the wig, grimacing in the mirror as she angled her head this way and that. After she finished primping, I led her onto the balcony and pointed out the house where her husband and daughter were living.

"It doesn't look like much," she offered, wrinkling her nose.

"It's cheap anyway," I said. "You did say you didn't think he had a helluva lot of cash."

"He must have some. He cleaned out our bank account before leaving." She pursed her lips thoughtfully. "Of course, if he's back on the bottle, he's probably blown most of it by now."

While she stayed out on the balcony, her gaze riveted to the front door of Brad's building, I moved my stuff out of the bedroom and hauled her bags in. The living room had one of those hide-a-beds and I figured I might as well crash there since I'd be going in and out while she stayed under wraps.

"Nothing?" I called over my shoulder.

"No, nothing." The voice was leaden with disappointment. She was leaning on her elbows on the balcony railing, her narrow shoulders hunched against her slim neck. Suddenly, her whole body stiffened and there was a sharp intake of breath.

"It's him!"

I pulled her back from the railing then jotted down the time in my notebook. Eleven forty-five. I guessed Brad was on his way to pick up the girl at school. Not good. It was obvious he wasn't letting Stacey out of his sight for a minute. We stood just inside the sliding glass door, looking down into the street.

"Aren't you going to do something," Diane asked desperately. "Aren't you going to follow him?"

"Nope. That'd be a waste of time – also too risky. The trick is to let him come to us."

And, shortly after noon, that's exactly what he – or rather, *they* – did. Stacey had a canvas tote-bag slung over her shoulder and she was wearing the same outfit she'd had on the day before. Diane had her face pressed against the glass and spotted them when they were still half-way up the block.

"Stacey." Her voice was low but charged with emotion. Her hands were clenched and shaking as she strained forward, trying to reclaim her child with her eyes.

"Stacey." A lost, strangled cry, repeated over and over again, long after Brad and the girl had disappeared into the rooming house. Diane finally turned away from the door, an expression of sheer terror on her face. She feared that having found her child, she was now on the verge of losing her again. I led her over to the couch and sat her down. But she wouldn't stay put. Within seconds, she was chain-smoking, pacing the floor, and bristling:

"That bastard! Why can't we just go down there and take her? She's mine! I have a court order. He has a absolutely no right –"

"That order's only good in Manitoba," I reminded her. "Besides, if we confront him, there's no telling what he might do. Do you want to chance that?" She shook her head. "O.K., then let me tell you a couple of facts of life. First of all, I'm not a cop so I can't arrest your husband and, even if I was, I still couldn't. And neither can the Vancouver police even if they showed an inclination to take their thumbs out. Under the law, Brad hasn't done anything illegal. Immoral, maybe. Cruel, for sure. But not criminal. As far as the law's concerned, it's just another husband-and-wife squabble with a kid caught in the middle."

Diane's eyes flashed with anger. "Well, if it's not against the law for someone to steal a child from her mother, it sure as hell should be!"

"Maybe you're right," I shot back. "But what are we here for? To try and reform the legal system or to get Stacey back? If you want to prod the public's conscience, write a letter to the editor but if you want to get your girl back, forget about everything but following my orders."

She glanced toward the balcony. "That bastard," she hissed. "He doesn't give a damn about her. He never did.

He just wants to punish me because –" She checked herself.

"Because what?"

"Nothing." She averted her eyes. She was hiding something alright. But I didn't waste my breath trying to pump her, figuring if she wanted to clue me in, she would. She didn't though, at least, not right then, and I went ahead with my briefing.

"The chances of intercepting Stacey on a week-day seem pretty slim. It looks like your husband walks her to school and back and, from what I've seen, he never lets her out of his sight in the evenings."

Diane Statten looked attentive but I knew at least a part of her mind and all of her heart were somewhere else.

"Now we can go about this two different ways," I continued. "We can drop down to the school and see if we can get the authorities to keep their mouths shut and cooperate or we can keep it in the family, so to speak, and put the grab on Stacey ourselves."

"Do you think they'd cooperate – the people at the school, I mean?"

I shrugged. "Maybe but then again they just might be like most people and not want to get involved. Even that wouldn't be so bad but what I'm afraid of is that they might tip Brad off and we both know where that could lead."

I guessed she was thinking of her husband's gun like I was and the frightened glint in her eye confirmed it.

"Then what do we do? What *can* we do?"

"Like I said, we can do it on our own but that's going to involve a lot of planning, patience, and legwork."

She sagged into an upholstered arm chair and buried her face in her hands. Her words were as muffled as her sobs but they came through loud and clear, stabbing right into my guts.

"I want my baby. I don't want to live without my baby."

I went over and patted her reassuringly on the shoulder.

Tears were seeping through the fingers masking her face. My throat felt like it had a golf ball stuck in it.

"We'll get her," I managed to croak. "We'll get Stacey back. I promise."

And after Diane went into the bedroom to rest, I started to prepare for the most important role in my entire career – one that had more riding on it than I cared to think about. It wasn't as though Brad Statten was my only worry though. Sure, I knew he could flip out if he learned his wife and I were planning to snatch Stacey back but there was a second factor as well: the Vancouver cops. After all, Brad Statten was a resident of the city and the natural father of the girl which would give him an edge as far as the authorities were concerned.

In addition, I, personally, didn't have a legal leg to stand on when it came to putting the grab on Stacey, although Diane certainly did. I'd have to set it up so she and she alone physically took possession of the girl if and when the opportunity presented itself, otherwise I could be laying myself open to a charge and that's something I definitely wanted to steer clear of. Maybe I was a little gun-shy about running afoul of the law because, as I mentioned earlier, the interior of a jail cell is not exactly foreign to me. Actually, that's not as dramatic as it sounds because it'd be stretching it quite a bit to call myself an ex-con and my prison memoirs would have to be padded to fill a single page. The only reason I'm mentioning it is that it goes to show what can happen when you least expect it and it can serve as a good lesson to private detectives who have a tendency to get carried away and think they're Richard Diamond or Mike Hammer.

Anyway, this is how it happened. I was on a surveillance job, checking up on a chick who was supposedly playing around on her husband. Well, after a couple of stakeouts, there was no supposedly about it. When hubby was away, wifey would play – and I don't mean bingo. On this one particular occasion, she took her act on the road to the home of a guy we'll call Bob Chester. After I put them to bed (private eye jargon for seeing them turn in for the night) I called my client and let him in on the bad news. And what does he do? He heads right down to Bob's place where I intercepted him and tried to calm him down.

What a night for my powers of persuasion to pull up lame. Said client could not be reasoned with and instead of waiting for morning and consulting a lawyer, he waits all of thirty seconds and puts the boots to Bob's back door, resulting in one splintered door and many curses and screams by all concerned. To prevent the mayhem that I figured was sure to ensure, I followed my client inside and, later, to the hoosegow.

I guess Chester didn't have much of a sense of humour because he filed a trespassing complaint against myself as well as that lunatic client of mine and after I showed up at the police station to explain matters, a kindly understanding sergeant had me placed in the lockup overnight.

The irony of the whole thing was that from my cell I could look up and see the window of my office which was located in a building just across the street from the Winnipeg Public Safety Building. Let me tell you, there's no lonelier feeling than looking out at somewhere you'd like to be but can't. I did get one laugh out of the deal though so, aside from having the charge against me dropped, there was at least one other bright spot.

After spending a sleepless night in the slammer, I was waiting to be brought before a magistrate so I could be sprung when a guard shoved a brush and some detergent into the cell and told me and the three other guys in there to get busy and clean the toilet. Well, that toilet bowl was so filthy and caked with crap that it should've been condemned rather than cleaned and there was no way I was going to come within ten feet of the damn thing. The other guys felt the same way and when the guard had turned and started away, one of them – a tough-looking guy with tattoos on both forearms and the look of a guy who'd seen more cells than this one – jerked his thumb toward the departing cop and sneered: "That's a screw for you. Too lazy to work and too scared to steal."

Well, I laughed so hard I almost had to use that god-damn toilet myself and I'll never forget either that comment or one of the most miserable nights I've ever spent. It was a lesson to me though. And I was thinking about it as I put the finishing touches on my plan to reunite Stacey with her mother.

I couldn't sleep that night. Neither could Diane and about three in the morning, she got up and fixed some coffee. We sat at the table in the dining nook, aimlessly stirring our coffee and listening to my alarm clock ticking the night away. Finally, the dam burst and all of her fear and uncertainty broke loose.

"Will it be alright? Are you sure it'll work?" She toyed with her thin gold wedding band then stopped abruptly and looked at it with distaste.

"If it doesn't, it won't be due to lack of planning," I said. She looked so downcast, I thought she needed some reassurance so I tried to sound more confident than I felt. "We won't go ahead unless everything's right. We won't gamble on . . . anything." Thank God, I caught myself before saying "your daughter's life."

She lit a cigarette and took a deep drag, exhaling slowly.

"I haven't been totally honest with you," she said, gauging my reaction out of the corner of her eye.

"Really?" I said, trying to sound surprised.

She butted her cigarette, took a deep breath and began. "The fight Brad and I had the night before he took Stacey away added up to quite a bit more than I told you."

My raised eyebrows seemed to be all the encouragement she needed.

"As I told you, we had a big hassle about his drinking and not wanting to look for a job."

She paused, taking on a distant look as though going back in time to that fateful evening, then continued. "I tried to get him to see a psychiatrist or alcoholism counsellor but he wouldn't even talk about it and I just couldn't see any way out. And it wasn't only himself he was destroying but me and Stacey. He was getting worse – more out of control – every day. And the beatings, they were getting worse too. Instead of the occasional slap like before, he started hitting me with his fists or a belt."

All of a sudden, I felt tired and about a hundred years old – like a father confessor who'd just got through working a double shift. You can only take so much of anything, including listening to other people's troubles and sins. After a while, all the violence, filth, and degradation that people lay on you builds up inside, poisons you mentally and spiritually, until you start to hate the entire human race, including yourself. You begin to forget that human beings are capable of nobility and decency and when something happens to remind you, it's like discovering a diamond in a mound of rotting, stinking, garbage. As a defence against reality, I only half-listened to Diane's recital. But my mind snapped to attention as she came into the home stretch.

"Maybe I should have kept quiet but I couldn't take his brutality any more. I wanted to hurt him the way he was hurting me and I lashed out the only way I could – with words."

She got that faraway look again and I waited for her to come back. Somewhere below us, a car door slammed and a dog began to bark. When Diane Statten spoke again, her voice was little more than a whisper.

"I told him he wasn't a man – that no man would beat a woman." She swallowed hard and bit her bottom lip.

"He said he'd show me who was a man." She gave a short, brittle, laugh. "And I guess he did that alright. And do you know how he did it?"

I shook my head.

"He raped me." She said it so simply and matter-of-factly, it was a couple of seconds before it sank in.

"And what did you do?"

"Oh, I thought of doing a lot of things," she said airily.

"Killing him. Laying a charge. Telling his dear mother what a fine boy she raised. A lot of things. But I ended up doing nothing except telling him he was even a lousy rapist."

She walked over to the balcony and stood looking down at the street. Her voice wafted over her shoulder. "I couldn't bring myself to tell anyone what happened. I felt dirty . . . ashamed. And the next day, he was gone. And so was Stacey."

I really felt sorry for her. Sure, you could say it was partly her own fault for marrying a guy who was two bricks shy of a load and then sticking with him even after it became obvious he was a total loss. But I guess Diane had had a dream that all the pieces would come together somehow and the ugliness would be no more than a distant memory. It didn't happen. In my world – a world of broken promises, homes, and lives – it seldom does. But I'm the last one to say people shouldn't go on dreaming.

After Diane went back to bed, I went out on the balcony. The night air was like a cool, soothing hand on my brow. It was clear and starry and the moon was reflected in the inky ripples of English Bay. Festooned with lights, the Burrard Street bridge looked like a giant Gothic arch. The sound of crossing cars rose and receded. The highrises fronting the beach were all dark except for the occasional rectangle of flickering blue light where some insomniac was watching the late-late or early-early show.

Burnaby Street was deserted and Brad Statten's place was lost in the shadows of neighbouring apartment blocks. Today's the day, I told myself. Phase one of my plan to reclaim seven-year-old Stacey Statten would be put into operation within a matter of hours. Then I came inside and tried to get some sleep.

By the time my alarm went off at seven-thirty, Diane was already stationed before the balcony door, staring down into the street with grim determination. I got up, put the coffee on, and spelled her while she put on the wig and got herself ready. At eight-forty, I called her to the balcony and together we watched Brad and Stacey leave their building. Diane turned and looked at me expectantly. I shook my head.

"Not today. Not 'til the weekend."

She didn't try to hide her disappointment as we headed downstairs and drove to a used-clothing store on Hastings. I let Diane drive. It was important that she get used to the vehicle because after we put the grab on Stacey, she'd be the one behind the wheel and I wanted to make sure she could handle it. If she let the car stall or had trouble manoeuvering it at a critical time, it might be game over in more ways than one. She wasn't a bad driver anyway. That was something in our favour.

At the store, I picked up some threads that looked approximately my size – some pants, a shirt, a maroon cardigan sweater that was stretched out of shape, and a pair of running shoes with the toes worn through. The middle-aged clerk looked at me questioningly, as though to say: "You sure you really want this stuff?" But she took my money and kept her trap shut.

Diane had her disguise and now it was time for me to put on mine. Like I said before, being a private eye means fifty percent investigation and fifty percent impersonation. And this was one role I couldn't afford to blow. In preparation, I'd allowed my beard to grow and I already had a quarter-inch of grey stubble. The grubby clothes I'd picked out turned out to be perfect. The dark brown slacks were baggy and a couple of inches too short. The checked lumberjack shirt was the right size and had a couple of buttons missing. The sweater was a real winner too. It looked more like a bathrobe. The elbows were worn through and the right side was particularly mis-shapen, with the pocket reaching almost to my knee. And those open-toed runners, well, they were the crowning touch. At one time, they were probably white but now they were a sickly grey. Of course, even if they were their original colour, they wouldn't have come close to matching the laces: one was black and the other brown.

I stood in front of the hall mirror, checking my image and running a hand over the bristles on my chin. While I was posing there, I heard Diane start to giggle then burst out laughing and it wasn't long before I joined her because I have to admit I was quite a sight. I looked like the kind of guy you'd cross the street to avoid for fear of contracting some particularly disgusting social disease.

My get-up was complete except for the most important prop and I drove down to a liquor store on Bute and Davie to get it. When I shuffled in, I could almost feel the sneers of the snotty white-shirted clerks who were pulling in a couple of hundred bucks a week and figured that entitled them to look down on whatever wino stumbled in for his daily fix of joy-juice. Of course, to be convincing, you have to do more than just look like an alky. You have to move and act like one which means always keeping your eyes downcast like you're looking for change someone might've dropped. Another reason winos study the sidewalk is because they don't want to risk looking someone in the eye and seeing their own reflections. You have to put on a whining tone as well because winos are forever putting the touch on people in the street and if they don't have pity going for them, they don't have a goddamn thing.

When I counted out the change for the cheap bottle of wine, to put the icing on the cake, I practised making my hands tremble. It worked like a charm, the clerk cracking:

"Looks like you need that stuff in a bad way."

I huffed like I'd just been grossly insulted and slurred: "My good man, I'd 'preciate it if you would confine your remarks to the price of your ver' ex'llent product which I use for medicinal purposes only."

Then I turned and lurched out of there with the towering dignity that only a wino can muster. Behind me, I could hear the clerks cracking jokes at my expense but it didn't bother me a bit. It was working. That was all I cared about. I had to be convincing and I was.

Then it was back to the apartment, making sure I went

in unobserved through the rear entrance. If the management spotted me looking like this, I'd have a lot of explaining to do and that was something I wanted to avoid. I'd just gotten in the door when Diane beckoned to me excitedly.

"It's Stacey and . . . him." It was as though she couldn't bring herself to say her husband's name.

She grabbed my binoculars and pressed them right against the balcony door as she peered into the street. It was a little after noon and I guessed Brad had just picked up his daughter at school. I looked over Diane's shoulder, watching them approach the walk leading to their building.

Abruptly, they stopped. Brad seemed to be yelling at her, then, all of a sudden, he slapped her hard across the face. We could hear Stacey's piteous howl all the way up to our eighth-floor perch. Diane dropped the binoculars and tried to claw the balcony door open. I held it shut, positioning myself between her and the balcony. Her mouth was twisted with helpless rage.

"Let her go, you bastard," she shrieked.

I put my hand over her mouth, not wanting some well-meaning neighbour to bring the law down on us.

"Easy. Take it easy," I soothed, holding her at bay until Brad had carried Stacey, kicking and screaming, into their building.

For the rest of that day, I didn't let Diane near the apartment door, fearing she might take off and confront her husband. I even coaxed her into taking a sleeping pill, telling her she had to be in top shape for the next day's work. So at least one of us looked half-way rested that Saturday morning. We kept watch on their place until after one p.m. before spotting them. Brad and Stacey came down the steps and turned left, heading west. Since it was a beautiful sunny afternoon, it was my guess they were going to the beach or Stanley Park. Diane was as jumpy as a cat and kept eyeing the door. If it'd been up to her, she would've gone tearing down into the street and scooped her little girl up in her arms.

"Let's move," I barked.

We made quite a pair – her with the wig and shades and me in my wino regalia complete with a wine bottle tucked inside my shirt. We rode the elevator down to the basement and left by the parkade. Jumping into the car, we caught up with Brad and the girl at the corner of Davie and Denman. Diane was behind the wheel with me slumped down on the passenger side.

We stopped for a red light and Brad and Stacey started to cross the street right in front of us.

"Don't even look at them," I cautioned.

She did as she was told, looking straight ahead, her face pale and drawn. They turned and headed toward Beach and it was my guess they were heading for Stanley Park. We headed down Denman and entered the sprawling complex through the Georgia Street entrance. From there, I gave Diane directions to the parking lot nearest the zoo, figuring the chances were they'd end up there sooner or later. From where we were parked, we had a clear view of the walk leading to the animal enclosures and as we waited, I tried to come up with a foolproof plan because I knew we'd only get one chance.

I didn't like the set-up. For one thing, we couldn't park close enough to the zoo to grab the kid and get back to the car safely. And for another, Diane would have a helluva time getting out of the lot, never mind the park, what with the heavy Saturday afternoon traffic. Of course, it would be my job to see that her getaway time was stretched to the limit. In that setting, it would be none too easy but we couldn't wait for Stacey to be dropped in our laps so I decided to set the wheels in motion and hope for a break somewhere along the way. It was a good fifteen or twenty minutes before they showed. As soon as I spotted them, I hopped out of the car, telling her: "Stay put. Don't move until I give you the word."

Even through the tinted lenses, her eyes looked wide

and frightened. I squeezed her hand and she managed a tight smile. I loped up the incline from the parking lot. Brad Statten was buying Stacey some popcorn from a pushwagon vendor and I managed to get ahead of them. I hurriedly reconnoitered the zoo to see if there was a parking area near any of the exhibits and came up empty. By this time, Stacey and her dad were at the monkey cage and the little girl was pointing excitedly at the inmates' antics. Her old man ignored her, preferring to give the once-over to a cluster of teenage chicks in shorts and skimpy halter tops.

So far it looked hopeless. Statten never so much as strayed from the girl's side and, even if he had, the place was so overrun with visitors that there was no way Diane could put the snatch on the kid and make her way through that mob before her hubby got wise. I shuffled past Brad and Stacey, heading back to break the bad news to Diane. And stopped dead in my tracks. There was Diane Statten advancing slowly toward us and she was no more than a hundred feet away. In my mind, I saw the whole caper collapsing like a house of cards. Without taking time to think, I lurched right into her path, muttering: "C'n yuh spare some change for a vet'rin? I ain't et all day, lady. Hones'. Can yuh help a guy out?"

That was for public consumption. Under my breath, I hissed. "If you don't get out of here right now, you'll never see your daughter again." It wasn't just an idle threat. I believed it and so, finally, did she. Brad and the girl had already moved on without so much as a backward glance. At least Diane had had the sense to keep her disguise on. I walked her over to a bench away from the main display area and sat her down.

"Do you realize what you almost did?"

She looked so miserable, I didn't have the heart to chew her out any more. She nodded, saying: "I couldn't help it. She's so close. I can't stand not being able to touch her, to hold her. Now that I've found her, I'll never let her go even if it means. . . ." Her voice trailed off pathetically and two big tears formed in the corners of her eyes.

"We'll get her back," I said, trying to convince both of us. "I promise. We'll get her back."

"But when?" The tears were starting to trace uneven paths down her cheeks.

"When the time is right and not before."

I noticed that her right hand was still shoved deep inside her purse. It had been there when I short-circuited her attempt to confront her husband. I took hold of her wrist and pulled it gently but firmly. Her hand slid out of the purse and with it, a wicked-looking butcher knife. I recognized it immediately as the one I'd seen in a kitchen drawer in our apartment.

I was too shook up to do anything but sigh and tell her how many kinds of fool she was. Passers-by stared at us. It must have been quite a sight, this wino laying down the law to a straight-looking, well-groomed young woman. This time, I think my words had some effect. She listened dutifully then headed back to the car while I resumed my stakeout. I was just going through the motions though. The place was wrong and Diane was too hyper for us to try and put anything together that afternoon.

Nothing was working and I wondered if it ever would. The pressure was like a cold hand around my throat and I even started to wonder if I was the right guy for the job. The longer the thing dragged out, the greater chance there was that Diane would go off the deep end and do something crazy. And the greater the chance Brad could get wise to us or take off for some other, unrelated reason.

Casing Brad and Stacey one last time, I joined Diane at the car and we drove back to the apartment in silence. It was another sleepless night with Diane and me taking turns pacing the floor. Sunday, we'd try again and maybe this time, Lady Luck would be in our corner.

Watching. From the first crack of dawn. Watching 'til my eyeballs ached. Until I felt the vertebrae in my neck start to fuse. At about nine, a middle-aged woman in a baggy housedress came out and made a few half-hearted passes at the steps with a broom. During the morning, other tenants left and returned but there was no sign of Brad Statten or his daughter. Until shortly after noon. When they emerged from the old, three-storey house, I signalled to Diane who bolted for the bedroom. She already had the wig and shades on by the time I tossed her the car keys and headed for the elevator.

We didn't speak on the way down. We'd rehearsed the caper so many times, there was no need for me to give her instructions. I felt a rush of adrenalin and said a silent prayer. It was short and not so sweet. Just: Dear lord, don't let me fuck this one up. Not this one.

Statten was carrying a wicker beach bag and the girl was lugging a plastic shovel and pail so there wasn't much doubt about their destination. The only thing that remained was seeing which part of the beach they'd stake a claim on.

We drove down to English Bay and Diane managed to find a spot beside the Sylvia Hotel. I told her to sit tight then hustled over to the little triangle of grass just below the intersection of Denman and Davie where I plunked myself down on a bench facing the bay.

It was a real picture postcard day, heavy on blue sky and fleecy clouds. The sun warmed the breeze off the bay and bounced off the water. Many more days like this and the B.C. Tourist Bureau would be able to give up lying. Far off in the distance, over in North Van, you could see a whole gang of bluish-grey mountains whose snowy peaks were half-shrouded in mist. It was quite a scene and I vowed that someday I'd come back just to let all that natural beauty seep into my bones. But not this time. This time it was all business and one panoramic look was all I allowed myself. My attention and nerves were keyed to other matters. No sign of them. I'd give them another couple of minutes then start to track them down. By then, there was a pretty good crowd and the beach was littered with reclining bodies in all shapes, sizes, and pigments.

Everybody wasn't there to worship the sun though. A lot of them came just to see and be seen, with tourists and locals mingling and passing each other on the long, mildly-rolling path running along the perimeter of the bay. Joggers of every description, decked out in everything from short-shorts to flannel sweat-suits, glided, thudded, and sweated by. Rollerskaters whirred past, vying with each other to see who was the biggest exhibitionist. At tall black girl in a red tank top and white gym shorts pirouetted on her skates right in front of me. The muscles in her heavyduty thighs glistened. She bent down, adjusting her kneepads and, at the same time, checking to see if anyone was casing her buns, half of which was spilling out of her shorts. Our eyes met and she turned away, a curl of distaste on her ripe lips. I hoped it was because my wino disguise was convincing and not because she could read my mind.

I craned my neck toward the sunbathers, some sprawled on blankets, others perched on telephone-pole-sized logs half-buried in the sand like giant pieces of driftwood. The scene was set against a backdrop of sailboats that tacked and wheeled, taking advantage of every gust of wind. Their sails, conventionally white or all the colours of the rainbow, gave the bay a festive look. But there sure as hell was nothing festive about the way I felt – even after I spotted Brad and Stacey.

They'd stopped at one of those old-fashioned popcorn wagons that have plastic bags of the pre-popped stuff piled on the roof. After picking up a couple of bags, they started toward the beach, heading directly at me. I went right into my wino routine, mumbling and singing to myself and Statten gave me an amused look as he passed by. I smiled and gave him an exaggerated salute and a garbled "How-ya-doin', Cap'n?" Perfect. Perfect. From this point on, I'd be just part of the surroundings to him – a harmless old drunk, a loser who couldn't help himself let alone anyone else. So much for step one.

Step two involved me getting back to Diane and orchestrating what was to come. It was important that she find a parking spot as close to the beach as possible, even if it meant stopping in a no-parking zone. The plan was for her to grab the kid, haul her into the car, and head back to the apartment. But, for it to work, two things had to happen. Stacey and her father had to be separated and Brad had to have his attention diverted long enough for Diane to do her thing. The latter was my job but I wouldn't be able to play my part unless Stacey and her old man got some distance between them first.

We lucked into a parking spot in a back lane that intersected with the foot of Denman Street. From there, it was only a matter of a couple of hundred yards to where Brad and Stacey were situated. The first hundred and fifty consisted of a grassy slope that led to the path that ran parallel to the bay. Beyond that, the terrain levelled out into about fifty yards of sand reaching right up to the water's edge. Two hundred yards. But they might just as well have been miles unless we got some sort of break.

Below us and to the east, there was a large combination change-house and concession stand that faced the bay. Fashioned of grey concrete, it fronted on the asphalt path and looked more like a mausoleum than a fish-and-chip stand. I laid out the scenario for Diane one last time, finishing up with: "Remember, when I take off my sweater, that's the signal for you to move and move fast. Got it?"

She nodded, her face clouded with anxiety.

I reached over and patted her hand, saying: "Don't worry. We're going to do it. We're going to get Stacey back. I promise."

Now, ordinarily, I never make promises because I've found that most of them are pretty hard to keep – even the ones you make to yourself – but I figured she needed something to get her through the caper.

She twitched a smile and quavered: "Be careful."

"That's one thing I can guarantee," I grinned. Leaving Diane, I shambled down the slope and leaned against the concession stand, watching Statten and the girl for a couple of minutes to try and pull out a pattern. Glancing back over my shoulder, I was relieved to see that Diane had followed my instructions to the letter. Stationing herself just west of the building and part way up the slope, she was lounging on the grass, going through the motions of reading a pocketbook.

Brad and Stacey had had bathing suits on under their clothes and, after stripping down, the girl played in the sand with her pail and shovel while her father lay on his stomach, sunning himself. Real father-daughter bliss. To some it would have been a heartwarming scene. But not to me. To me, it was a disaster. Stacey was never any more than a half-dozen yards from her old man and I started to get the same sinking feeling I had the day before.

Christ, I told myself, if we strike out again, Diane is sure to go off the deep end. Keeping up my wino routine, I weaved down onto the beach and flopped down on a log right next to a middle-aged couple who were taking snapshots of each other against a variety of backgrounds.

"How 'bout takin' my pic-shur," I slurred, smiling crookedly.

Well, that was enough to make them pack up their camera and stick their noses in the air like they'd just smelled something and I was it. They made tracks out of there in no time flat and just as I was congratulating myself on getting a better vantage point from which to observe Statten and his daughter, I sensed rather than saw someone approaching. I saw his shadow first but didn't want to look up for fear it was a cop with a penchant for rousting bums. As it turned out, it wasn't the law but what it was turned out to be almost as bad. A wino. A real one. And he was smiling at me like he'd just discovered a kindred spirit – no pun intended.

"How ya doin', partner," he crooned, plunking himself down beside me and treating me to a gust of fermented breath.

"Not so bad," I muttered, wishing I could tell him to bugger off.

"Ya got anythin' to drink?" He pointedly eyed the bulge in my shirt where I had the bottle stashed. "Ya got a li'l taste?"

I averted my face and tried to hold my breath but it didn't work. He kept on yammering, spattering the side of my face and neck with saliva. Running a grubby hand through his long, greasy hair, he tugged at the sleeve of my sweater with nicotine-stained fingers. I turned back and studied his leathery face. The nose was cobwebbed with thin red veins and the eyes bloodshot and watery. And not a goddamn thing in those eyes but his maniacal thirst. Christ, what a way to live, I thought.

"Jus' a taste, pal," he implored. "Whattaya say? I'm gonna get me some bingo later on. No kiddin'. My partner's gonna pick it up later soon as we score 'nough change. An' I'll share with ya, hones'." He made an exaggerated show of crossing his heart that put him off balance and almost sent him tumbling off the log.

I had no choice. If he kept hassling me, it was liable to bring down the law and I couldn't think of any way to get rid of him, so I fished out the bagged wine bottle and handed it to him. He unscrewed the top and, without even looking around to see if anyone was watching, he took a hefty pull then wiped his mouth with the back of his hand. I grabbed the bottle before he tried for seconds. He smiled at me hopefully, his hand and lips smeared with purple. I figured I'd take a short slug myself just to make it look good and just when I had the bottle to my lips, Brad Statten sat up and spotted me. He laughed and gave me a perfunctory wave.

That was all the invitation I needed. I hauled myself up and started toward him with the wino still clutching at my sweater and begging for another drink. Without even looking at him, I brought my heel down on his instep as hard as I could. He yelped in pain, then slunk off, muttering curses.

I made my way over to Brad who was stretched out on his back, resting on his elbows and checking out the bikini'd flesh along the beach. My open-toed sneakers had filled with sand and my feet felt as though an army of ants was crawling all over them. I squatted down next to him and pointed conspiratorially to the half-filled wine bottle that was poking its neck out from inside my shirt.

"Ya wanna drink?"

He smiled and shook his head. "I'm not much on that stuff."

"Me neither," I said. "I'm a champagne man, myself, but I'm a li'l down on my luck."

He chuckled mirthlessly. "I know how you feel. My luck hasn't been all that shit-hot lately either."

"Then what ya need is some o' this," I said, pulling out the bottle.

He waved it and me away. I ignored the rebuff.

"Zat your girl?" I flicked a thumb toward Stacey who was busy planting a piece of driftwood in the sand like a cross.

"Yeah, that's right." His voice took a hard edge.

"Bee-yoo-ti-ful girl. Bee-yoo-ti-ful."

He stared at her intently, without saying anything. Somehow, she must've felt his gaze on her because she looked up, saw his expression, and kind of flinched. It was his eyes. Cold and angry. The tip of an iceberg of hatred. He was looking at his daughter but seeing his wife.

"C'mon," I urged, poking the bottle at him, "have a drink jush for ol' times sake. Whattaya say? Have a li'l smash with me."

"What happened to your drinking partner?"

"Him?" I snorted. "He's no partner o' mine, nossir. He's a goddamn mooch that's what he is. Whenever he's got a bottle of his own, it's like he's the goddamn divisible man or somethin' but let 'im get a sniff o' yours and he's like a goddamn bloodhound."

"A real leech, eh?"

"Ya better b'lieve it." I took a pull on the wine and set it down between my legs. "By the way, ya wouldn't have a smoke on ya, would ya, buddy?"

He had a package lying next to him. He fished one out and handed it to me. I dug a book of matches out of the misshapen cardigan and my hand was shaking when I lit it. Only this time, it was no act. I was starting to sweat heavily too. I glanced up at the grassy slope next to the concession stand. There was Diane, still making like she was engrossed in that pocketbook. I wondered how long she'd be able to keep her cool. She'd been quiet today. Too goddamn quiet. And I wondered what was going through her mind at that moment. I could have kicked myself for not checking out her purse to see if she was packing anything.

Brad squinted down the beach, trying to ignore me.

Stacey's attention was held by a couple of hippies playing catch with a Frisbee.

And me? I just watched and waited and sweated. I could feel puddles forming in my armpits but there was no way I could get rid of that heavy cardigan. Not yet.

Back up the slope, Diane was getting restless. She'd put down the book and was staring fixedly in our direction. The hair prickled on the back of my neck. I sensed she was getting ready to crack. I had to do something. I couldn't wait for fate to throw a horseshoe into my lap.

"I had a li'l girl like that once," I muttered.

Brad cocked his head toward me. "What'd you say?"

"Jush sayin' what a pretty li'l girl ya got there. Had a girl o' my own once. Jush like her – same hair, same eyes. I wunner if. . . . Nah, I don' s'pose you'd. . . ."

"What are you trying to say?" He was trying to be patient but a note of irritation had crept into his voice.

"Well, I was jush wunnerin' if maybe you'd lemme buy your li'l girl a treat."

Stacey was sitting next to her father, tracing a circle in the sand. She stopped and eyed me questioningly.

"Ya like ice cream, li'l girl? Sure ya do. All li'l girls like ice cream."

She nodded shyly. I pulled a couple of quarters from my pocket and held them out to her. "G'wan, take it. Go get yourself some ice cream. Go ahead."

She started to reach for the coins then abruptly pulled back, looking anxiously at her father.

"Zat O.K., buddy?" I asked him. "Zat O.K., if I buy your sweet li'l girl a treat?"

I held out the coins with a trembling hand. Statten looked at the girl then at me, sighed as though my company was wearing a little more than thin, and said: "If you're sure it won't leave you short."

"Hell, no – oops." I clapped my hand over my mouth and apologized for my indiscrete language.

Brad yawned while Stacey looked at the quarters as if they were a cobra getting ready to strike. It looked to me like Statten was getting a kick out of seeing her hanging there mid-way between desire and fulfillment. It also looked like that little girl had an intense fear of her father.

"Daddy?" She looked at him imploringly.

"Yeah, O.K.," he said grudgingly.

Her hand shot out and snatched the quarters from my hand. I wondered when was the last time her old man had bought her anything. Even after she had the coins tightly clenched in her little fist, there was still uncertainty in her eyes as though she was afraid her happiness could still be pulled out from under her, and she double-checked with her father.

"It's really O.K. if I buy an ice cream?"

Brad had long since lost interest in the entire transaction and was watching a tawny beachnik caress her shoulders with suntan lotion.

"Huh? Oh, yeah. Sure. Go ahead."

The girl hurried off, her heels kicking up plumes of sand. I looked up toward Diane. She was starting to get to her feet. I peeled off my sweater, rolled it into a ball, and dropped it on the sand. My heart was going like a trip-hammer. I took a deep breath, put the wine bottle to my lips and took a giant swallow. But this time, it wasn't entirely for show. It coated the inside of my mouth with a sickeningly sweet film.

I watched Stacey out of the corner of my eye. She was just approaching the concession stand. There were people waiting at each window and she got in line. Diane was on her feet by now and starting down the hill. Brad had turned back from the chick he was eyeing and looked at me as though he wished I were somewhere else. I proffered the bottle, feeling large beads of sweat forming on my forehead. He waved it away without saying anything. I watched his eyes. They were looking toward the snack bar, searching for his daughter. I hoisted myself up and lurched into his line of vision.

"Well, I guess I better be on my way," I said. "Lots to do. Lots to do. But 'fore I go, won't ya jush have one li'l drink with me – just to be sosh'ble?"

I thrust out the bottle, at the same time glancing toward the concession stand. Diane had made the connection. She was leaning down, talking to Stacey. Brad shook his head, then stiffened. He'd spotted them – just as Diane was leading her daughter out of the line. He scrambled to his feet in a spray of sand. Diane and Stacey were halfway up the slope. They were running now – or at least Diane was. The child was pretty well being dragged behind. He'd spotted them too soon. There wouldn't be enough time. I had to make some. As Brad shot by, I shoved out my leg and tripped him. He fell face down into the sand and, without wasting a second, I yelled: "For Chrissake, watch where you're goin'!" and plopped my not-inconsiderable bulk right on top of his prostate form, pinning him flat. He writhed and struggled beneath me, clawing at me and the sand while I moaned about him spilling my wine.

"For Chrissake, it took me all mornin' to get enough scratch for that bottle!"

He had a helluva lot of strength for a guy his size or maybe it was just the desperation that allowed him to buck me off and squirt free. But, at least, I'd given Diane another ten precious seconds. I hoped it'd be enough. For everyone's sake, including Brad's and my own. We'd gone too far to turn back now and, even if it meant getting physical, there was no damn way I was going to let him get his hooks on Stacey again. One good thing, with him being in just a pair of swim trunks, I knew he wasn't packing his gun.

By the time Brad reached the concession stand, Diane and her daughter had disappeared over the crest of the hill. I charged after him as fast as I could but weight and age made me no match and I was steadily losing ground. By the time I hit the path, he was almost to the top of the slope. I was puffing like a steam engine and fear alone kept my legs going. My heart pounded fiercely and I prayed I wouldn't have a heart attack or stroke, at least until the caper was over.

I was about halfway up the incline when I heard the shrill screech of rubber and the continuous blasting of a car horn. With a final, desperate, gasp of energy, I covered the last dozen yards in nothing flat and staggered to the top in time to see Brad making a broken-field run through traffic to get to the other side of the street. He was waving his arms and screaming at the top of his lungs. It was like the cry of a wounded animal – rising on a tide of anger and futility.

The rented car was gone from its spot in the lane. Diane and her daughter had gotten away. I felt weak. My heart was trying to bang its way right through my rib cage. I sagged onto a bench and watched Brad Statten. He was about to re-cross the street when, all at once, he lashed out and smashed his fist into a telephone pole again and again, as if he was incapable of feeling pain. A number of people stopped, gaping at him in shock and disbelief. Finally, his fury spent, he crossed the street and started back to the beach, his battered and bloody hand swinging limply at his side.

I kept out of sight, just to be on the safe side, but he wouldn't have noticed me anyway. He seemed to be walking in a daze. The last I saw of him, he was pulling on his clothes with his one good hand and scooping up his daughter's things. If he hadn't been such a rat bastard, I might have felt sorry for him because, in some twisted way, he may have loved his daughter as much as he hated his wife but just wasn't capable of separating the two emotions.

There was another reason why I didn't feel sorry for him though. Even after all we'd gone through, I knew it wasn't over. I knew Diane and Stacey would never be safe from him. He'd never be content to just poison his own life. He wanted company and he'd never be happy until his wife was as sick and tortured as himself, even if it meant sacrificing his daughter.

Playing it safe, I kept to the back lanes on my way back to the apartment. It was a good ten blocks and I was dragging my ass by the time Diane let me in. But all the fatigue drained away and I felt light as a feather when I spotted Stacey. Decked out in an outfit her mom had brought with her, she was sitting in the middle of the living room, hugging Theodore Bear. It also felt pretty good when Diane threw her arms around me and thanked me over and over while her tears blotted into the front of that grubby lumberjack shirt. When she finally drew away to wipe her eyes, Stacey pointed at me wide-eyed and piped:

"Mommy! Mommy! That's the nice man who gave me the money for ice cream!"

"I know, honey," she smiled through the tears. "I know."

And damn it if I didn't have a delayed reaction from the wine I'd guzzled because, you know, my eyes started to get a little watery too.

We packed up and left that evening, driving to Seattle where we spent the night. In the morning, I booked passage for Diane and her daughter on a flight to Winnipeg. I drove them to the airport that afternoon and at Stacey's bidding, kissed Theodore Bear good-bye right on the tip of his button bazoo, in full view of about fifty by-standers.

After seeing them off, I returned to Vancouver and caught a plane back home.

You see, knowing what kind of screw-loose guy Brad Statten could be, I didn't want to take a chance on him staking out the Vancouver Airport and heading off his wife. Paranoid? Maybe. But as it turned out, it was with some justification because when I showed up at the airport on Monday night, there he was seated in the terminal, his eyes glued to the departure gates for Winnipeg flights.

By this time, I was clean-shaven and well-dressed and he didn't even give me a second look, which made me breathe a little easier. He certainly would've given Diane a second look though – not to mention something else. He never got the chance though. Not then and not ever.

A couple of weeks later, Bradley Statten was just another entry in the daily obituaries. What happened was he'd borrowed his buddy, Kaves', car once too often. He'd been on his way to Winnipeg when the car left the road, somersaulted a couple of times, and ended up in one of those deep canyons along the Trans-Canada near the B.C.-Alberta border. He'd died instantly.

The R.C.M.P. had found some booze in what was left of the vehicle and it looked as though he'd been juiced or had fallen asleep at the wheel. Or maybe his desperation and hatred had gotten the better of him and he'd no longer been able to live with himself and without his wife and daughter. Who knows? All I know is that Stacey and her mom are making it alright now. Diane calls me every now and then just to shoot the breeze and every Christmas, she sends me one of those personalized cards with a photograph of her daughter on the front. The girl looks great which is exactly the way I feel when I look at her picture.

NINE

Dead on Arrival

Now, IF there's anything I'm not it's a teetotaller. During the War, I learned to knock back the booze pretty good and I still tie one on every now and then. But one thing I no longer do is drink and drive and it's because of a case I had a few years back and the image of a beautiful young woman whose life ended in pain and horror in a roadside ditch.

Her name was Kelly Edwards and although I never met her, I got to know her pretty well, as a matter of fact, too well for my own peace of mind. As I said earlier, a guy in my line of work should never get emotionally involved in a case but saying it and making it stick are two different things.

Kelly was eighteen years old on that summer night in 1976 when the life was crushed out of her body by a speeding van. It was the end for her and the beginning of a living nightmare for those who loved her.

It happened in a little municipality just outside of Winnipeg. Once a haven for market gardeners, it's now starting to take on an urban look thanks to some developers who think a tract of land is obscene unless it has about six hundred identical bungalows squatting on it.

Since I have fictionalized the names of the people in this caper, I'll do the same for the locale and call it Castleton even though a lot of people will probably know who and what I'm talking about.

Now, most of the cases I get involved in never see the light of day since, as a private investigator what I see and hear goes no further than my client. But the death of Kelly Edwards was a completely different matter. It was front page news almost two years before the Edwards' lawyer contacted me. But only one version of the story hit the press. The real story is locked away in the minds of those who were most directly involved and will probably never be known. I've got a damn good idea what happened though and that's what this chapter is all about.

In solving a case – any case – your chances are better the closer you are to the event and that's why I wasn't overly optimistic when I was asked to look into the Edwards fatality. In two years, witnesses can leave the area or forget what they saw or heard. And if anyone is trying to cover anything up, they've had a helluva long time to fill in the loopholes in their alibis.

But even though the case was as cold as yesterday's coffee, Kelly Edwards' parents had no intention of letting it drop and, in a way, I could understand it. They'd lost their daughter and the guy who'd hit her had gotten off without so much as a slap on the wrist. It was probably a combination of frustration and revenge but Terry and Anita Edwards were obsessed with finding out how their daughter died and nailing whoever was responsible. But there was more to it than that. They also wanted a spotlight turned on the way the case had been investigated by both local and provincial authorities.

It wasn't as though the thing had been swept under the rug. An inquest had been held a few months after the death. But in spite of the fact that a judge had found the driver of the van partly to blame for the tragedy, no charges were laid.

By the time I came on the scene, the Edwards had already gone through three lawyers and a good chunk of dough in an attempt to get the case reopened but without any luck. After more than two years, they were still obviously shook up by their daughter's death and the last thing I wanted to do was to trade on their grief. I felt for them though so I agreed to at least give it a shot.

After hitting the library and checking out the press clippings on the accident, I got a copy of the inquest transcript from the Edwards' current lawyer, a young street-wise guy called Marty Dodson. Marty was a good guy and a good lawyer and there were two things about him that I particularly liked. One, as far as I knew, he never screwed a client and, two, and more important, he never screwed me.

I spent a whole day going over all the paper I could get on the case, including the police reports and the autopsy results and, by the time I got through, I was convinced that the Edwards had been royally shafted. Through my research and talking to Terry and Anita, I was able to draw a pretty clear picture of what had happened.

Kelly and her friend, Barbara Frater, who was a year younger, got together at about five p.m. on June 18th, the last day Kelly would spend on this earth. It was a Saturday and they stayed together all evening, right up to the very second Kelly was killed. After watching TV at Barbara's house at 872 Harrison Road, the pair decided to go for a walk, heading east to the junction of Harrison and Garvin. They killed some time at a park, sitting on the swings and shooting the breeze, before starting back for Barbara's. By then, it was about a quarter to eleven and starting to get pretty dark.

The girls were walking west on Harrison along the edge of the two-lane asphalt thoroughfare. Barbara was on the fringe of the westbound lane while Kelly was beside her on the narrow gravel shoulder that gave way to a sharply sloping ditch.

Shortly before eleven, when dusk had settled in and the streetlights blinked on, a small car came up behind them. The driver had no trouble spotting them and veered to give them a wider berth. Within minutes, they again heard the sound of a motor and, looking over their shoulders, saw another, larger vehicle coming up behind them, a white Ford van owned by Foster Catering and driven by thirty-year-old Barry Reynolds who, besides driving for Foster part-time, had the good fortune to be married to his boss's daughter. In the passenger's seat was Paul Stasiak, eighteen.

As the van drew nearer, the girls switched places at Kelly's suggestion. Much the taller of the two at five-feet-nine, she felt she'd be more visible than her five-foot friend. The truck loomed larger, its headlights cutting through the darkness. Nervous or just cautious, the pair moved further off the roadway. The truck roared closer. It seemed to be headed directly at them and the girls started to think the driver must be playing some sick joke. They started to descend into the ditch. But not soon enough. The fateful switch meant the difference between life and death for the two friends. Struck from behind, Kelly Edwards was hurled into a sodden ditch where her lifeless body was found moments later, her skull turned to a bag of bones by the impact of the van.

Fighting off hysteria, Barbara Frater ran to a nearby home and summoned help. Two constables from the Castleton police force arrived some twenty minutes later with an ambulance hot on their heels. One of the officers accompanied Kelly to the hospital while his partner remained at the scene, directing traffic around the crowd of gawkers that always shows up at fires or accidents or anywhere they can shake their heads and say: "Thank Christ, it didn't happen to me." But it did happen to Kelly Edwards. At 11:40 p.m. on June 18th, 1976, she was pronounced dead at Winnipeg's Health Sciences Centre. And it would only be a few minutes before Terry and Anita Edwards saw a good chunk of their hopes and dreams come crashing down around them.

Meanwhile, at the scene of the accident tragedy had turned to farce. The Castleton police would've made the Keystone Cops look organized. After a fatality involving a motor vehicle, it's common practice to check out the driver to see if he's been into the sauce. And the Castleton cops did that with Barry Reynolds, going so far as to haul him in for a bloodtest. Now, in Manitoba, the impairment level is anything over .08 and Barry Reynolds weighed in with a whopping .12 which should have made him a prime candidate for the slammer. Except there was a king-sized fly in the ointment. You see, Reynolds wasn't tested immediately after the accident as one might have expected. Instead, he was allowed to go home and wasn't taken in for a reading until more than three hours after the mishap.

So, even if he had been impaired at the time of the accident, he'd been given an out on a silver platter. And I was of the opinion that he'd used it. When the Castleton cops called at his home at 1:40 in the morning of June 19th, Reynolds didn't deny he'd been into the booze but his story was that he'd taken a couple of good stiff belts after getting home to help him get over the shock of smacking into Kelly Edwards. He flatly denied he'd been drinking before the collision and swore he definitely wasn't impaired when he was behind the wheel and, in spite of a lot of suspicions, no one could prove otherwise because of the way the Castleton cops had fucked up.

I could see why the Edwards felt that justice wasn't only blind but deaf and dumb as well. They figured that the Castleton police were at best, incompetent and, at worst, collusive. They also thought that municipal and provincial authorities lacked the brains and/or guts to reopen the case and conduct a proper investigation.

They were probably right which left me in the position of trying to lift a lid that a whole lot of other people were trying to hold down. I knew it wouldn't be easy – maybe not even possible. But I knew I had to give it a shot. There were just too many damn questions that needed answering. And when I got to the end of a trail that began in 1976 on a lonely stretch of asphalt, I could readily understand the Edwards' sorrow, frustration, and anger. In fact, in spite of telling myself over and over again that professionals do not get emotionally involved in their cases, it wasn't long before I began to share them.

Like I said before, an inquest had been conducted into Kelly's death. But after reading the transcript, I got the feeling that the authorities had just been going through the motions. More questions than answers had surfaced and no one had seemed particularly concerned about answering them.

Now, that was my job. At least the inquest transcripts gave me some leads to follow. I had a hunch that some of the witnesses could have filled in some pretty important gaps if they'd been asked the right questions. There were just too damn many loose ends and if those Castleton cops had been able to tell their asses from their elbows they would have realized it.

For example, one of the witnesses at the inquest, Sarah Turner, gave some particularly intriguing testimony. Mrs. Turner lived almost directly across the road from the scene of the accident. She'd heard Barbara's screams and had run outside to see what the matter was. Learning of the accident from the semi-hysterical girl, she had called for the police and an ambulance.

A key witness, Sarah Turner saw the driver of the death van frantically tying to free the vehicle from the ditch on the south side of the road. Her testimony sure as hell lit a fire under my curiosity. Why had the driver been in such a hurry to get mobile? If you smack into someone, surely the first thing you'd do is get out and check on the victim. But that was only one of the many mysteries which emerged as the case went on.

Mrs. Turner saw something else that made me even more curious though. She testified that after failing to free the van, Reynolds and Stasiak clambered up onto the road where they got into a furious tussle, grabbing each other's shirts and swearing up a storm. What had provoked it? What came next was even more bizarre though. According to Mrs. Turner, Reynolds and Stasiak cooled down, and chatted with some unidentified third party for a couple of minutes after which they ran off into the night hollering and swearing. The whole thing made no sense at all. Had they been in shock? And why hadn't they shown the slightest concern for the girl who'd just finished bouncing off the hood of their vehicle?

Sarah Turner wasn't the only one to come up with some pretty provocative testimony. Another key witness, fifty-three year old Bill Mandiuk also said some things that shifted my curiosity into overdrive. Mandiuk had been driving west on Harrison, no more than a couple of minutes after the accident. A white van had been blocking the westbound lane and he had pulled up behind it. And when he mentioned that it had been a Foster Catering truck, the crown counsel who was questioning him seemed more than just a little confused. I didn't blame him because that was the first time anyone knew that there had been either an eye witness or the next best thing to it to the accident. Who'd been driving the second van? And why hadn't he come forward to tell what he knew? Just another couple of questions to rattle around in my head and keep me awake nights. According to Mandiuk, he'd seen Paul Stasiak behind the wheel of the second van. But that couldn't be. He'd been in the death van with Reynolds. Or had he?

There was certainly no doubt that he'd seen Barbara Frater though. As he passed the stationary van, he was flagged down by the crying girl and together they'd found Kelly's sprawled and broken body. Shortly after, he'd also encountered Barry Reynolds who told him he'd hit "a squirrel or something." Mandiuk laid the bad news on him and asked him how his van had ended up in the ditch on the south side of the road some distance from the point of impact. According to the middle-aged mechanic, Reynolds replied that when he felt his truck hit something, he immediately swung the vehicle to the left and ended up in the ditch.

Up to that point, I think I was still pretty objective but that was the straw that broke the camel's back. I mean, this guy actually expected someone to believe he veered into a ditch because he thought he hit a squirrel? Somebody had to be kidding. And a whole lot of somebodies had to have had their heads in the sand and their fingers up their kazoos if they bought his story.

But Mandiuk insisted that that was what Reynolds had told him and he was certain about something else as well. Like Sarah Turner, Bill Mandiuk testified that shortly after the death van had hit the ditch, the driver had gunned the motor in a desperate attempt to extricate it.

Taken together with Mrs. Turner's testimony, this convinced me that Barry Reynolds – assuming it was he who was gunning the motor – had been a helluva lot more concerned about getting out of the ditch than about seeing how much damage he'd done to either the van or the "squirrel."

Still, there are sometimes logical explanations to illogical behaviour especially when people are under stress so I tried to suspend my judgement until I studied all the inquest testimony. After all, who knows, Reynolds and his pal, Stasiak, might have fully explained what to me was some pretty far-out behaviour.

Paul Stasiak preceded his buddy to the stand and gave his version of what happened on the night of June 18th, 1976. According to Stasiak, he and Reynolds had been working for Foster Catering that evening. At five p.m., they'd met at the catering centre and later headed to the Southport Community Club in Transcona, another suburb of Greater Winnipeg. There they had supplied food and utensils and stayed until about nine or nine-thirty. They then got into their company van, a 1975 Ford with one of those short, snub-nosed hoods, and went to another social a short distance away where they picked up some equipment and cutlery that were no longer needed.

According to Stasiak, they remained at this second social for about half an hour, leaving shortly after ten p.m. Their next stop was the catering centre at Harrison and Garvin which was no more than about half a mile from the scene of the accident. They got there at about a quarter to eleven and, after unloading the van, Reynolds was going to give Stasiak a ride home. Still using the company van, they set off west on Harrison at around eleven o'clock.

There'd been a beer garden at the Castleton Community Club about a half mile west of the accident scene and Crown Counsel Tom Gates, homed in on the booze issue but Stasiak insisted that neither he nor Reynolds had been into the sauce and testified that he didn't visit the beer garden until after the accident. Again nobody, neither the crown attorney, the judge, nor the Edwards' lawyer followed up to find out exactly when Stasiak showed up at the beer garden and what he was doing there. Maybe they were all double-parked and had to get out of there in a hurry or something but somebody sure as hell should have been asking some questions.

As for booze, Stasiak testified that he'd had three or four beers while working at the social in Transcona. He also said he'd seen Barry Reynolds with a beer in his hand but didn't know how much his buddy had had to drink.

It was his testimony about the accident itself that set off a whole stampede of question marks though. He stated that while they were driving west on Harrison on the way to his place, he and Reynolds were talking when all of a sudden they hit something. He said Reynolds immediately cut the wheel to the left and went into the ditch on the south side of the road. He added that his partner had told him that he thought he'd hit something. He also confirmed that Reynolds had tried to get out of the ditch before they crossed the road to see what they'd struck.

But while he admitted one thing, he strongly denied another saying there was no way he and Reynolds had been fighting, which was directly contrary to Sarah Turner's testimony.

That struck me as about as fishy as an over-ripe mackerel. Why would Mrs. Turner make up a story like that? Or if it was true, why would Stasiak lie about it? That was for him to know and me to find out. I also had to find out why he denied knowing the van was damaged in spite of the fact the windshield directly in front of the passenger side was cobwebbed with cracks from the impact of Kelly's body.

What was also incredible was that Stasiak stated he wasn't aware they'd hit anything until his buddy mentioned it. A five-foot-nine-inch woman had bounded off the hood and smacked into the window a couple of feet from his face and he hadn't noticed it? That was plain, unadulterated bullshit. I knew it. And Crown Attorney Tom Gates should have known it as well. But if he did, he'd done his damnedest to keep it a secret, dropping what I thought was a key line of questioning.

But if Stasiak had failed to notice a little thing like a young woman slamming into the windshield, he was very emphatic about some things he did pick up on. For example, he made no bones about declaring that Barry Reynolds had been sober and driving carefully and at a moderate speed before the accident. He also said that the van's lights were on and visibility was good, adding he was certain the van had not strayed onto the shoulder of the road at any time.

And why was he certain? His story was he would have felt the three-inch drop from the pavement to the shoulder. He would have felt a three-inch drop but hadn't felt the impact of over a hundred pounds of flesh and blood careening off the windshield? Yeah, sure. If you believe that, I got some stock in De Lorean Motors you might be interested in.

Once again, Stasiak's testimony contradicted that of a previous witness. Barbara Frater had stated that she'd definitely heard the sound of tires on gravel before the impact. Was she lying? Or was Stasiak.

I had my own ideas and they were confirmed when I got a little further into his testimony. You see, he stated that as soon as Reynolds thought he hit something, he immediately cut the wheel to the left but if that was the case, why had the van ended up a couple of hundred feet west of the accident scene? Also when you think you've hit something, wouldn't you jam on your brakes? Wouldn't that be the instinctive thing to do? But there were no skid marks at the accident scene. In fact, all the evidence seemed to indicate that Barry Reynolds had been interested in only one thing – getting the hell out of there as quickly as possible.

Of course, the only one who knew what Barry Reynolds' intentions were was Reynolds himself and he didn't give much away when he testified. But although the part-time van driver and full-time appliance salesman came across as a pretty cagey customer, he let a few things drop that to me, at least, didn't seem quite kosher. As a matter of fact, the more I studied his testimony, the surer I became that there was more to Kelly Edwards' tragic death than met the eye.

Under questioning by Crown Counsel Gates, Reynolds revealed his activities in the hours leading up to the accident. It'd been Father's Day and he'd visited his parents before starting work at 5:00 p.m. He denied having a drink with his dad to celebrate the occasion, however.

Now, that struck me as a little strange since I'd heard that both Reynolds and his old man liked the sauce. But what was even stranger was that Father's Day has always been on a Sunday so if he'd visited his dad like he claimed, it must've been the day after the accident. But that did nothing to explain where he'd been earlier in the day on Saturday which was what the crown attorney was trying to find out. Had Reynolds lied to the crown counsel about his whereabouts and if so, why? And if he wasn't at his old man's just before heading to work, where was he and what was he doing? More gaps to fill in. And each one of them could have been the one to blow this case wide open.

And what had Reynolds had to say about drinking any booze on the day of the accident? He testified that he'd consumed only "half a beer, three-quarters of a beer" at one of the halls where he'd been working.

And then, there was his version of the accident. He said that he and Paul Stasiak had finished their work at the catering centre at about eleven p.m. and started west on

Harrison. He was going to drive Paul home. Shortly after crossing a set of railway tracks, he heard a thud at the right side of the van and veered to the left, crossing the eastbound lane and ending up in the ditch on the south side of Harrison Road.

Insisting that he'd been paying close attention to the road, he couldn't explain why he hadn't seen the two girls walking beside it. He was equally shaky in his recollection of what happened immediately after the collision, only admitting that he "might've" tried to free the van from the ditch. He did make one important admission though, stating that he had at no time applied his brakes.

By this time, my notes and my cynicism had both grown a helluva lot. I could understand why someone would crank his wheels to *avoid* hitting someone but why do it after the fact? It didn't make any sense. At least, not if you believed Reynolds' story which, by this time, there was no damn way I did.

I also didn't fall for his line that he and his buddy had scoured the ditches on both sides of the road for about a quarter of a mile looking to see what they'd hit. He and Paul Stasiak had taken off east on Harrison alright but it hadn't been on any search mission. They'd hauled their asses out of there for a totally different reason – one that had more to do with losing themselves than finding what or who they'd smacked into.

But if there were a lot of questions concerning Reynolds' testimony, there were even more about the way the Castleton cops handled the whole caper. Maybe "handled" isn't the right word though. It was more like they sleepwalked through it and only woke up when it was too late for them to even pretend that they knew what the hell they were doing.

According to Barry Reynolds, the cops told some friends of his who came upon the accident that it was kosher for them to take him home. So he took off without so much as a single cop speaking to him or checking him out for any signs of impairment. This was probably the greatest single indication that the case had been botched from square one but there were others: so many that I soon came to understand the Edwards' frustration and anger.

And what did Reynolds do when he was driven home by his friend, Bonnie Simmons, without having had to suffer the inconvenience of taking a breathalyzer test? Claiming he'd been hysterical and in a state of shock, he said he did what anyone else would've done under the circumstances: he took a good stiff shot – he estimated it at from five to seven ounces – of hard liquor, knocking it back in a single gulp. Funny thing was he remembered all that but claimed he couldn't remember what kind of booze it was.

Although Crown Counsel Gates strongly suggested that the driver of the death van had jumped into the sauce to cover up the fact he'd been juiced at the time of the accident, Reynolds stuck to his story. He also stuck to the line that he couldn't understand why he hadn't seen the two girls at the side of the road in spite of the fact that Harrison was a narrow thoroughfare and his lights should have illuminated not only the westbound lane but the bordering shoulder.

The other witnesses who testified at the inquest weren't much more helpful, including the Castleton cops who were supposed to be professionals and should have known how to gather evidence. But instead, constables Peter Sandor and Fred Lauchlan came across as a couple of guys who would've needed an instruction manual to take a leak.

It's a wonder those bozos ever took Reynolds in for a blood test at all. Of course, by the time they did, it was game over and Reynolds had an alibi that was tighter than a seventy-year-old virgin. It was no wonder these officers had been out to lunch considering the kind of leadership they got from their chief. As it turned out, Victor Dakin, the chief of the Castleton police force, had happened upon the accident scene shortly after his men showed up. But did he take charge of the investigation? Not on your life. He just told Sandor and Lauchlan that he was going to pick up his wife and couldn't spare the time to help out a scene that was rapidly going from disorganization to complete chaos. If these three police officers – and I use the term loosely – had entered a "Bungler-of-the-Year" competition, you could safely predict there would've been a three way tie for first place.

That's why Barry Reynolds, who had absolutely no explanation for failing to see and running into Kelly Edwards, wasn't taken for a blood test until three hours after the accident. And that was also why no one took a statement from him until several days later by which time he'd been able to put together a story that would've made the Brothers Grimm look like pikers.

Those weren't the only instances of incompetence though. Even the police report of the accident wasn't completed until a month later and in explaining why, Chief Dakin outdid himself, saying: "The reason for the delay is that we were working on other things and there were shift changes and the statements from the witnesses took a long time to get. And the officer who had the file was on the night shift."

It wasn't surprising that Crown Counsel Gates didn't follow up to see if he could get an explanation that made sense. The funny thing is that Chief Dakin was capable of straight talk as he showed in the report he finally put together on the fatality. In it, he left no doubt that he believed a serious crime had been committed. Part of it was what the Castleton police chief had to say about the circumstances leading to Kelly Edwards' death:

It appears that the catering truck driven by Reynolds was steered at the girls to impress or frighten them. The driver probably intended to steer away at the last moment but due to his condition (blood sample showed an alcohol level of .12), the slope of the ditch and the slippery grass, Reynolds misjudged the distance and was unable to steer away in time, striking and killing Kelly Edwards.

It was a bombshell alright. If the chief's theory was correct, Reynolds was guilty of anything from manslaughter to criminal negligence causing death. But for some unknown reason, the chief had never carried his conclusions past the theory stage. No charge had been laid. Nothing. Not even careless driving. And at the inquest when Dakin was asked who he felt was responsible for Kelly's death, he completely backed off, saying: "Well, I'd rather not go into that."

As always, the question was: why? What had changed him from a lion to a lamb? I'd heard that Mel Foster, Barry Reynold's father-in-law had a lot of clout in Castleton. Could he have used it to kill the investigation? Was that why the thing went in the dumper and no charges were laid?

By now, I was so caught up in the whole caper that I didn't give a damn how many cans of worms had to be opened. The story had to be told. I owed it to the Edwards. But more than that I felt I owed it to a girl who paid a helluva price for being in the wrong place at the wrong time.

I had my work cut out for me that was for sure. When the inquest wrapped up, the judge ruled that Kelly Edwards' death was "due in part to the wrongful act or culpable negligence of Barry Reynolds in not observing and avoiding a collision with the deceased under the circumstances of the accident as they happened."

But in spite of this finding, no charges were laid. That didn't sit too well with Terry and Anita Edwards. They'd lost a child they'd loved. They wanted to know why. But they also wanted something more and wanted it so bad they could taste it. They wanted whoever had shattered Kelly's body and their lives to pay for it. I wanted it too.

The death of Kelly Edwards hadn't just affected her family. Castleton was a small, close-knit community and the shock-waves of the girl's death were felt in a lot of homes and hearts. It also left scars that will never be healed. I know. I've got some of them myself because even a hard-bitten type like me didn't get away without a little wear and tear on the emotions.

But that came later – after the smell of something rotten grew into the stink of lies, incompetence, and cowardice; a stink that reached right up to the ivory towers of Manitoba's law enforcement establishment.

Filling in the Gaps

TERRY AND Anita Edwards are a couple in their late forties. He's slim, average height, with salt-and-pepper hair combed straight back and she's plump and motherly-looking. Nice people. The kind you'd like to have as neighbours. He's a construction foreman, a hard-working guy who isn't afraid of getting his hands dirty. She's a housewife who does volunteer work when she isn't keeping their ranch-style bungalow all spick and span.

They have two children: twenty-two-year-old Kevin and Sandra who's a year younger. Once they had three but that all changed in one shattering moment when a family of five became four and a suburban bungalow turned into a storehouse of tragic memories.

Outwardly, Terry and Anita still look like typical middle-aged parents in a typical middle-class home but you just have to talk to them to see that Kelly's death had left a king-size hole in their lives.

For them, June 18th, 1976, had become a reference point for almost everything else that had ever happened to them. For instance, one time I mentioned having had a gall bladder operation and Anita commented that she'd had one too. It'd been in 1975. But that isn't how she put it. She phrased it in a way that showed how much her daughter's death filled her thoughts, saying: "It was in the summer, just about a year before Kelly died." I guess you could say that on Terry and Anita's personal calendars,

there was only one date that counted any more: June 18th,
1976.

I mentioned before that the death of Kelly Edwards had
a considerable impact on the municipality of Castleton. In
the wake of the accident, rumours flew thick and fast and
many residents drew conclusions, most of which weren't
based on fact. The upshot was that there were two different bodies of opinion concerning the tragedy. One held
that the girl contributed to her own death by walking on
the wrong side of a poorly lit road. The other maintained
that, thanks to a rotten job by the Castleton police, a
scumbag by the name of Barry Reynolds had killed one of
the nicest girls you could hope to meet and gotten away
with it.

The rumours didn't die with time either. When I took
on the case in May of 1978, I ran into a few of them
myself. I heard, among other things, that the cop who
allowed Reynolds to go home was a buddy of his and that
was why he gave him a break that kept him from being
nailed for Kelly's death. That was one rumour I followed
up; however, it turned out to be unfounded like so many
that are spread by people who have axes to grind.

I also heard that there was a cover-up in place – that a
close-knit group of politicos didn't want the true facts of
the case brought out because they'd show the Castleton
and provincial authorities in a poor light.

In my business you have to be a good listener and I
heard out anyone who might have had even a sliver of
information. I also asked a whole gang of questions, being
careful not to come on too strong since, in my business, I
have to play it cool because unlike cops, I can't lean on
people to make them talk. I have to string them along, get
all buddy-buddy and hope they open up.

Most of the time it works because, if I say so myself, I'm
one of the best bullshitters I know. It paid off for me in the
Edwards case too. All kinds of doors and people started
opening up and by the time I put the pieces together, I was
more sure than ever that the case had to be reopened and

that this time, the authorities had to have a fire lit under them to keep them from falling asleep.

The original investigation was full of more holes than a swiss cheese with acne. And although Crown Attorney Tom Gates did a pretty fair job at the inquest, he'd had one arm tied behind his back because the cops hadn't given him enough ammunition. For example, if they hadn't done such a half-assed job, they might've discovered the identity of the driver of the second Foster van – the one Bill Mandiuk spotted on his arrival at the accident scene.

Considering the sequence of events, the driver of this vehicle would have had to have been one of the first at the scene. He could even have been an eyewitness. Who was he and what had Paul Stasiak been doing in his van? And why had he taken off in such a hurry? These were questions that the cops should have dug up answers to.

Another reason why the inquest came up empty was that some people who should have been called as witnesses weren't. You'd think that by the law of averages the Castleton cops would have done at least something right but if they did, they sure as hell fooled me. Maybe they flipped a coin to see who they'd interview but however it was done, it was a strictly hit-and-miss proposition.

The cops weren't the only ones who were out to lunch though. During the inquest, witnesses constantly made references to persons who, to some degree or other, had some significant involvement in the matter. But were these fresh leads followed up? Not on your life. They should've been though. The Crown should have been flexible enough to expand its witness list as new names came up. It didn't happen, however, and that's one of the reasons the inquest was a poor imitation of a genuine inquiry.

Now it was my turn and in early May of 1978, I began my investigation with a visit to the accident scene. As I traced the route taken by Kelly Edwards and Barbara Frater, my feet crunched on the gravel shoulder the way Kelly's had almost two years before. Even though it was broad daylight, instinctively, I looked over my shoulder when I heard a car come up behind me.

Relying on a police diagram and hoping it wasn't as fucked up as everything else they'd done, I located the spot where her body had been found. Looking down, I had a mental image of her lying there, twisted and broken. As corny as it sounds, I had a strange feeling she knew I was working for her. Yeah, not just for her family but for her too. And I also felt that she approved. I still didn't know if any wrongdoing had been involved in her death but I promised her – and I said it right out loud – that if anyone had been criminally responsible for the accident, I'd do my damnedest to see that he got what was coming to him.

I started with Barbara Frater. She was a pretty, dark-haired little thing. Looked a lot younger than nineteen too which was probably due to the fact she was so tiny. She and Kelly must have made quite a pair; one five-nine and the other barely five feet. They had been great friends. Terry Edwards had said they'd been inseparable.

It turned out that she had been acquainted with both the driver and the passenger in the van that killed Kelly.

"Barry and Paul were at some socials I went to and just about every time I saw them they were drunk or at least feeling good," she told me.

So they were a couple of pisstanks. That was interesting. And what she told me next was even more so.

"After Kelly got hit, I remember screaming real loud, trying to get someone to help her. Barry and Paul were on the road and I was screaming so loud they had to have heard. But instead of helping, they started fighting with each other, pushing and grabbing and swearing really loud."

"Then what did they do?"

She frowned and thought as though still trying to make some sense out of what had happened almost two years before.

"They took off. They just started running east on Harrison and it was quite a while before they came back. That was after Gerry went to look for them."

"Gerry" was Gerry Salter who was also working for Foster Catering at the time. He was off duty on the night of the accident. He'd been coming from the beer garden at the Castleton Community Club just down the road when he happened on the accident. I guessed he'd probably knocked back a few too many and was afraid to stick around in case the cops picked up on it. Considering the competence of the Castleton cops, the chances of them picking up on anything ranged from slim to none but maybe he didn't know that.

To cover all the bases, I asked Barbara if it was true that some of the local geniuses played chicken with pedestrians, aiming their vehicles at them, then cutting away just when the latter started to feel something wet and warm running down their legs.

"Oh yeah, there's some guys around here who do it all the time. They think it's a big joke. One time I was walking down Harrison just like Kelly and I were doing . . ." she paused, biting her lip ". . . that night. And this jerk – one of Paul Stasiak's friends – came so close that his mirror brushed against me. It's a good thing he wasn't going very fast, not like. . . ."

She looked away, unable to complete the sentence. After talking to Barbara, I knew it was important that I interview this Salter guy. He could've been the one Reynolds and Stasiak were talking to immediately after the accident. If so, he knew something and I was going to do everything I could to make him spill it. I just wondered why the cops had shown no interest in doing the same thing.

The next day, I spoke to another key witness. Harry Belsky lived a couple of houses east of the accident scene. He'd just tuned in the eleven o'clock news on T.V. when his door bell rang frantically. It was Barbara Frater. She was in tears. She told him Kelly had been hit by a truck. They rushed to the ditch where, with the aid of a flash-

236 If It Weren't for Sex

light, they found Kelly Edwards' crumpled body in about ten inches of water. Harry lifted her head free of the water then called the Castleton police and an ambulance just as Sarah Turner had done.

The police and ambulance arrived almost simultaneously. And, according to Belsky, so did Reynolds and Stasiak who started to fight with each other right in front of the cops and several other onlookers. I wasn't sure that he had the sequence of events right since others stated that the pair had started scrapping almost immediately after the accident. When they started scrapping wasn't that important though. At least, not as important as why. And why had they flatly denied doing what at least three people had witnessed?

I next interviewed Peter Sandor who, by this time, was no longer on the Castleton police force. I wondered why. Maybe he was unable to maintain a satisfactory level of incompetence and had accidentally done something right.

Sandor was the constable who'd allowed Reynolds to take a hike after the accident. He told me he hadn't been able to detect any liquor on the Foster driver's breath and, because of this and the confusion at the scene, he'd allowed him to leave. He admitted he'd made a serious mistake by not detaining Barry.

"It took a while for the mounties to come to our assistance and traffic was backed up for a quarter of a mile. I was afraid we might have some more accidents on our hands because a lot of people were coming from the beer garden and they weren't any too sober."

This was the first caper I had where a company played such a big part in an investigation. Housed in a long, low frame building that's seen better days, Foster Catering is pretty well an institution in Castleton. Owned by Melvin Foster and his wife, Alice, it employs quite a number of people on a part-time basis, most of them from the Castleton area. The outfit caters banquets, receptions, and socials, supplying food and serving personnel and from what I'd heard, did a pretty good business.

In investigating the Edwards case, it seemed that everywhere I went, I heard the name Foster. At the accident scene, there'd been a couple of other Foster vehicles present at various times that night besides the van that had taken Kelly Edwards' life.

Many of the onlookers at the scene were past or current Foster employees and Bonnie Simmons, the person who drove Reynolds home, had been employed with the catering firm as well. They were a pretty close-knit group alright. They not only worked but partied together and I had a hunch some of them knew a whole lot more than they were letting on.

Since Castleton is a place where everyone seems to know everyone else, it didn't surprise me that the Edwards were acquainted with many Foster employees. I got their names and set about trying to locate those who might've been working on the evening of Kelly's death. The object of the exercise was to trace Barry Reynolds' movements on the evening of the accident to see if any of them had involved booze. At the inquest, he'd testified he hadn't had more than three-quarters of a bottle of beer during the entire day and had consumed hard liquor only after he was driven home from the accident.

Q. BY MR. GATES: *I ask you, prior to the accident is it your evidence that during the entire day you had at the most three-quarters of a bottle of beer?*

A: *That night, yes it is because I didn't drink during the day.*

Yeah sure, and Pierre Elliot Trudeau has a Ph.d. in humility. As far as I was concerned, there was no way a cold sober driver could have hit Kelly Edwards, given the prevailing conditions. Granted the lighting wasn't that great on Harrison but there was also some illumination from the houses along the road and, besides, the van's headlights would've picked up anyone walking on either the road or the shoulder.

Even Reynolds himself had been unable to come up with an explanation for hitting the girl. It was my feeling he'd downed a lot more than three-quarters of a bottle of beer before the accident. All I had to do was prove it which I didn't kid myself into thinking would be easy.

The first Foster employees I interviewed were of little help. They were both middle-aged Ukrainian ladies who'd worked for the catering outfit for several years. Neither one appeared particularly overjoyed to see me. I could understand that. Nobody wants to rock the boat particularly when the guy who's in it happens to be your boss's son-in-law.

They said they knew all of the people involved and didn't want to cause trouble. That didn't surprise me since if there's one thing that most people are good at, it's copping out. But when something happens to them or their families, it's a different ballgame. Then they bitch that everyone is out for themselves and the world's going to ratshit.

To be honest, I expected the same treatment from the Simmons although I hoped that wouldn't be the case since Bonnie Simmons was the one who'd driven Reynolds home after the accident and I considered her a key witness. Like herself, her husband, David, had been a part-time employee at Foster's during the summer of '76. Slim, bespectacled, with dark bushy hair, David Simmons was cutting his lawn with a power-mower when I drove up. I told him why I was there.

He stiffened and I figured he was going to clam up like most of the others. But instead, he invited me inside where I met Bonnie, a dark, medium-sized woman carrying a few extra pounds. Both she and David looked to be in their early thirties.

Throughout the interview, David, who looked at me warily and chose his words carefully, did most of the talking. His wife just listened and threw in the occasional brief comment but there was something in her eyes that made me think she knew something. It was a couple of days before I found out what it was, though.

On this initial visit, it was strictly a fencing match and,

at one point, David came right out and hit me with: "We don't have to talk to you."

"That's right, you don't," I agreed. "But how would you feel if it was one of your kids who got run over? Wouldn't you want some answers?"

Earlier, I'd noticed a tricycle and some other toys in the yard. He thought for a moment then slowly nodded. "O.K., what do you want to know?"

"A lot of things. But for know, I'd like to get a line on what Barry Reynolds was doing before he went to work on the day of the accident."

"That's easy. He was here. He had a couple of beers then took off to get ready for work."

There it was. The first real break in the case. I was pretty excited but tried not to let it show because I didn't think the Simmons were aware of the significance of that bit of information and I didn't want to tip them off. For the time being, I was content to let it drop and go on to another line of questioning. It too paid off.

David told me he'd been at the catering centre on the night of June 18th, 1976, when Reynolds and Stasiak had taken off, heading west on Harrison. Both of them had testified under oath that they were heading for Paul Stasiak's when the accident occurred. But David Simmons had a different version. He said the pair were on their way to the community club's beer garden.

I also found out how Bonnie Simmons happened to show up at the accident scene just in time to haul Reynolds' ass out of there. David said that he too had been on his way to the beer garden and had come upon the accident shortly after it happened. My guess was that it had been *very* shortly and that would account for the Foster van that Bill Mandiuk had to pull around when he got there within minutes of the fatality.

According to David, when he saw what had happened, he drove to the beer garden, found his wife whom he'd arranged to meet there and sent her to the accident scene to look after Barry. Accompanied by her cousin, Karen,

Bonnie drove her station wagon to the scene by which time the police and ambulance were in attendance. She spotted Reynolds and Stasiak in the crowd of bystanders. According to her, Barry was hysterical and there was a lot of confusion. She stated that a policeman (presumably Constable Sandor) then asked her to drive Barry home.

"What time did you leave?" I asked.

"About one a.m."

"How was he? I mean, was he drunk . . . feeling good?"

Her husband jumped in before she could answer. "He was hysterical. How the hell can you tell anything about anybody when they're in that condition?"

I then asked David if Barry had been drinking on the job that evening but he couldn't say since they'd been working at different halls. It was important that I find out who was working with Reynolds and Stasiak that night and Bonnie Simmons was a big help. She said that a Dorothy something-or-other from Transcona or a lady who lived in Tyndall, about twenty-five miles east of Winnipeg, would have been at one of the halls Reynolds delivered food to. I already had these two women on my list of potential interviewees and now I had even more reason to contact them.

Finally, as I was preparing to leave, David Simmons said something that made me more sure than ever that he and his wife knew where some skeletons were buried. His parting comment was: "I sure wouldn't want to be in Barry's shoes."

After talking to the Simmons, I knew that I was finally getting somewhere – somewhere the police and Crown should've been two years earlier. And it seemed that the more I learned about the case, the more obvious it became that the Castleton police had been completely out of their depth. When I asked David and Bonnie why they hadn't come forward to tell what they knew, the young housewife's answer pretty well summed up the way Chief Dakin and his crew had botched the entire caper.

"Nobody ever asked us."

Nobody had ever questioned David and Bonnie even though it was common knowledge that she had driven Reynolds home and could have either supported or discredited his story about chalking up his .12 blood alcohol level *after* the accident. The failure of the police to take statements from Bonnie and David was more than an oversight: it was a disgrace.

The Crown hadn't exactly covered itself with glory either. During the inquest, Reynolds himself revealed that Bonnie Simmons had driven him home but did Crown Attorney Gates try to find out what she knew? No goddamn way. Christ, she wasn't even called to testify! Had she been, she could've put an entirely different slant on things, perhaps different enough for the judge to find that Barry Reynolds was more than just *partly* responsible for Kelly Edwards' death.

It wasn't as though the cops didn't take any statements. The trouble was that even when they did take them, they didn't have enough brains to understand their significance. There were all kinds of clues but maybe the Castleton police were waiting for a formal introduction.

For example, in Paul Stasiak's statement, the passenger in the death van revealed that he had called Apex Towing Services after the accident, requesting that a tow truck be sent out. A truck had subsequently showed up but everyone had figured that it must have been sent for by the cops.

According to Stasiak, he called Apex about an hour after the collision, advising them that "there is a truck in the ditch on Harrison Road and we need a tow."

Fred Lauchlan, the cop who was questioning him, must've been as floored by that answer as I was when I read it almost two years later because he pressed him for an explanation, asking: "Can you tell me why you called Apex Towing for a truck knowing that the truck which was stuck in the ditch had been involved in an accident?"

If Lauchlan had hoped for a straight answer, he must

have been disappointed, for Stasiak replied: "I didn't know what I was doing."

I could understand Lauchlan's confusion. It didn't make any sense. According to Stasiak, he phoned Apex around midnight. By that time, both the Castleton cops and the mounties had shown up and Kelly had been pronounced dead at the Health Sciences Centre. There was no goddamn way that van was going anywhere unless the cops authorized it. Something didn't smell any too fragrant and it got even ranker when I paid a visit to Apex Towing Services.

The manager was very cooperative. He checked his records and came up with the card covering the call.

"Here it is. June 18th, 1976."

"The call came in about midnight, is that right?"

He peered at the card. "Nope. 11:15, it says here."

"You sure?"

"See for yourself," he said, handing me the card.

That's what it said alright. Not midnight but 11:15, less than fifteen minutes after Kelly Edwards had been hit. It just about knocked me on my ass. And there was more. According to the towing company manager, the caller, who identified himself as Paul Stasiak, was in a panic and said he needed a towtruck right away. The manager had thought this a little strange since he couldn't see some van stuck in a ditch as a matter of life or death. Still, he hustled his buns and dispatched a truck at 11:16 p.m.

This rush job ended up taking over two hours. When the tow truck got to the van it was being photographed by the mounties and when it was finally pulled out of the ditch, it wasn't handed back to Foster Catering. On instructions from the cops, it was taken to Apex Towing's garage.

Since all of the statements taken by the cops had presumably been turned over to the Attorney-General's Department prior to the inquest, I couldn't figure out why somebody hadn't spotted the discrepancy between Stasiak's statement and the towing company's records. The explanation was that nobody had had the brains to go down to Apex and check out Stasiak's story.

Nor did the Crown try to fill in some of the other gaps even after it became painfully clear that the Castleton fuzz had blown it. If the people in the A.-G.'s Department had taken their thumbs out long enough to read what passed for police reports, they'd have known a lot more work was needed and could have called in somebody who had some moxy, like the R.C.M.P.

I'm sure that if the mounties had gotten on the case, they'd have asked the questions I was asking myself. Like, just where had Stasiak phoned Apex from? Had he run back to Foster's after the accident? Witnesses had seen him and Reynolds running in that direction. Had he seen or spoken to anyone at the place he'd phoned from?

The police had not only the right but the duty to ask Stasiak these questions. The same went for the Crown when the Foster employee took the witness stand. They didn't and it was left to yours truly to try and piece together still another mystery that the authorities had ignored.

Continuing my investigation, I called at Foster Catering. I'd heard that Mel Foster wasn't exactly in love with his son-in-law. The buzz was that he'd opposed the marriage, saying Barry Reynolds was a bum who was looking for someone to live off. I hoped what I'd heard was true and that I could use Foster's hostility to my own advantage. It turned out that Barry Reynolds wasn't the only one Foster didn't care for. It didn't take me long to see that I fit into that category as well.

Short, wiry and balding, the catering firm owner had the stiff posture of a British officer. He was also unbending when it came to talking about the accident. I could understand that. After all, Barry had been driving a company truck at the time and if he was nailed with a drunk driving rap, it might well be that Foster Catering could be hit with a heavy lawsuit. So to protect his own ass, Mel

Foster had to protect his son-in-law's as well, even if there was bad blood between them.

I asked him if he could tell me who the supervisor was at the hall Barry worked at that night and he said he'd check it out and get back to me. I wasn't about to make book on that happening but I said I'd be back in a couple of days.

I had other fish to fry and one of them was a guy by the name of Brian Elkin, another person who wasn't interviewed by the police but should've been. A slim, good-looking dude I took to be in his early thirties, Elkin had also been a week-end employee at Foster's. He'd been working on the evening of June 18th, 1976, but at a different hall from Barry and Paul. I knew from the inquest transcript that he'd been at the scene of the accident shortly after Kelly was hit and wondered what he knew.

It sure as hell wasn't easy finding out. Although he talked a lot, I had the feeling he was just blowing smoke. He said he'd been working at the catering centre when, at a few minutes after eleven, a "stranger" arrived and told him a Foster van had been involved in an accident just down the road.

His story was that he'd gotten a ride to the accident scene with this anonymous informant. The police and ambulance hadn't yet arrived. He spotted Reynolds and Stasiak and the three of them found Kelly Edwards in the ditch, lying in some water.

Somewhat later, the police and ambulance arrived and a crowd began to gather. Barry Reynolds was hysterical and Elkin, being a good friend of his, held him in his arms trying to calm him down. There was no smell of alcohol on Barry. During the confusion, one of the policemen asked that Reynolds be driven home. Elkin accompanied him in a station wagon driven by Bonnie Simmons who was with a girl-friend (actually, her cousin, Karen). They took Barry to his new house on Pembina Highway. Elkin didn't enter the house and was driven back to Foster's but was unable to remember by whom. When he got there, he and Paul Stasiak went to work putting some catering equipment away.

As far as I was concerned, Elkin's story was as phony as a politician's smile. A "stranger" just happened to drop into Foster's and tip him off to the accident? That's the kind of stuff you sprinkle over gardens. And he didn't know who'd driven him back to work? If he thought I believed that, he must've been smoking those funny roll-your-owns.

If only some half-way zealous cops had been on the case. They'd have sweated the truth out of him. But zeal was a scarce commodity in Castleton so, once again, a potential key witness was totally ignored.

Things were looking up in some other areas though. I'd succeeded in tracking down the woman who'd supervised the catering at the Southport Community Club where Reynolds and Stasiak were working for the better part of the evening of June 18th and I lost no time in paying her a visit.

Pauline Losinski was living in Garson, twenty-odd miles east of Winnipeg. In her early fifties, she seemed to be a bright, alert woman and when I told her the reason for my visit, she was quite open. She told me that the social at the Southport hall had been in honour of a couple of relatives of hers, Nick and Jean Balan. She recalled that Barry Reynolds and his helper, Paul Stasiak, showed up at around seven p.m. with the food which they then unloaded. Later in the evening, they helped with the dish-washing and re-loaded the catering equipment for return to Foster's. I hit her with the key question.

"Did you see Barry or Paul drinking any beer or liquor that evening?"

"Oh sure. They each had at least two shots of whiskey. Maybe even more. I wasn't watching them all night."

It was music to my ears. A couple of shots of whiskey didn't add up to impairment but they sure as hell spelled perjury when you considered what both Reynolds and Stasiak had testified to under oath. And there was more.

Mrs. Losinski related an incident involving a bottle of rye whiskey which had been given to her by Nick Balan. Even at this late date, she remembered that it'd had a red label and a picture of a horse on it. She'd placed it in the refrigerator in the community club's kitchen and thought no more about it until a fellow worker, Mary Cizick, told her Paul Stasiak was trying to put the grab on it.

Later in the evening, Pauline caught Stasiak red-handed at the fridge. He had poured about half of the twenty-six of rye into a 7-Up bottle. Pauline told him she would report this to Foster's but never followed through on the threat, preferring to let sleeping dogs lie. She said the rye was taken at about ten p.m., after which Paul and Barry left with the dishes in the van. As far as she knew, the rye went with them.

You didn't have to be a genius to guess what had happened to it next. And you didn't have to be any mental giant to know that some of the key witnesses at the inquest had lied through their teeth. And the police and Crown would both have known it if they'd done their homework and talked to the people I interviewed.

As a matter of fact, the inquest transcript shows the police did consider the question of whether Reynolds had been drinking prior to the accident to be of considerable importance. But if they tried to find out, they sure as hell didn't do much of a job if the following excerpt is any indication.

Q. BY MR. GATES: *Did you determine if Mr. Reynolds had been drinking prior to the accident? Did you carry out an investigation to find out?*

A. BY CHIEF DAKIN: *We checked the place where he worked and also the beer garden at the community club but we couldn't find out. Nobody knew.*

Nobody knew? What the hell were the Simmons and Pauline Losinski? Chopped liver? And how about Mary Cizick? When I interviewed her it was no trick at all to get her to confirm that Barry and Paul had been drinking on the job.

According to Crown Counsel Gates, Chief Dakin hadn't had any kind of report ready as late as August 5th, some seven weeks after the accident, when the Deputy Director of Criminal Prosecutions finally asked for it.

Now, this raised a couple of important questions. First, why did Dakin wait seven weeks before checking to see if Reynolds had been juicing it up before the accident? And, second, considering the Castleton cops were on the case while it was still warm, why hadn't they come up with the witnesses and information I managed to dig up two years later?

Oh yeah, Pauline Losinski told me something else that might have interested the cops as much as it did me. She said Reynolds and Stasiak always drank on the job at the functions they catered but, after the accident, Mel Foster warned them that from then on, this was strictly taboo.

While I visited a number of witnesses more than once, some, like the Simmons, I contacted several times. I had a hunch they were the key to breaking the caper open.

When I dropped by their place the second time, David was alone. He didn't exactly greet me with open arms but agreed to talk. He told me that Barry Reynolds had dropped in the afternoon of the accident and had stayed there from about three to five p.m. There'd been four of them: Barry, David, Bonnie, and her cousin, Karen. They'd knocked back a dozen beer and when the party broke up, Barry left for work.

By now, it wasn't exactly a revelation that Barry Reynolds had committed perjury at the inquest. He'd lied about how much booze he'd had before the accident and I was sure he'd lied about getting smashed *after* the collision. Now, I had to prove it. I figured Bonnie Simmons was the person who could help me to do just that.

It seemed to me that Bonnie had a tendency to clam up when her husband was around so I made sure that David's car wasn't in the driveway when I called. She was a helluva lot more open without her husband around throwing her warning looks.

"So there were the four of you drinking that Saturday afternoon, is that right?"

She nodded.

"Do remember how much Barry drank?"

"About the same as the rest of us, maybe three or four bottles."

"And you're sure that was on June 18th?"

"I'm sure," she said softly. "I've thought of that day a lot over the past couple of years."

I then steered her toward that evening. According to Bonnie, she and Karen had been at the beer garden. Some time after eleven, David rushed up and reported that Barry had been involved in an accident. He suggested that she go down and look after him. She and Karen drove to the scene, getting there about 11:30 p.m. Barry Reynolds and Brian Elkin then joined the two women in their station wagon and, shortly afterward, Constable Sandor asked Bonnie to drive Reynolds home. So far so good. It was time to get the good stuff.

"Was anyone home when you got there?" I asked.

"No. The house was empty."

"What happened then?"

"Well," she said, "we just kind of sat around in the living room. Not really talking or anything. Nobody felt like saying much."

"And Barry, what was he doing?"

"He was just slumped down in an arm chair, sort of holding his head."

I tried to sound casual when I hit her with the next question. "Did you or Karen go and get him something to drink, some liquor?"

"No, the only time I left the room was to go to the bathroom. And Karen stayed with Barry in the living room the whole time."

"So Barry never left the room either?"

"That's right."

Strike one. I went into my wind-up for another high

hard one. "How about booze? Was there any in the living room?"

"If there was, I didn't see it."

"So Barry didn't have anything to drink while you were there?"

"Not while we were there," she shook her head emphatically. "He couldn't have."

Strike two.

Bonnie recalled that she and Karen had stayed with Barry for one-and-a-half to two hours, after which Reynolds' wife and father-in-law had shown up. She said Mel Foster had blown his stack at Barry and she and Karen thought it best that they left. I asked her if Barry could've had something to drink after they left.

"No way," she emphatically, "Nancy – that's his wife – would have gone up the wall. She doesn't let him drink around her and he doesn't push it because her dad's got a lot of money and I think he'd like to get his hands on some of it."

When I left this woman who knew so much but had never spilled it simply because no one had ever questioned her, she said: "You know, I've had a feeling all along that someday the accident would be re-opened."

"Yeah, and chances are you're going to be smack dab in the middle," I said.

She shrugged her shoulders and gave an uncertain smile. "Maybe I should've been there a lot sooner. Maybe a lot of us should've."

By now, my investigation was getting down to the short strokes. One of the last people I interviewed was Gerry Salter, another of Foster's part-time employees and one of the first to arrive at the accident scene.

Tall, dark-haired, and slim, he was like a lot of those unisex types who flounce around with tight pants and limp wrists. If this guy wasn't out of the closet it was probably because he wasn't strong enough to turn the door-knob. Although he'd probably turned a few others in his time.

I spoke to him at Manitoba Hydro where he was then working. He seemed jumpy as hell. In spite of a large "No Smoking" sign, he lit up a cigarette and chain-smoked right through our talk.

He confirmed he'd been at the accident scene shortly after eleven and his story was as follows: He and a male friend had spent at least two hours at the Castleton beer garden on Harrison, during which he drank four beers. They left at about eleven, with Salter planning to drive his buddy home. Although he hadn't been working for Foster that evening, he was driving a company van. They were heading east on Harrison when they spotted another Foster van in the ditch. Shortly after, Barbara Frater flagged them down and told them Kelly'd been hit. Neither Barry nor Paul was in sight at the time. Salter checked out the van in the ditch and found it empty.

Because he'd been drinking, he figured he'd better make tracks before the cops showed up. He and his pal drove to the catering centre, left the van, and returned to the scene on foot. By this time, the police and ambulance had arrived and Brian Elkin was looking after Reynolds. Salter and his unnamed friend left a short time later.

Most of what he told me made sense. But not all of it. I could understand why Salter and his buddy hadn't spotted Barry and Paul at the accident scene since the driver and his partner had taken off like a pair of scared rabbits. But they'd headed east and so had Salter, so why hadn't their paths crossed? Or had they?

Monday, May 28th, 1978. Back at Foster's. Mel Foster had promised to get some information for me. It was a good thing I hadn't held my breath. The guy was about as communicative as a mute with lockjaw. He said he'd been advised (by his lawyer, presumably) not to tell me anything. He added that it had all come out at the inquest anyway. If it hadn't been such a bad joke, I would've laughed.

Sweet piss-all had come out. Nothing about Reynolds drinking beer and whiskey in the hours leading up to the accident. Nothing about his partner bringing a 7-Up bottle full of hard stuff into their van. Nothing about eye-witnesses who could testify that Reynolds lied when he said he'd downed five to seven ounces of liquor almost immediately after getting home.

By now, I was pretty sure what'd happened. Barry Reynolds had been half-gassed and feeling playful. He'd seen the girls walking along the road and decided to scare them. The booze had affected his driving and he'd strayed onto the shoulder slamming Kelly Edwards into eternity.

After the impact, the wheels on the passenger side left the shoulder and began to slide into the ditch. Panicking, Reynolds gunned the motor and fought the steering wheel to the left. This accounted for both his failure to hit the brakes and his ending up in the ditch on the opposite side of the road, a helluva long way from the point of impact.

I also had a pretty good idea why Reynolds and his partner had started scrapping. Stasiak had probably been so pissed off at the dumb stunt his buddy had pulled that he'd blown up at him. Then, closing ranks, they'd buggered off to the catering centre where Paul frantically called for a tow-truck. It was an emergency all right. They wanted to get rid of the evidence, which in this case was the van, before the cops came on the scene.

It'd been a half-baked idea like most of those born of desperation and someone, probably David Simmons or Gerry Salter, had convinced them to go back to the accident scene and face the music. They were in luck. The cops at the scene were so dumb they would've needed diagrams to find their asses.

Monday, June 18th, 1978. The second anniversary of Kelly Edwards' death and the last stop for me as it had been for her. Intending to recreate the conditions at the time of the accident, one of my operatives, Dennis Steele, and I arrived in Castleton at 10:30 p.m. At 10:55, I had Steele follow in Kelly's footsteps. Sticking to the gravel shoulder on the north side of Harrison Road, he walked west toward the spot where Kelly had been struck.

As had been the case with Kelly, Steele was wearing dark clothing. During the time he walked on the shoulder, close to the slope of the ditch, a total of four westbound cars appeared. None of the drivers seemed to have any trouble seeing him and each of them pulled over to the left before passing.

I drove west on Harrison at 11:03 p.m. at the posted speed. My headlights reflected off the light-coloured gravel bordering the road. Even though I was a good thirty or forty yards away, Dennis' form was clearly visible. I was now more sure than ever that Barry Reynolds had seen Kelly before the van crushed the life out of her and sent her best friend screaming into the night.

ELEVEN

The Trial

THE DRIVER of the van which struck and killed Kelly Edwards on the night of June 18th, 1976, finally went to trial in mid-October of 1978. Over two years had passed since the tragedy but finally, it looked like the Edwards' might get something that at least bore a faint resemblance to a fair shake.

The road to justice hadn't only been long. It'd been bumpy and filled with a lot of dead-ends. One was the Castleton police commission which in the spring of 1977 had the goddamn nerve to tell Terry and Anita that in its opinion "the Castleton police acted in a responsible and professional manner." Pardon me while I toss my cookies.

The Attorney-General had been equally prepared to slough off his responsibility, saying: "I know that it was a matter of concern to you that your daughter's accident was not investigated by the R.C.M.P. I sincerely do not think that any useful purpose can be served by having them look into the incident at this late date."

And that was where the matter stood in May of 1977. I already mentioned how I got involved in the caper and how I had to do the cops' work for them because they figured they were risking nervous breakdowns if they did anything more challenging than handing out speeding tickets.

After I wrapped up my investigation in June of 1978, I handed the reports over to Marty Dodson, the Edwards' lawyer. He in turn turned them over to the Attorney-General's office and I assumed they'd follow up the leads I uncovered. But that wasn't quite the way it happened.

The A.–G.'s Department continued to drag its feet and it wasn't until mid-July of 1978, that the Crown Prosecutor's office was dragged kicking and screaming into doing what it should've done a helluva lot earlier.

Some heavy prodding by lawyer Dodson coupled with the thinly-veiled threat of cluing the media in on the Crown's piss-poor performance finally paid off. But the pay-off wasn't quite what I expected. I didn't know whether to laugh or cry. Instead of having the R.C.M.P. conduct the investigation, the A.–G.'s office almost guaranteed failure by giving the Castleton cops another shot at what they'd already screwed up so badly. I believe in the motto, "If you don't succeed, try and try again" but this was becoming a little ridiculous.

Actually, in a way, it scared the hell out of me. Given their past performance, it wouldn't have surprised me if those cops ended up tossing Kelly's parents in jail and making Barry Reynolds an honourary constable.

It didn't turn out quite that bad. Of course, it didn't turn out all that good either. During my investigation, I interviewed more than a dozen people, most of whom had never previously been contacted by the police in spite of the fact that they could've been valuable witnesses. But even these additional witnesses were just the tip of the iceberg. There were others I would've liked to interview but there was no way the Edwards' could have afforded to keep me on the case for as long as it would've taken me to chase every lead.

I assumed that once my reports were handed over to the A.–G.'s Department, the Crown would follow up the leads I'd dug up. I was dreaming. Rather than initiate any investigative work of its own, the Crown was content to be spoon-fed on what I'd uncovered.

By mid-August of 1978, nothing seemed to be happening so I got on the blower to the A.–G.'s office. I was told that the Crown was having some trouble deciding which if any charges should be laid against Barry Reynolds. I was also advised there was more chance of a perjury charge being laid than one relating to the accident itself.

It came as something of a surprise then when I got the word that Reynolds had been charged with causing death by criminal negligence, driving while impaired, and driving with a blood-alcohol level in excess of .08.

The case didn't come to trial until late that fall. It was held before County Court Judge Harold Michaels, a relative newcomer to the bench. Veteran Crown Counsel Walter Mallory appeared for the Crown while Richard Isaacs, a young but seasoned mouthpiece from a stable of high-powered criminal lawyers, fronted for Barry Reynolds.

The courtroom audience was pretty well divided between friends and relatives of the Edwards and Reynolds. Although Anita Edwards seemed to be keeping her cool, Terry was a bundle of nerves. And as the trial unwound, he got even more wired up as he saw the way the Crown presented its case.

R.C.M.P. Constable Phillip Wright was the lead-off witness for the prosecution. He arrived at about 11:50 p.m., some forty-five minutes after the accident and photographed the accident scene. There was only one problem: the shots he'd taken of the north side of the road where the impact had occurred were mysteriously missing. I began to wonder whether incompetence was contagious and some of the mounties had gotten too close to the Castleton cops.

Wright testified he gave the film to the Castleton police and that was the last he saw of it. What a beginning! And what came next wasn't any better. Next up was Peter Sandor the cop who'd let Reynolds fly the coop. Sandor, who was no longer with the Castleton force, testified that he took notes at the scene of the accident and handed them over to Chief Dakin. So far, so good. The only thing was that, in the next instant there was another bombshell when it was revealed that these notes, like the critically important photos of the north side of Harrison Road, had vanished into thin air!

The ex-cop explained that the notebook containing the information he recorded at the accident scene had been kept in a police locker with several others belonging to him. Surprise, surprise! Only the one with the info relating to the Edwards' fatality had gone a.w.o.l.

The disappearing act was only one of the things he couldn't explain. He also couldn't come up with a decent excuse for failing to detain Barry Reynolds until the mounties arrived (about twenty minutes later) so a statement and blood-alcohol reading could be taken.

One thing he could say, however, was that there was no evidence Reynolds had been drinking. He said he'd been "not more than six inches" from the defendant's face and hadn't got a whiff of booze fumes.

Sandor's story was pretty convincing, at least a lot more convincing than it had been at the inquest where he only remembered that he'd stood in front of Reynolds. Now, more than two years later, he was able to recall that they'd been separated by "not more than six inches." Amazing what the passage of time can do for a person's memory especially when what he remembers helps to keep his ass out of the meatgrinder.

Equally amazing was Sandor's testimony that he didn't try to get the names of the people who went home with Reynolds and couldn't recall whether he'd tried to locate the passenger in the van.

One thing you could say about Peter Sandor: he was consistent. There was no way you ever had to worry about him doing something like being half-way competent.

If you think that's too harsh, listen to this. Among other things, the former Castleton constable testified that when he came on the accident scene, Barbara Frater had been hysterical so he placed her in the back seat of his police cruiser. But while he claimed he didn't take a statement from Reynolds because the latter was all shook up, he had no compunctions about prying one out of Barbara who'd just seen her best friend blasted from her side and later found her sprawled in a ditch with part of her brain spilling out of her skull. Yeah, this guy was a real winner alright.

He pulled more boners than an attendant at a gay bathhouse. But he really topped himself when Crown Counsel Mallory asked him about the Apex tow truck that showed up after the accident. In a statement to the Castleton cops on July 10th, 1976, Paul Stasiak admitted that it was he who called Apex and asked that a truck be sent out. He'd said he made the call about an hour after the accident but I discovered that it had actually come in at 11:15 p.m., no more than ten or fifteen minutes after Kelly was struck. The tow truck had been dispatched at 11:16.

This information was contained in one of my reports and was turned over to the A.-G.'s department long before the trial. Yet for some unknown reason, Mallory had felt compelled to ask the ex-constable if *he* was the one who'd summoned the Apex truck. And I almost dropped my load when Sandor cleared his throat, looked the crown attorney straight in the eye, and replied: "That's correct."

It was one goddamn screw-up after another. The next one surfaced when the mechanic who was supposed to examine the death van to see if it'd been operating properly testified he wasn't able to do a proper job. Seems someone walked off with the keys and the cops hadn't had the brains to get another set from Foster Catering.

Then it was Bill Mandiuk's turn and he related how he'd been one of the first on the scene. "I came up to Barry and asked him if he was the one driving the van. He said 'yeah' and I told him he hit a girl and she looked to be in pretty bad shape. That was when he started pounding on the hood of my truck and yelling: 'Why couldn't it have been a rabbit or a squirrel I hit? Why did it have to be a girl?'"

The thing is, Reynolds was carrying on about rabbits and squirrels well after he knew his van had incurred considerable damage. In fact, at the inquest, he'd testified that when he veered into the ditch on the south side of the road, "the whole window actually looked like it was smashed."

So could he really have believed that his victim was a rabbit or squirrel rather than a young woman who stood five feet nine inches and weighed one hundred and twelve pounds?

The fact that Reynolds had been able to carry on a conversation with Mandiuk at all was pretty surprising since Peter Sandor testified that he'd tried to speak to Barry a half hour after the accident and the latter had been totally incoherent and incapable of answering any questions. Had something happened to turn him into a basket case or had he been putting on an act? I had a pretty good idea what the right answer was. I hoped the judge did too.

Comedy turned to drama on the second day of the trial when Barbara Frater took the stand and painfully recounted the events surrounding her best friend's death.

Her story was much the same as it'd been at the inquest. Originally, she'd been walking on the edge of the road and Kelly'd been on the gravel shoulder. During this time, a small white car with only its parking lights on, came up behind them, veering slightly to the left as it passed. Shortly after, they heard the clatter of a vehicle going over the tracks a couple of hundred yards to the east. Spotting its headlights and guessing it to be a large vehicle going at a pretty good clip, the girls decided to change places so that the much taller, and hence more visible, Kelly would be closer to the pavement.

As the vehicle roared down on them, Kelly moved off the pavement onto the shoulder while Barbara edged over into the ditch. They looked back and were able to make out the shape of a light-coloured van. The racing motor drowned out their voices. The headlights seemed to be coming straight toward them and they concluded it was some friend trying to scare them.

They had moved further from the roadway, with Kelly having one foot on the shoulder and one in the ditch. Barbara was to her right, further down the incline, when she heard the sound of tires on gravel. She grabbed Kelly's arm but it was too late. The van struck her friend, catapulting her ahead into the ditch, then swerved across the road, ending up in the ditch on the south side.

Barbara then ran to the nearby home of Harry Belsky who called the police and helped find Kelly's body. Barbara saw Paul Stasiak on the road and told him Kelly was in bad shape. Stasiak subsequently spoke to Barry Reynolds and the pair scuffled and swore at each other. Barbara was later placed in a police car with Sarah Turner and a statement was taken from her by Constable Sandor.

In cross-examining Barbara, Richard Isaacs lost no time going for the jugular. It always amazes me how lawyers get away with browbeating witnesses and in general, treating them like shit. A lawyer can accuse a witness of anything from setting fire to little old ladies to indecently assaulting potted plants and the poor schmuck's got to sit there and take it. And if he loses his temper and politely suggests that maybe his tormentor should take a flying fuck at a rolling bagel, he stands a helluva good chance of being cited for contempt of court and having his ass slapped in the pokey.

Anyway, Isaacs must have figured he could get kicked out of the bar association if he didn't come on like a combination of Perry Mason and Attila the Hun so he pulled out all the stops.

At the inquest, Barbara testified that the van took a few minutes to reach her and Kelly after it crossed the tracks. It couldn't have taken that long and it was obvious she hadn't said what she'd meant, saying "minutes" in place of "seconds." Of course, Isaacs immediately made a federal case of her verbal miscue.

Hammering her apparent confusion over the elapsed time, he tried to use it to challenge her recollection of other pertinent facts such as whether the van's wheels had actually left the pavement as she'd claimed. When the dust settled, however, even Isaacs' slashing interrogation failed to shake the young woman's testimony and her evidence remained largely intact.

Next up for the Crown was R.C.M.P. Constable Peter Janzen, who had arrived at the accident scene at about 12:30 a.m. on June 19th, or about an hour and a half after the collision. He'd helped Sandor take measurements and testified that he had been unable to tell whether the point of impact had been on the shoulder or the paved portion of the road.

On cross-examination, Richard Isaacs suggested that there'd been no tire marks on the gravel shoulder on the north side of the road to indicate that the van had left the pavement. Janzen agreed, saying that the tire marks he observed started on the road rather than the shoulder.

However, at the inquest, he'd told a different story, saying he had, in fact, seen "what appeared to be tire tracks" on the north shoulder and that they had definitely been "within the accident scene."

A sharp crown counsel would have picked up on the discrepancies in Janzen's testimony. Walter Mallory was asleep at the switch though and let the R.C.M.P. constable off the hook. Now, I'm not a lawyer, but it seems to me that if a witness saw some tire marks on the gravel shoulder at the accident scene, the judge should have heard about it. But because Mallory was out to lunch, Judge Michaels never got the chance.

When court recessed that afternoon, the spectators milled in the hallway for a while before forming into two well-separated groups. One of them was composed of friends and relatives of the Edwards while the other was made up of Reynolds-Foster partisans. There was certainly no love lost between the two factions. The atmosphere between them was strictly sub-zero and I recalled the stories I'd heard about the tragedy causing a rift in Castleton.

As for Barry Reynolds, he seemed as cool as a cucum-

ber. A short, well-built guy, he had a boyish face and a
mop of wavy, light-brown hair. But that boyish look was
probably pretty deceptive because I'd heard he was pretty
good with his fists. While out in the hall, he kibitzed with
his buddies but, in the courtroom, he gazed stolidly ahead
or down at his hands. His only sign of animation was
some heavy-duty blinking.

His wife, Nancy, physically at least, was a good match
for him. She looked to be little more than five feet and,
facially, bore a strong resemblance to her father. She was
a hard-looking broad with black roots showing through
her short blonde hair. There was something about her that
made me think she was used to getting her own way. I
guessed that the fact her old man had a few bucks had
something to do with it.

After the break, the court heard from Harry Belsky.
Although for some strange reason, he was never called to
testify at the inquest, the slight man with thinning dark
hair had a lot to say at the trial and some of it was
dynamite.

Belsky's home fronted on the accident scene and that
was where Barbara Frater had run for assistance. Harry
had helped her find Kelly in the ditch and, at the trial, he
testified that, immediately after the accident, he saw a
man running up and down the road, yelling: "Where is
she? Where is she?" He couldn't say who the guy was but
it had to have been either Reynolds or Stasiak. Since
neither had as yet come across Kelly's body, the only way
this guy could have known they'd run into a girl was if
they'd seen her *before* the collision.

Belsky was a helluva witness all right because that
wasn't all he saw and heard. He also testified that he'd
witnessed an argument between Reynolds and Stasiak
during which a third man told them to shut up. He stated
that the defendant cried: "Oh, no! I killed her! I killed
her!" adding that after this outburst a scuffle ensued
between the Foster driver and his helper.

And, if that wasn't enough, he also told the court he'd

seen Barry Reynolds at the Castleton beer garden at about
4:30 p.m. on the day of the accident and the latter had
been holding "what looked like a beer."

Defence Counsel Isaacs ran true to form, doing his
damnedest to discredit the witness. He homed in on the
fact that Belsky had never been interviewed by the cops
and hadn't testified at the inquest, implying that this was
because his story wasn't worth a pinch of coonshit. Of
course, the real reason Belsky had been ignored was
because the cops hadn't taken the time to track him down.

The same went for Brian Elkin who could've been the
Invisible Man for all the attention the Castleton cops and
the Crown paid him during the initial investigation. Walter Mallory did call him as a witness for the prosecution at
the trial. However, you can lead a witness to the stand but
you can't necessarily make him talk. You could see Elkin
was keeping something back, trying to protect his friend
Barry. Still, the Crown did manage to pry a couple of
things out of him and one of them, at least to my way of
thinking, was pretty significant.

Although he was close-mouthed about a lot of things,
including the identity of the person who had driven him to
the accident scene, he did volunteer that he had a conversation with Barry while he was consoling him in the wake
of the accident. He testified Reynolds had been emotionally upset and one of the first things he said was: "How
am I going to be able to tell Nancy I killed a girl?"

That told me and should have told the judge two things:
one, Reynolds had known whom he'd hit; and two, the
Foster driver had conversed with at least two different
persons before allegedly becoming too incoherent to
answer Constable Sandor's questions.

The next day saw Paul Stasiak take the stand. Tall and
raw-boned, he looked like a big farm-boy in spite of the
mod, tinted shades he was sporting. He'd been with the
accused before, during, and after the accident and if the
defence chose to keep Reynolds off the stand, he would be
the only one who could testify about his friend's actions

during those fateful seconds before the van Barry was driving slammed into Kelly Edwards.

After Stasiak testified that he and Barry Reynolds had taken a load of food to the Southport Community Club on the evening of June 18th, 1976, Crown Counsel Mallory, hit him with a biggie.

"While you were working at that community club, did you and your supervisor, Pauline Losinski, have some words about a bottle of rye?"

Stasiak paused and looked down at the floor before answering: "I don't remember."

This was the booze that Pauline said Stasiak had ripped off, pouring half of it into a 7-Up bottle which he apparently took with him when he and Reynolds headed back for the catering centre. Where it ended up, nobody knew and Paul Stasiak's memory lapse meant there was little chance of anyone finding out.

Paul's powers of recollection improved a helluva lot when it came to what happened later on that night, since he recited chapter and verse what he said at the inquest a couple of years earlier. He testified that, after unloading the van at Foster Catering, Barry agreed to drive him home and they started off west on Harrison shortly before 11:00 p.m.

They were shooting the breeze when, suddenly, they felt a bang and Barry swerved the truck toward the opposite side of the road and into the ditch. Reynolds then commented: "Paul, I think I hit something."

Crown Counsel Mallory went on the offensive. "What did you do then?"

"We climbed out of the van, then started walking through the ditches to see if we could find what it was."

"And did you find anything?"

The witness took a deep breath. "No. We were still looking when someone – I don't remember who – came up and told us Kelly Edwards was lying in the ditch up the road and looked like she was hurt pretty bad."

"Did you see or speak to Barbara Frater?"

"No," he replied, then added quickly, "I don't remember."

After establishing that Stasiak went back to the catering centre for an hour or so after the accident and later dropped by Barry's place, getting there at about one a.m., Mallory homed in on one of the key issues.

"From the time of the accident until the time Barry was taken home, did you or he consume any alcoholic beverages?"

"No."

"Did you see Barry consume any alcohol at home?"

"No."

"Did he say he'd had anything to drink?"

"No."

"Did you smell any liquor on his breath?"

"No."

On cross-examination, Paul Stasiak declared that Barry Reynolds had been cold sober at the time of the accident and driving in a normal manner at a speed of thirty to thirty-five miles per hour. The only thing was that, at the inquest, he told a different story, saying the van had been clipping along at thirty-five to forty miles per hour.

By now, I wasn't particularly surprised when Walter Mallory failed to pick up on this discrepancy. As a matter of fact, I'd have been more surprised if he had.

It's no wonder Stasiak felt safe in changing his story time and time again. For example, at the trial, he testified that the van had definitely been on the pavement when it struck Kelly Edwards. However, at the inquest, mere months after the tragedy, he hadn't been nearly so sure.

Q. BY MR. GATES. *At the time of the accident where was the vehicle in relation to the road?*

A. *I can't really say. I wasn't watching where we were going.*

This was a far cry from what he said at the trial but, once again, his doctored testimony went unchallenged. The result was that although Paul Stasiak appeared as a witness for the Crown, to a large extent, his testimony ended up assisting the defence.

Stasiak's testimony was of the utmost importance, for if Judge Michaels bought it, it virtually assured an acquittal for Barry Reynolds. Consequently, Paul's credibility was a key issue and one that certainly should have been explored by the Crown. But if Mallory was up to the challenge, he sure as hell kept it a secret. It made me wonder if he'd taken the time to read the inquest transcript and the statement Stasiak gave to the cops. I couldn't figure it. The guy had all kinds of ammunition yet ended up shooting blanks.

And he did it again when he failed to follow up a response Stasiak gave Crown Counsel Gates at the inquest. Gates had tried to find out whether there was any significance to the fact that a beer garden had been operating in Castleton on the night Kelly was killed. He put some questions to Paul Stasiak and the following exchange took place.

Q. BY MR. GATES. *There was a beer garden in Castleton that weekend, wasn't there?*

A. *Yes. That's right.*

Q. *And were you involved with that?*

A. *No, no, I wasn't at the beer garden.*

Q. *You were not at the beer garden?*

A. *Afterwards that night, yes, I was.*

Q. *After the accident?*

A. *Yes.*

The question that should've been asked by Gates and, later Mallory, was: when exactly had he been at the beer garden? Both at the inquest and trial, Stasiak testified that he went back to the catering centre after Barry was taken home and that, about an hour later, he walked over to the Reynolds', getting there about 1:00 a.m. No mention had been made about any visit to the beer garden yet he'd testified under oath that he'd been there sometime after the accident.

It may not seem like a big thing but it looms pretty

large when you tie it in with something else that the Crown failed to bring to Judge Michaels' attention. That something was Paul Stasiak's bizarre phone call to Apex Towing.

There are a couple of strange things about this information. One, the Crown didn't see fit to use it at the trial and, two, it directly conflicts with what he said in a statement he gave the Castleton police which contains the following exchange.

Q. *Did you call anybody by telephone from the scene of the accident?*

A. *About an hour later, I called Apex Towing and told them that there was a truck in the ditch on Harrison Road and we needed a tow.*

If he expected anyone to swallow that, he needed his head read. An hour later? That was when the Castleton cops and the mounties were photographing the scene and taking measurements. I could just picture some tow truck jockey showing up on Harrison and saying: "Excuse me, officers, but I just got a call to come and tow your evidence away." Unfucking-believable!

There's no way Mallory should have ignored this incident because it went right to the heart of Stasiak's credibility. But here was a guy who had done his damnedest to tamper with key evidence and nobody had the balls to ask him why. Oh yeah, he gave some half-assed explanation about not knowing what he was doing but that made about as much sense as taking sincerity lessons from Brian Mulroney.

And if he didn't know what he was doing an hour after the collision, when did he regain his senses? Two hours after? Three? If the guy'd been that shook up, how much weight could be placed on his recollection of the event? These were things that should've been brought out at the trial but weren't.

The notorious rye-filled 7-Up bottle was though and it sure as hell didn't do much to boost Stasiak's stock. When Pauline Losinski told the story of how half her bottle of booze had been ripped off by Paul, it became obvious that Reynolds' helper wasn't the most trustworthy guy in the world.

As the trial drew to a close, the Crown called David Simmons, the guy who'd played a key role in whisking Barry Reynolds away from the accident scene before the cops got their act together and decided to take Kelly's death seriously. Mallory wasted no time in getting to the good stuff, asking: "Did you see Barry Reynolds on Saturday, June 18th?"

"Yes."

"When?"

"Shortly after the lunch hour."

"Who was present?"

"My wife, Barry, Karen (his wife's cousin), and myself."

"Was any alcoholic beverage available in your home?"

"There was a case of beer."

"And who was drinking this beer?"

"Myself, my wife, and Karen, before Barry came."

"And after Barry arrived?"

"All four of us."

"That includes Barry Reynolds?"

"Yes."

David Simmons went on to say that, to the best of his recollection, Barry had a couple of beers and left at about four o'clock. That wasn't the last he was to see of his buddy that day, however, although the next time, it would be under very different circumstances.

David had also been working for Foster Catering that Saturday night. According to him, he got back to the catering centre at about 11:00 p.m. He said there were no lights on so he decided to head down to the Castleton Community Club where he planned to meet his wife.

He was heading west on Harrison and, upon reaching the tracks, noticed lights in the ditch up ahead. He passed two people along the way. They were in the ditch and

running east. He identified them as Barry Reynolds and
Paul Stasiak.

Simmons proceeded to the accident scene and went
over to the truck in the ditch. He then spoke to a man on
the opposite side of the road, at which time he spotted
Kelly Edwards' body in the ditch. David then started back
to the catering centre, meeting the ambulance on the way.
After staying at the centre for two or three minutes, he
headed for the community club, arriving at about 11:10
p.m. (David's times appear to be a little off since the
ambulance didn't arrive until 11:24 p.m.) He located his
wife in the beer garden and told her what'd happened. She
and her cousin, Karen, then drove to the accident scene
and David didn't see his wife again until about 1:00 a.m.
when she was at the Reynolds home.

In cross-examining David Simmons, lawyer Isaacs gave
it his best shot but he couldn't shake the witness's story
about seeing Barry drink a couple of beers. And he wasn't
the only one who'd seen the Foster driver knock back a
few before reporting for work.

Following her husband to the stand, Bonnie Simmons
confirmed that Barry Reynolds had been drinking beer at
her home that Saturday afternoon, from about 12:30 p.m.
to 4:00 or 4:30.

At some point, she and her husband agreed to meet
Reynolds at the beer garden that night after he and David
got off work. She and Karen were having a beer when her
husband showed up shortly after 11:00 p.m. and told her
what had happened. On his instructions, she drove to the
accident scene with her cousin, getting there about 11:20.
She was standing next to Barry Reynolds when, at about
11:45, a policeman asked if there was anyone who could
drive Barry home. She volunteered to do so and they left
shortly after.

In the station wagon with her, Karen, and Barry were
Brian Elkin and Paul Stasiak, both of whom were
dropped off at the catering centre. The others arrived at
Barry's house shortly before midnight. There was no one

in the house when they got there and Bonnie, Karen, and Barry went into the living room where they sat until Reynolds' wife and father-in-law arrived at about 1:00 a.m. Mr. Foster asked Barry if he'd been drinking and the latter replied: "No, I just had a couple of beer."

At this point, Bonnie and Karen joined Nancy Foster in the kitchen, leaving Barry and Mel Foster alone in the living room. The women drank coffee in the kitchen and, at about 1:30 a.m., David Simmons came by to see his wife. They had a brief conversation on the back porch and he left. About ten minutes later, Bonnie also left, arriving home at 1:45.

Having set the stage, Crown Counsel Mallory proceeded to try and demolish Reynolds' claim that he'd downed about five ounces of whiskey *after* the accident, asking Bonnie: "From midnight until the time you went into the kitchen, did you see Barry drink anything?"

"No, nothing."

"When you saw Mr. Foster with him, were they drinking anything?"

"No."

"Did you see anyone in that house drinking anything but coffee?"

"No."

"Did you see Barry Reynolds leave the living room from the time he got home until the time you left?"

"No. He stayed in the living room the whole time."

"From what you could see, were there any alcoholic beverages in the Reynolds home?"

"No."

Although Bonnie looked nervous, she was a powerful witness and Isaacs knew he'd have to defuse her testimony. On cross-examination, he pulled out all the stops, alternately badgering her or spooning out sarcasm in an attempt to rattle her.

Attacking her ability to remember something that had happened more than two years earlier, he suggested Bonnie was mistaken about arriving at Barry's at midnight and that, in fact, she'd gotten there somewhat earlier.

Slapping on a sneer that he'd probably spent three years in law school perfecting, Isaacs asked: "You may want to think about this for a minute but isn't it true that Constable Sandor asked you to drive Mr. Reynolds home at about 11:30 p.m. rather than 11:45 as you previously stated?"

She frowned in concentration. "No, I'm sure we didn't leave until about a quarter to twelve because we were waiting for Paul."

"And where was Paul?"

Her answer was the icing on one of the craziest cakes I'd ever seen. "He was trying to drive the van out of the ditch."

All that courtroom needed was the theme music from the "Twilight Zone" or maybe Porky Pig stuttering: "Th-th-th-that's all, folks."

Just picture it. A van that has just taken the life of a girl is stuck in the ditch. The cops are at the scene. One is directing traffic a couple of dozen yards away. Others are taking photographs and measurements of the accident scene. And here's this guy, a buddy of the driver of the death van and a passenger in the vehicle, busting his ass trying to take off with the incriminating evidence. It could only happen in Castleton.

Now, it didn't surprise me when Richard Isaacs dropped this line of questioning like a bad habit. But I've got to admit it threw me when neither the prosecutor nor the judge seemed to think there was anything unusual about Stasiak's behaviour. I don't know, maybe they were both members of some religious cult that considered curiosity a cardinal sin but neither Mallory nor Michaels so much as raised an eyebrow. As a matter of fact, they looked so goddamn dead-assed you'd have thought they were auditioning for senate appointments. In a way, I kind of admired them. It's not easy to sleep with your eyes open.

Isaacs wasn't sleeping though. During his cross-examination of Bonnie Simmons, he let fly with both barrels. It was a virtuoso display of browbeating and bullying and Bonnie was at his mercy since neither Mallory nor Judge Michaels had the balls to intervene.

Isaacs wrapped up his interrogation by going back to Bonnie's statement about taking off into the kitchen when Barry's father-in-law arrived.

"You couldn't see into the living room from the kitchen, could you?"

"No."

The implication was quite clear. Since Barry had been out of her sight for some forty minutes, he could have downed some booze without her seeing. This was a theme that Isaacs would go back to again and again.

The next witness, Dr. Jerzy Palovcik, testified about the blood samples taken from the accused and Isaacs wasted no time in suggesting that they could have become contaminated, yielding an erroneously high reading. Palovcik disagreed, saying his methodology and equipment had both been beyond reproach.

The day ended on that note and the following morning, Sarah Turner was called to the stand. The slim, young housewife testified in a composed, articulate manner, telling the court about the scuffle between Reynolds and Stasiak immediately after the accident.

"They were jostling. They had one another by the shirts."

She told about how she heard them swearing and saw them run east on Harrison Road. She also recited how she'd observed smoke coming from the back wheels of the van as the driver frantically tried to free it from the ditch. On cross-examination, Isaacs confined himself to getting Mrs. Turner to agree that Reynolds and Stasiak might have been in a state of shock after the accident.

Although I'd heard Mel Foster considered his son-in-law a real loser, the catering company owner's testimony proved to be largely favourable to the accused. Not that

that surprised me since, in the courts as well as anywhere else, blood is usually thicker than water. On direct examination, he testified that he got to Reynolds' home at about 1:00 a.m. on the night of the accident and Walter Mallory went on the offensive.

"Who was there at that time?"

"Barry, my daughter, Nancy, and Paul Stasiak."

"Where was Barry?"

"He was sitting in the living room by himself."

In so testifying, Mel Foster directly contradicted the evidence of Bonnie Simmons who swore she'd been in the living room with the defendant when his father-in-law showed up. Foster flatly denied asking Barry if he'd been into the sauce before the accident, saying he'd only tried to console him. He added that he was in the Reynolds home for about fifteen or twenty minutes, only five of which were spent with Barry. Mallory then zoomed in on the main issue.

"Did Barry have anything in his hands?"

"No."

"Did you at any time see him drink anything?"

"No."

"While you were in the house, did anyone offer you a drink of liquor?"

"No."

"While you were with your son-in-law, did anyone offer him a drink?"

"No."

On cross-examination, Richard Isaacs opened the door to Reynolds' defence. Through some well-orchestrated questioning, he tried to emphasize that Foster had been with his son-in-law for only five of the twenty minutes he spent in the house. The message was clear: if he hadn't been with him at all times, how could Foster be expected to know if his his son-and-law had knocked back some hard stuff?

Next to be heard from was Constable Fred Lauchlan who was still a member of Castleton's finest. He was the one who showed at least a little intelligence by thinking that it might be a good idea to at least talk to the driver of the vehicle that killed Kelly Edwards.

He testified he arrived at Barry's place at about 1:40 a.m. on June 19th and found Reynolds sitting in an armchair in the living room. Smelling liquor on his breath, he asked him if he'd submit to a blood test. When Reynolds agreed, he hauled him to the Health Sciences Centre, arriving there at about 2:00 a.m. Before the blood test was administered, Lauchlan questioned Barry about whether he'd been drinking that night and the latter told him he'd had between three and five ounces of liquor at home after the accident but couldn't say at what time.

When had Reynolds become impaired? That was the key question and the Crown tried to get to the bottom of it by calling an R.C.M.P. expert on blood-alcohol analysis. Slightly built and boyish-looking, Steve Carter testified that he'd carried out a blood analysis on the sample of Reynolds' blood taken by Dr. Palovcik some three and a half hours after the accident.

He said that the sample contained 120 milligrams of alcohol in 100 millilitres of blood, yielding a reading of .12, and added that all persons would show some symptoms of impairment by the time they reached a reading of .10 which "is recognized as the international level at which all persons are impaired in their ability to operate a motor vehicle."

After establishing that Barry Reynolds was legally impaired at the time the blood sample was taken, Mr. Mallory tried to show that his condition was a result of liquor consumption *before* rather than *after* the accident.

He asked Carter to assume that a blood sample was taken at 2:27 a.m. from an individual involved in a motor vehicle accident at 11:00 p.m., that the reading was .12, and that there was no evidence of any consumption of alcohol between 11:00 p.m. and 2:27 a.m. He then asked the R.C.M.P. expert if he could determine what the individual's blood level would have been at 11:00 p.m.

The witness responded that between 11:00 p.m. and midnight, the individual would be on a plateau and his level would remain the same but between midnight and 1:00 a.m., he would be in a decreasing phase and the decrease in his blood alcohol level would be between 10 and 20 milligrams of alcohol per 100 millilitres of blood per hour. Therefore, the blood sample taken at 2:27 a.m. recorded at 120 milligrams of alcohol per 100 millilitres of blood would be twenty to forty milligrams of alcohol lower than it would have been at 11:00 p.m. when it would have been 140–160 milligrams of alcohol per 100 millilitres of blood.

The conclusion the crown attorney was attempting to draw for the court was pretty obvious. If, as the prosecution contended, Reynolds hadn't had anything to drink after the accident, he would've had a reading substantially above .12 at the time of the collision and been even more bombed than he was when the cops finally wised up and took him for a test.

Mallory also tried to shoot down the defence argument that the booze in Reynolds' system when the sample was taken was solely due to his drinking at home after the accident.

"Suppose an individual drank five ounces of liquor shortly before 1:40 a.m. and was tested at about 2:30 a.m.," he asked Carter. "What blood-alcohol reading might that person be expected to yield?"

The police expert replied that the blood-alcohol level of a person of average weight (such as Reynolds) would be raised by a maximum of 100 milligrams of alcohol per 100 millilitres of blood, giving a reading of .10. He stated that if the person had nothing of an alcoholic nature to drink other than these five ounces of liquor, there was no way he could have a concentration of 120 milligrams of alcohol per 100 millilitres of blood (the reading chalked up by the accused).

In answer to further questions by the Crown, Carter testified that if the person had consumed a couple of bottles of beer during the afternoon and another in the evening, there would've been no residual alcohol left to affect the level caused by the five ounces consumed at approximately 1:30 a.m.

The inference was obvious. Even if Reynolds had downed five ounces of liquor shortly before Lauchlan showed up, this alone could not have accounted for all of the alcohol in his blood. He would've had to have consumed something else – something aside from the couple of beers he was alleged to have drunk at the Simmons and the single beer Stasiak said he saw him with at the Southport Community Club. I had a hunch that "something else" had been guzzled out of Paul Stasiak's infamous 7-Up bottle.

Continuing his examination, Mallory had Carter discuss the "sobering effect" of an accident on an impaired person and the witness testified that a person with a blood-alcohol content over the impaired level could temporarily appear to be sober through experiencing fear or shock. He'd still be drunk though and when the fear or shock wore off, he would once again show it.

The way I figured it, that was exactly what happened with Barry Reynolds and why he hadn't appeared hammered at the scene of the accident.

On cross-examination, Richard Isaacs dragged in a red herring that was big enough to stock a fish market, suggesting that the vial into which Reynolds' blood sample was placed could have been contaminated. Carter conceded that this was a possibility but said he had no reason to believe the vial wasn't sterile.

Isaacs also tried to undermine the Crown's scenario by suggesting that, contrary to the prosecution's hypothesis, five ounces of liquor, if consumed between 1:00 and 1:15 a.m., could yield a reading of from .075 to .125 at 2:27 a.m.

Carter rejected this contention, however, stating that a person's body would have eliminated for one hour prior to testing, getting rid of one of the five ounces. Consequently, only four ounces would be left at the time of testing, yielding a reading of from .06 to .10.

The defence counsel then argued that, even if a person could have registered no more than a reading of .10 from five ounces he consumed at 1:00 a.m., if a sample were taken at 2:27 a.m., but ultimately weighed in with a reading of .12 (that registered by the accused), the additional .02 wouldn't have been a factor as far as any impairment at 11:00 p.m. was concerned since all it proved was that Reynolds might have had, at the most, two drinks before the accident which was far from enough to render him impaired.

By the time Isaacs wrapped up his cross-examination, therefore, it was clear that there was only one major issue as far as the trial was concerned: had Barry Reynolds knocked back some booze between the time of the accident and Constable Lauchlan's visit at 1:40 a.m.? There was, of course, one person who could have thrown quite a bit of light on this but when the Crown rested its case, Richard Isaacs chose to keep Barry Reynolds off the stand and call no evidence.

When court reconvened the next morning, all that was left was for both sides to deliver their summations. Walter Mallory led off, emphasizing that lighting conditions at the accident scene – though not perfect – were adequate and that if the accused had been driving properly, he would certainly have observed Kelly Edwards and Barbara Frater at the side of the road. He pointed out that the road was straight and even and there had been nothing in the weather or time of night to interfere with anyone driving a motor vehicle on that stretch of road.

He also suggested that some of Paul Stasiak's evidence was a pile of horse pooky and questioned how the accused and his passenger could possibly have been unaware that the van had struck a pedestrian, considering the jarring impact and the resulting damage.

He told the court that Barbara Frater had stated that she definitely heard the van's tires on the gravel shoulder and, consequently, the court should make a finding that the accused was not driving on the paved portion of the road when the accident occurred. He noted that Barbara, unlike Paul Stasiak, was a disinterested witness and, therefore, her testimony should be given greater credence than that of the accused's friend.

Mr. Mallory argued that the van had a wide windshield affording good visibility and contended that the damage to the vehicle was a good indication of the speed at which it had been travelling prior to the accident. The crown attorney then raised two critical questions: why had the van swerved into the oncoming lane instead of braking and why had Reynolds and Stasiak been jostling and swearing at each other after the collision?

In answer to the latter, he suggested that Stasiak had been furious at his friend for driving dangerously and causing the accident. He contended that this fit in with other facts, all of which pointed to the excessive speed of the van and the negligent driving of the accused.

And why had Reynolds been driving without due care? Because, the crown attorney argued, he had been under the influence of alcohol. He pointed out that if Reynolds had a blood-alcohol reading of .12 at 2:27 a.m., at 11:00 p.m. (the time of the accident) it would've been .14 to .16 if he had nothing to drink after the accident as was the Crown's theory.

Mallory referred to Steve Carter's testimony that, under the influence of alcohol, fine judgement and motor control are the first faculties to be diminished, affecting both the field of vision and reaction time. He suggested that this was what happened in Barry Reynolds' case and the end result of his inability to control the van he was driving was the death of Kelly Edwards.

In recounting the events following the accident, Mallory tore a strip off Peter Sandor, saying: "Constable Sandor allowed the most incredible thing to happen. He committed an incredible blunder by allowing the accused to be taken home."

Then, anticipating the defence counsel's arguments, he focused on the post-accident period with a view to demonstrating that Reynolds' opportunities to drink without being seen had been almost non-existent.

Reviewing the testimony of Crown witnesses, he stated that Reynolds did not drink at the scene of the accident. Nor did he consume any beverages – alcoholic or otherwise – from midnight until 1:00 a.m. while he was in the presence of Bonnie Simmons and her cousin, Karen. He added that when Bonnie left Barry, the latter remained in the living room with Mel Foster who also testified that he didn't see Barry drink anything.

Even though Mr. Foster testified that he didn't see Bonnie at Reynolds' residence, Mr. Mallory asked the court to find that she had, in fact, been there, saying that her husband, David, had gone to the accused's home at 1:30 a.m. and spoken to her. Becoming impassioned for one of the few times during the trial, the crown counsel declared: "Bonnie Simmons was there. She is an independent witness and she was there! Why would she submit to the kind of cross-examination she was put through in this courtroom, if she weren't telling the truth? She is not an enemy of the accused. She is not out to get him. She merely wants to tell the truth."

Pausing to check his notes, Mallory referred back to earlier testimony, saying: "Brian Elkin was in the car that took the accused home. He testified about who else was in the vehicle and he stated under oath that Bonnie Simmons was one of them." He pounded the air with his fist. "She was there! Bonnie Simmons was in the car and she was also in the house. And while she was there, Barry Reynolds didn't have a drop to drink. Not a drop."

He turned and looked straight at Reynolds who was seated in the front row next to his wife. Barry quickly dropped his head and started studying his clasped hands. His wife, Nancy, put on a really snotty look and glared at the crown attorney.

"When did the defendant drink the five ounces of

liquor as he claimed?" he boomed. "It couldn't have been when he was with Bonnie Simmons. We have already heard her testimony on that point. It couldn't have been when he was with his father-in-law since Mr. Foster testified that there was no liquor in evidence. Not five ounces. Not three ounces. Not one ounce. Nothing."

"When did he drink this liquor then?" Mallory raised his eyebrows and gave an exaggerated shrug of his shoulders. I hoped he was a better prosecutor than he was an actor. "When did he drink this phantom liquor that came from nowhere and was seen by no one except the accused?

"At the inquest two years ago, Barry Reynolds testified that he drank the liquor in a single gulp within minutes after arriving home as an antidote for shock. This is what he testified under oath. Bonnie Simmons' evidence totally refutes this claim, however. And he couldn't have drunk it when his father-in-law was there because Melvin Foster would have observed it and he did not. This proves that his story at the inquest was a complete fabrication.

"His story is not only refuted by the testimony of a number of witnesses, however. Scientific evidence also gives the lie to his claim. The scientific recording of Mr. Reynolds' blood-alcohol level of .12 at 2:27 a.m. proved beyond a shadow of a doubt that the only drinking the accused did was *before* rather than *after* the accident.

"If he had nothing to drink before the accident as he claimed and drank five ounces of liquor at about midnight, this amount would have produced a maximum blood-alcohol level of .10 and, between midnight and 2:27 a.m., he would have eliminated at least an ounce and a half of alcohol, resulting in a blood-alcohol level of approximately .07. It would have been a scientific impossibility for him to come up with a level of .12.

"There is only one way to explain a reading of .12 at 2:27 a.m. and that is if he had drunk the five ounces of liquor after Bonnie Simmons left at 1:40 a.m. and did not eliminate any of the alcohol between the time of consumption and the time the test was taken at 2:27 a.m. But this would mean that he downed the alcohol not when he came home and needed a stiff drink to help him compose himself but almost two hours later, after he had sat in his living room and been comforted by his friends and relatives.

"Does that sound reasonable? And does it sound reasonable that he could have gulped down five ounces of liquor in those few minutes between Bonnie's leaving and Constable Lauchlan's arrival? The evidence indicates otherwise. When Constable Lauchlan got there, there was no evidence of any liquor having been consumed. No bottle. No glass. Nothing. Just Barry Reynolds' story which I suggest is a total fiction designed to cover up his criminal negligence in causing Kelly Edwards' death.

"Barry Reynolds' story is not capable of belief. He had a clear, unobstructed view of the road and his headlights would have clearly revealed the two girls. Yet he claims he failed to see them. If he could not see them, I suggest this was due to his impairment and the wanton and reckless operation of his vehicle.

"Barry Reynolds is, beyond the shadow of a doubt, guilty of criminal negligence and the included offences of dangerous driving and driving while impaired and I urge the court to find him guilty as charged on all counts."

Not surprisingly, Reynolds' mouthpiece saw it somewhat differently. In his summation, Richard Isaacs pointed out that no charges were laid until over two years after the fatality.

"Why weren't charges laid a week after? Two weeks? Even a month?" He smiled condescendingly, like a mother clucking over the minor misdeed of a wayward child. "Simply because there was no evidence that a crime had been committed."

My blood pressure which is pretty high at the best of times started to rise. But not as much as my temper. The only goddamn reason charges hadn't been laid earlier was because those dull normals they had for cops couldn't find cowshit if they stepped in it.

"This long time lapse had to do something to the memories of the witnesses," he continued. "After two years, how could anyone be expected to remember what or when someone drank?"

He then went on to hammer the piss-poor investigation carried out by the cops.

"The photos of the north side, the missing notes, the lack of a blood test immediately after the accident, were all colossal blunders but I suggest that these blunders have hindered the case for the defence as much as they have the case for the prosecution. If a proper investigation had been conducted, my client would have been completely exonerated and there would have been no need for this trial."

"It was a tragedy. There is no doubt about that. But I suggest that it was unavoidable. It had been raining that day and was overcast. Visibility was poor as evidenced by the fact that flashlights were required to locate Miss Edwards' body in the ditch. The girls were not walking facing traffic as they should have been. That's the terrible tragedy of it all.

"There is no evidence to substantiate the Crown's case that the impact took place on the shoulder of the road. Barbara Frater may have thought she heard the van on the gravel – nobody is saying she lied – but it may have, in fact, just struck a raised patch of asphalt on the pavement. Surely, she's no authority on the sound tires make when they come in contact with various surfaces.

"Barry Reynolds was alone from 1:15 to 1:40 a.m. and had ample opportunity to drink. He didn't say he drank as soon as he got home."

That, of course, was pure bullshit because at the inquest, Reynolds had said just that under oath. But like many lawyers, Isaacs probably figured telling the truth was O.K. as long as you didn't overdo it. Then, figuring it was time for a giant-sized red herring, he tossed out a dandy.

"The court must also have grave doubts about accepting the accused's blood sample. The vial used in the blood extraction procedure was not the type recommended by the R.C.M.P. It could also have been contaminated. Therefore, the court must consider whether the alcohol level in the sample was solely a result of ingestion or partly attributable to contamination."

Reiterating his main argument, Isaacs suggested that Bonnie had left at 1:10 rather than 1:40 and that Barry Reynolds could have drunk the claimed five ounces of liquor between 1:25 and 1:40 a.m. to get the required reading of .12. In conclusion, he stated that the incident was "as consistent with an accident as with anything else. Therefore, justice demands that the accused be acquitted on all counts."

And so, on the morning of October 16th, 1978, concluded the trial of Barry William Reynolds. All that remained was the most significant part of the judicial process: the verdict. Judge Harold Michaels reserved judgement until October 23rd and, after more than two years, the final chapter of a case that had been botched, buried, and belatedly resurrected was but one week away.

TWELVE

The Verdict

OCTOBER 23rd, 1978. Court wasn't set to convene until ten a.m. but by nine-thirty, there were quite a few people milling around in the marble hallway. I spotted Terry and Anita standing off to one side. They were staring out a window, their faces expressionless. I walked over.

"Good morning," I said.

They turned and game me tight little smiles.

"Well, it's finally here," I continued, trying to make small talk and ease the tension.

Terry looked grim-faced. "Yes, finally. I just hope. . . ." He was so shook up, he couldn't finish the sentence. His wife reached over and took his hand.

"It'll be O.K.," I assured him. "Mallory didn't exactly cover himself with glory but the evidence spoke for itself. There's no way Judge Michaels is going to buy Isaacs' b.s. Reynolds is going up the river, take my word for it."

Time seemed to stand still. The people going in and out of the courtroom looked like they were moving in slow motion. Finally, the courtroom was called to order. I watched Judge Michaels stride to the bench, searching his face for any tell-tale signs but he wasn't giving anything away. His smooth, pink face was about as expressive as a comatose bowling ball. That didn't surprise me. Like private eyes, judges have to park their feelings in the bleachers.

So what if some poor bastard's crapping his drawers waiting to find out if he's going to go to the slammer for a zillion years. For a judge, it's all in a day's work and playing God comes with the territory. After being directed to stand, Barry Reynolds got to his feet, his head cocked slightly to one side as he waited to hear his fate. Michaels didn't try to build any suspense, I'll say that for him. Reynolds had no sooner scrambled to his feet than Michaels said: "Mr. Reynolds, I have decided to acquit you on all three counts in the indictment. That will be a verdict of Not Guilty on each and every count."

Reynolds just stood there for a few seconds without moving a muscle, then he turned and looked at Isaacs who flashed him a thumbs-up sign. A buzz ran through the courtroom. I turned and looked at Terry Edwards. His jaw muscles were working and he was gripping the back of the seat in front of him with both hands. I kept watching him, afraid he might go off the deep end. But a couple of seconds later, the shock and anger seemed to give way to resignation and he slumped back into his seat. Anita reached across and grabbed his arm but he didn't seem to notice. He just kept staring at the judge with this hurt look in his eyes.

It was over. Barry Reynolds had been cleared of any wrongdoing in the death of Kelly Edwards. A tragedy had officially been declared an accident. A teenage girl had just been in the wrong place at the wrong time. Neat. Clean. All the loose ends finally tied up. At least that's what the court would have liked everyone to think.

From square one, nothing about the death of Kelly Edwards had been either neat or clean. Not the way she died, sprawled in a ditch with her skull crushed in. Not the piss-poor way her death was investigated. Not the way the Edwards' tried for years to get the case reopened and had doors slammed in their faces. And not the way the case was finally presented in court.

And now, the case went full circle and what began with police incompetence ended with judicial bungling. As

Barry Reynolds sank relieved back into his seat, Judge Michaels read his reasons for acquitting the accused into the record. It was a lengthy recitation and most of it was pretty straightforward. But not all. And when he came up with a couple of observations that were in total opposition to the facts, it was all I could do to keep my trap shut.

You see, from some of his findings, it became obvious that Michaels had either dozed off during some of the most important testimony or his hearing aid had picked a helluva time to go on the blink. For example, he concluded that: "In very large measure, I was forced to base my decision on the credibility of the witnesses and, in particular, those who were eye-witnesses to the accident. Barbara Frater was such a witness. She was with Kelly when the latter was struck down and killed and her evidence was of critical importance. If she were believed, it would follow that the van left the pavement and, when it struck Kelly, was on the gravel shoulder. Unfortunately, I have had to reject Miss Frater's testimony as being totally unreliable.

"Barbara testified that, at the point of impact, Kelly Edwards was walking at least partly on the grass at the top of the north ditch, having just moved off the pavement. She further testified that she herself was then walking on the shoulder with Miss Edwards to her right.

"It is my finding that this evidence is not to be believed. If the girls had been walking as Miss Frater testified, immediately prior to the impact, with Miss Edwards partly in the ditch and she herself on the shoulder nearest the pavement, there is not possible way that Miss Frater could have escaped serious injury herself. If Miss Frater's testimony was accurate, the vehicle would have had to run over her to reach Miss Edwards. This did not happen. Miss Frater was not injured whatsoever. Therefore, I cannot accept her evidence as to the van leaving the pavement and driving onto the gravel shoulder.

"As to the matter of Barry Reynolds' blood-alcohol level of .12, I am convinced that this level was attained

after rather than *before* the accident. It seems perfectly
logical that he would have consumed some liquor at home
following the accident to steady his nerves and calm his
emotions.

"In addition, I am convinced there is some reasonable
doubt about the blood sample of the accused being uncon-
taminated. The vials used were not ideal for the taking of
blood for the purpose of a blood-alcohol test as there were
other more preferable types currently in use.

"All of these factors conspire to lead me to believe that
Barry Reynolds was not intoxicated at the time his van
struck Kelly Edwards. But they do not stand alone. Constable Sandor whom I believe to be a frank and truthful
witness testified that he stood no more than six inches
from Reynolds' face and could detect no odor of alcohol.
As a former law enforcement officer, Constable Sandor
realizes the importance of telling the truth at a criminal
trial and I am fully convinced he has done so in this
instance. He is a disinterested witness and would have no
reason to lie."

The learned judge read out a number of other reasons
for acquitting Reynolds but they were just window-dress-
ing. The bottom line was that he'd taken Stasiak's word
over Barbara Frater's because he thought her testimony
wasn't truthful. But the fact is that it wasn't Barbara who
screwed up. It was hizzoner himself who got the facts ass-
backwards.

You see, Barbara didn't come within a country mile of
saying what Michaels said she did. She didn't say Kelly
was in the ditch to her right when the impact occurred.
She clearly stated that she and Kelly changed places
before the accident, with Kelly moving to the shoulder and
she, Barbara, moving further into the ditch. The van in no
way had to go through Barbara to hit Kelly and that's
why when Kelly was hit, Barbara managed to avoid
injury.

Hell, of course there was no way Barbara could have
escaped being flattened if their positions were as described

by Judge Michaels. But where he got his information from was beyond me. He sure as hell didn't get it from Barbara. And he didn't get it from any of the other witnesses at the trial. Still, simply because he pulled some facts out of thin air and was using a one-cylinder brain to do an eight-cylinder job, Michaels tossed Barbara's story on the scrap-heap and chose to believe the fairy tale cooked up by a buddy of the accused.

Isn't that great? Doesn't that make you want to jump up and salute the flag? Christ, with this kind of justice and a nickel, you can make a down payment on a cup of coffee. Judge Michaels covered himself with just as much glory when he commented upon Reynolds' understandable need to have a quick shot of booze to calm his emotions. The fact is, when he got home and appeared to be shook up, he didn't touch a drop. Just sat there with his head in his hands. Witnesses testified to that. Or didn't Michaels believe them either? Did he think these witnesses who, like Bonnie Simmons, were totally independent, lied? Why the hell would they lie? And why would Reynolds wait well over an hour, long after he'd already calmed down, to sneak a quick drink in those few minutes when no one was looking?

It didn't make any sense. But where does it say common sense has to be a consideration when you've got judges who believe what they want to rather than what is backed up by a ton of facts? Christ, judges make a good buck. So is it too much to ask that they stay awake for an entire trial instead of just a few minutes here and there?

And then politicians and court bigshots wonder why so many people think the justice system is such a Mickey Mouse operation. When you've got lawyers who've spent all their lives drawing up wills and mortgages presiding over criminal cases, it's a wonder there aren't more foulups. And that's one of the biggest problems with the justice system: too many lawyers get appointed to the bench because they belong to the "right" political party and have kissed the "right" asses rather than because they know what the hell they're doing.

And this business about the "contaminated" vials which contained Reynolds' blood samples. Maybe the vials weren't the most up-to-date containers available but the same type had been used by the R.C.M.P. for years without any evidence that they were susceptible to contamination. And, as a matter of fact, there was absolutely no evidence that any such contamination had taken place in this case. Still, Judge Michaels somehow bought Isaacs' argument hook-line-and-sinker and made sure no facts got in the way of his conclusions.

It was that way all through the judge's lengthy rationale for his verdict. He believed those who supported the defence's case and dumped all over those whose evidence showed the accused in a bad light. For example, take a look at what he said about Peter Sandor, the cop who did the most to screw up the case. He said Sandor was a "frank and truthful witness" who had no reason to lie when he said he was within six inches of the accused and couldn't smell any booze.

Sandor didn't have any reason to lie? This was a guy whose main priority was to cover his ass because of the way he let Reynolds off the hook. Other witnesses said Sandor never spoke to or got close to Barry before letting his friends take him home. Were they lying? Or was it this "frank and truthful witness" who was playing fast and loose with the truth? Look at the evidence and make up your own mind. I've sure as hell made up mine.

I wasn't the only one who was pissed off though. Terry Edwards was just about climbing the walls while the judge went through his song and dance. He rocked back and forth in his seat and a couple of times, he muttered out loud: "You're wrong. You're wrong."

And it wasn't just what the learned judge said that frosted me. It was also what he didn't say. For example, he didn't so much as make a single reference to Stasiak's behaviour at the accident scene. Remember, he was the genius who tried to drive the evidence away right from under the cops' noses. If that isn't evidence of guilty knowledge, what is? And this is the guy he chose to believe over Barbara Frater?

When Michaels finished his spiel and court adjourned, I followed Terry and Anita into the hallway. Terry looked like he was sleepwalking. Finally, he snapped out of it and started ranting about how they'd been shafted again. Spotting Crown Attorney Mallory, coming out of the courtroom with his briefcase tucked under his arm, I steered Terry toward him and together, we buttonholed him.

"What the hell happened?" Terry pleaded. "How could the judge have made such an error? My God, even the papers got it right. Even they knew where the girls were positioned when that son-of-a-bitch killed Kelly!"

Mallory looked like he wanted to be anywhere but there. He looked around for an escape route before saying: "Judges make mistakes but usually they're not serious enough to affect the course of justice."

"Justice?" Terry flared. "You call this justice? He threw out Barbara's evidence simply because he didn't pay proper attention to the testimony."

"That's one way of looking at it, but in a legal sense. . . ."

"In a legal sense, my ass," Terry snorted. "Can't you do something? Can't you appeal?"

Mallory glanced away uneasily. "Yes, of course an appeal is always a possibility but, given the circumstances, I don't think we'd stand much of a chance for a reversal. It all boils down to credibility and Judge Michaels chose to believe Paul Stasiak rather than Barbara Frater."

"Yeah," I cut in, "but he made that choice because he didn't have the facts straight. And he didn't have them straight because his brain was in neutral for most of the trial. Isn't that grounds for appeal – the fact that a god-damn judge couldn't tell right from left and drew the wrong conclusion from the right evidence?"

"Mr. Manweiler," Mallory said curtly, "Judge Michaels is well respected among his peers. I know you feel strongly about this matter but there is no need to become abusive. The decorum of the halls of justice must be maintained. This is a court of law not a pool room."

"Yeah, sure. One of your brother lawyers blows it and you have to help cover it up because someday he may be able to do you a favour. If some poor punk makes a mistake, he goes to the slammer. If a judge makes one, everybody rolls over and plays dead. That's some game you guys are running here."

He glared at me. "Maybe you won't think it's such a game when your license comes up for renewal." Then he turned on his heel and strode away.

This may not come as the biggest surprise of all time but there was no appeal. And none of the papers had the guts to print the story of the way Judge Michaels screwed up. They knew it too. I know because I talked to a couple of reporters and they checked it out. And still they wouldn't print it. Maybe they or their bosses figured they might need some favours from the province's tight little legal fraternity sometime and didn't want to step on anyone's toes.

So one cover-up led to another. And this wasn't the first one I'd come across over the years. I've run into more of them than most people would want to know about. But I like to think that it all evens out somehow and that for every guilty s.o.b. who gets sprung there's some innocent schmuck who gets packed off the slammer.

Kelly Edwards' death was a tragedy, there's no doubt about it. But there was another tragedy too: the breakdown of a justice system that could give the Canadian senate a run for its money as far as buck-passing and copping out are concerned.

We've got to stop kidding ourselves. In spite of what a lot of lawyers and politicians (usually, they're the same thing) would like us to believe, Canada's justice system doesn't work all that well. Oh sure, it looks good from a distance with its granite palaces filled with oak and marble, the black robes, and the fancy language with a lot of two-dollar words and Latin phrases that nobody but the legal fraternity can understand. That's part of the gimmick. The lawyers make up the rules and then sock it to you and your bankbook if you're curious enough to want to find out how and why you're being screwed by a system that seems as foreign as the Great Wall of China.

You can't really blame the lawyers for the mess though. They just take advantage of it, the same way accountants exploit income tax regulations that make Einstein's theory of relativity look like kid stuff. It's because people don't understand the legal system that they throw up their hands and say "what's the use?" And even though I've had a lot of experience with it, there are still a lot of things I can't figure out.

In the death of Kelly Edwards, the system went in the dumper because the judge looked like he was doing his damnedest to have the important testimony go in one ear and out the other without disturbing anything in between. As far as I was concerned, he succeeded and a scumbag who should have been nailed to the cross came away smelling like a rose. But Kelly was just one victim of a system that doesn't seem to give a damn. Barry Reynolds wasn't the first guy to take a drink and then get behind the wheel of a three-hundred horsepower guided missile.

These days, it seems like every second driver is tanked to the eyeballs and the only kind of defensive driving that can guard against these creeps is to leave your car in your garage. But even then you're not safe because these jerks have been known to drive over sidewalks and through people's bedrooms. In one case, a couple were doing the dirty deed when a car slammed right through the wall of their bedroom and tossed them onto the hood. I bet they didn't know if they were coming or going.

Sometimes it seems that if it weren't for fatalities caused by drunken drivers, the crime reporters would have nothing to write about. Try and remember when you last heard of someone being killed or crippled by some mobile piss-tank in your town. Chances are it wasn't that long ago.

It may not be any news to you but things are getting out of control. It's common knowledge that alcoholism is on the upswing and a lot of bread is being spent trying to combat it. Don't get me wrong. I think that's the way it should be. A lot of lives are being destroyed by booze. But those lives don't just belong to the ones who're getting bombed. They also belong to those poor slobs who happen to be around when these juiceheads come barrel-ling along like ninety-proof Mario Andrettis.

What bugs my ass is that when these scumbags run over some poor kid whose only crime was to be in the wrong place at the wrong time, they have their lawyers cry the blues and try to get them off the hook with any bullshit they can lay their hands on.

One case I can remember, this guy had a blood-alcohol level of .18 and was so high, he probably thought he was flying a 747. The only thing is, he came in for a landing on a six-year-old kid who was riding his tricycle on the side-walk in front of his home. There was a red light. Instead of pressing the brake pedal, this drunken scumbag tromped on the gas. The car went out of control. One little boy went out of this life.

But in court, from listening to the bullshit his lawyer was shovelling, you'd have thought the poor little kid had attacked the car. This fine upstanding legal counsel told the judge that his client had been under a lot of stress due to marital and business problems. He'd taken a few drinks (turned out it was about a dozen) to calm his nerves and then had taken off to pick up a little boy for whom he was acting as a Big Brother. Weather conditions had been bad. The day was too clear and the sun had created a glare on his windshield.

He went on to say that if the judge for some perverse reason found his client guilty, he should remember that the guy was the sole support of his family and if he got sent to the pen, his family would have to go on welfare.

This argument often hits judges where they live because if there's one thing most of them are cheesed off at it's people going on welfare. Maybe they figure that if welfare costs go up, so will their taxes and they'll have to pull in their belts and trade their Mercedes in on Caddies. So, often it comes down to a judge being more concerned about some pisstank keeping his job than in seeing he gets punished for crippling or killing someone.

And, of course, lawyers usually pull out that old chestnut about prisons not rehabilitating anyone anyway, so why send their clients to the slammer. Great argument isn't it? One part of the criminal justice system doesn't work, so why don't we screw up the rest of it?

It's not strange that lawyers use these arguments. They've got a job to do which is to try and get their clients off no matter how guilty they may be and what the consequences are for society. What blows my mind is that so many judges swallow this crap. In the Edwards caper, Judge Michaels ate it up with both hands. And in the case of the little kid on the tricycle, the judge did likewise, giving the driver six months in the joint on a reduced' charge of dangerous driving.

In case you didn't know, they almost always reduce serious driving offences. That way, the Crown and the defence can make cozy little deals that spare the court's time and spare the public from knowing just how fucked-up the justice system really is. And when judges hand out these little pitty-pats on the wrist, they usually come out with the same cop-out, saying something like: "While there may be some strong feeling about a child's life being snuffed out, revenge has no place in a court of law and no matter how severe a sentence is imposed, it will do nothing to bring the victim back."

Isn't that great? Nothing but a bunch of mealy-mouthed bullshit to cover up the fact that the justice system, all the way from the police to the courts and the jails, is in big trouble. Revenge has no place in a court of law? Tell that to some poor bank teller who gets caught with

her hand in the cookie jar and gets sent up for two years.
Ah, but that's different, say the judges. We're talking
about money here not something so insignificant as a
human life. And, of course, revenge has nothing to do
with it. It's strictly for deterrence. But where's the deterrence for drunk drivers? The kind of sentences being
handed out sure as hell aren't.

And, even when some judge has the balls to hand one of
these scumbags a stiff sentence, the way the system works,
the creep's out on parole in a couple of months or ends up
serving his sentence on weekends. Pretty soon, they'll have
it so criminals will be able to serve their time on their
coffee breaks or maybe from three to nine in the morning
when none of the bars are open and they've got some time
to kill.

What's the answer? I'll tell you. When some creep is
sentenced to two years, make damn sure he serves it otherwise the whole caper turns out to be a joke, kind of like
the way it is now. And if the poor, misguided soul comes
out and commits another offence, sock it to him harder. It
may not do much for rehabilitating him but it'll sure make
the streets a lot safer for people who don't feel the need to
get tanked up and run over or beat up on their fellow
citizens.

The funny thing is that if you get drunk and hit someone over the head with a baseball bat and they cash in, you
can get nailed for non-capital murder or manslaughter.
But if you get bombed and start making U-turns all over
some poor bugger's frame, the worst you can get hit with
is dangerous driving or driving while impaired. And the
damage you do to the victim doesn't seem to count for a
pinch of coonshit.

I'm no social scientist but I've got a couple of ideas
about that. I think that crimes involving motor vehicles
are treated lightly because of the way our society feels
about cars. In a way, cars are our gods. We worship them
not only as a means of transportation but as status symbols. Some shrink or other even says that guys subcon-

sciously see them as phallic symbols but I don't think that's why I drive an eight cylinder instead of a four and have a hard-top instead of a sedan.

It's kind of like you're a somebody if you have a car and if you're a somebody, killing or maiming someone isn't as bad as it would be if you're a nobody who has to use a knife or tire iron. Let's face it, we live in a free enterprise society where big business has big influence. And car manufacturing and auto repairs and maintenance, not to mention oil, are big business.

Since this whole car industry makes the wheels of our economy turn just a little bit faster, automobiles are seen as a good thing and this positive feeling rubs off on everyone, including judges, some of whom have themselves been known to take an occasional nip before getting behind the wheel.

Booze has become a way of life in our society. And driving while half in the bag only trails by a nose. Maybe that's why judges and, for that matter, defence lawyers and prosecutors, seem to have an underlying sympathy for drunk drivers. Maybe they realize that they've done the same thing but were lucky enough not to get caught.

Frankly, I think the same thing goes for wife-beating because I know damn well that there's a helluva lot more of that going on than most people want to believe. But what happens when some macho man takes a few rounds out of his missus? She's put in the spot of having to charge him which is the same as setting herself up for another main event.

In Manitoba a while back, Attorney-General Roland Penner took the long overdue step of directing the cops to lay charges in cases of wife-beating. It was a good idea but, thanks to a court system that is about three inches removed from the dark ages, a good plan went into the dumper.

You see, even though the cops started laying charges, the judges still put the onus on the wives for having the cases prosecuted. This put the whole caper back to square one with the women once again having to carry the can for deciding whether their sparring partners should be tossed in the jug.

What it boils down to is that, in cases like this, you've got a system dominated by men handing out justice to women and a lot of guys on the bench still have the attitude that wives are possessions rather than people.

It's funny. If some guy walks up to a strange woman on the street and gives her a shot, he gets hauled up for assault with no sweat. But when a guy does the same damage to his wife, the cops, crown attorneys, and judges, all look for someplace to hide as if life had suddenly gotten too complex for them.

What the hell's the difference? A person's a person. No woman should have to take that kind of shit whether she's married to her assailant or otherwise. It's strange the way the courts look at domestic assaults though. It's not as if husbands can do whatever they want to their old ladies, like, they can't kill them. That's a definite no-no. If they do that, they can get as much as six months. No, it's more like guys have just a limited license when it comes to roughing up their spouses, one that entitles them to cuff them around a bit but not do any permanent damage. At least, not in a physical sense.

Emotional damage is something else again. Over the years, I've seen what it can do to a woman's head when she's treated like a punching bag. She starts to think of herself as less than human and somehow starts to believe that getting the shit kicked out of her is the way things should be.

To tell you the truth though, I don't know why I'm bitching about the justice system since it's exactly *because* it's so screwed up that I make a good living. A lot of people come to me for help because they've come up dry with the police and courts. Parents whose kids get run over and can't get anyone to give a damn. People who've had their children snatched by estranged husbands or wives. Guys who can't get divorces because their old ladies' lawyers will take them for every cent they've got. Women whose estranged husbands are hiding their assets so they won't have to pay support. People who are being bled by creeps who've got some dirt on them.

Where do people like this go when they don't want to lift the lid on their lives and let everyone poke around in their secret sins and weaknesses? They come to me. I'm their father confessor, their shrink, their shoulder to cry on and, sometimes, their whipping boy for all the shit they've ever taken in their whole miserable lives.

The pay isn't that great but I've got a lot of fringe benefits: high blood pressure, a broken marriage, a terminal case of cynicism, and the most god-awful nightmares you've ever seen. These nightmares are always different, at least the settings and characters are, but the theme is usually the same: someone or something is chasing me and, lately, I've been getting the feeling that whatever it is is gaining.

I don't have to go to a dream analyst to get the scoop on these nightmares either. I've got a pretty good idea they stem from some kind of fear of being caught or found out because, like I said before, I spend half my life bull-shitting and pretending to be someone I'm not so I can get the goods on people.

I'm a professional watcher. I watch people doing what they shouldn't and not doing what they should and what I see and do has a hell of an effect on their lives. Sometimes, it even *means* their lives. So I take some lives apart and put some together and every morning when I play back the calls on my answering machine, I wonder where the next desperate voice is going to take me. Like they say, it's a dirty job but somebody's got to do it and, who knows, maybe one of these days, I'll even run out of nightmares.

JAMES BURKE was born in Winnipeg where he currently resides. A graduate of the University of Winnipeg, he has been a freelance or full-time journalist for over a dozen years. Among other things, he has been a researcher for W-5 and a reporter for CKY-TV in Winnipeg. He is the author of the controversial *Paper Tomahawks: From Red Tape to Red Power* (Queenston House) and has also had fiction published. When not writing, Burke is involved in political organization and community development work.

ARNOLD MANWEILER was born in Latvia in 1920. In 1929, the Manweiler family immigrated to Canada, settling in Southey, Saskatchewan, where they engaged in farming. Enlisting in the Canadian Army at the outbreak of World War Two, Manweiler served overseas in Britain, France, Belgium, Holland, and Germany. A winner of the British Empire Medal, he began his career as a private investigator in 1947. He opened his own agency – "Arnold's Private Investigators of Canada Ltd." – in 1958, and shows no signs of slowing down, continuing to investigate cases from one end of the country to the other.

WE HOPE YOU HAVE ENJOYED THIS
KNIGHTSBRIDGE BOOK.

WE LOVE GOOD BOOKS JUST AS YOU DO,
SO YOU CAN BE ASSURED THAT THE
KNIGHT ON THE HORSE
STANDS FOR GOOD READING, EVERY TIME.